JOURNEY TO THE EDGE OF TEXAS

A MEMOIR OF LOVE, TRAVEL, NATURAL BEAUTY, WRITING, AND ONE MAN`S BATTLE WITH BIPOLAR DISORDER

CARLTON LEATHERWOOD

Journey to the Edge of Texas

For information about this title or to order other books and/or electronic media, contact the publisher:
Carlton Leatherwood
P.O. Box 561, Terlingua, Texas 79852
carltonleatherwood@yahoo.com

ISBN: 978-0-692-82739-0

Printed in the United States of America

Cover: Anna Oakley (Mercury Graphics), Terlingua

Interior Design: 1106 Design

For

James Vowell,

who edited this volume.

He was among the best of my colleagues at the *Houston Post*. Later he was an editor at the *Los Angeles Times*. He and wife Codette then published the *LA Reader.*

Photo by Carlton Leatherwood

James and Codette in Greece

Other Titles from Carlton Leatherwood

Why Terlingua: Adventure on the Edge of Texas

Big Bend People: Terlingua Edition

Big Bend People: Terlingua, A Desert Oasis

TABLE OF CONTENTS

INTRODUCTION

THIS NARRATIVE TELLS of my odyssey through the wonders and beauties of Texas, a journey of heart, but the book also follows a parallel rail, a journey into the mind. The story was begun 35 years ago, finished, and has rested out of sight on a book shelf for 15 years—until I felt I had contributed to my small community and had something to contribute to the community with mental illness at large.

As I write this introduction, I am content in a social celebration of Christmas in my 75th year, The years have been as rocky as the river canyons where I have chosen to end my days. There were an estimated 20 episodes of bipolar disorder for which I was hospitalized—before a psychiatrist 600 miles away in my old hometown of Houston successfully treated me outside a hospital, by way of television.

Terlingua, in far West Texas, is where I hang my hat. On the walls of my small frame house are the river canyon photographs of Jim Bones, who guided my first Texas journey outing in 1981. There are also the paintings of another friend, Bonnie Wunderlich, whose work of the Chisos Mountains and blooming ocotillos dominates the living room. And another friend, photographer Alexa Walker, has contributed out-of-state art highlighting trees.

With this book I mostly wanted to offer something steeped in nature, outdoor recreation, and history. But the dark moods that interrupted my efforts to create a fireside "chat" thundered to be heard as well. Hopefully, readers will go with me beyond the darkness to share in an exaltation of our landscape and thrill to the awareness in our nature of flora and fauna that overcomes the evil wind.

My mental journey took me to three state hospitals, a county, and three private ones. It is almost fondness with which I remember the state one in East Texas. It was more like a wooded college campus than a stereotypical "nut" house. Its treatment, take heart, was on the cutting edge. There a miracle drug, Risperdal, came my way, and I improved—significantly. Advancement is not a panacea, however. The drug has caused a neurological side effect, tremors.

I have not taken much note of things before age 40, about the time of the confluence of bipolar disorder and the odyssey, though I do include aspects of my being, such as touching on marriage (why I didn't) and death (its coming to the fore in more frequent funerals).

Midway with this writing project, I enrolled in a course on memoirs at Rice University, and the instructor gave the class an assignment to relate our earliest childhood memory. I obliged.

I was four, and we were living in an orange frame apartment over a store that sold lumber and hardware. This was in McCamey, Texas, in the Permian Basin President George W. Bush is so proud to include in his childhood history. My one sure recollection is a sand-storm that billowed into our residence. I remember the thickness of the air. I don't know how he—or we—survived.

Stairs led from the front door, trimmed in white, to the ground, and off to the side was a tin roof, over the lumber yard. We had a pet, a white-and-black fox terrier, which my paternal grandfather had given me, and we named her "Lady."

She had one trick. She may have had others that I don't remember.

When there were passersby, she would jump from the stairs onto the tin roof and then run to the edge—it had a pitch—hang her head over, and bark. She was genuinely on the edge.

My thoughts of those days, though, are fleeting.

I found inspiration to finish this writing task in the award-winning autobiography of Christopher Nolan. A quadriplegic, he wrote *Under the Eye of the Clock* by having someone hold his head while he tapped at a typewriter with a stick attached to his forehead.

My family helped me. My parents' final Christmas gift when I was down and they were going down, was a computer. My mother never accepted my disability as permanent. "What a waste," she said, pausing before adding "of money."

What of the old word processor I had started the journal on? A friend suggested I "bronze it like baby shoes."

CHAPTER 1

FIRST JOURNEY

THOSE WERE THE DAYS, the ones in which I roamed and romanced Texas—despite serious mental illness.

Chaps slapped cacti.

With J-strokes, our canoe rounded bald cypress knees.

Awesome canyons called.

Then I was surrounded by tamer walls and introduced to Monet and to Imax.

And the old term for a girlfriend—squeeze? Well, we breathed new life into it. With mountaintop kisses, we squeezed every drop of crimson out of splendid sunsets, later to stumble down rocky paths in the dark.

At the same time, I and the medical profession were stumbling down a rocky path toward a better treatment for manic depression (the early name for bipolar disorder). But the mania came less often then. Thoughts about it—the horrors of waking nightmares—trailed in river wakes and desert duets.

MY TEXAS ODYSSEY BEGAN on a raft in the state's outback. Cruising alongside heavy vegetation, we leisurely paddled the Rio Grande toward Santa Elena Canyon, the quintessential canyon to traverse in Big Bend

National Park, 600 miles west of Houston. Naturalist photographer Jim Bones told us to ease up as he began his explanation.

Tamarisk (or salt cedar), a frilly exotic introduced into this country from North Africa for windbreaks and ornamentals, edged the river. Tubular yellow blooms of tree tobacco announced it was spring.

"You'll notice that what we have got here is called a ribbon oasis," Bones said. "It is a linear oasis right along the river. If you go back thirty or forty feet, you're in the desert vegetation since the roots can't get down to the water. From the air, it is really beautiful to see. It's just a green ribbon along the river for as long as it flows through the land.

"OK, let's paddle forward again."

Common and giant reed (another import) thickened along the banks. Beyond them spread honey mesquite.

"OK, we can ease off again," Bones said. "What we will do is paddle like that for a little bit and rest, and paddle and rest—eventually, fall asleep. Try to fall into the boat.

"The water we are floating on is all from Mexico," he added. "No water (from the upper Rio Grande) gets past El Paso. Elephant Butte Reservoir north of Las Cruces impounds that mountain snowmelt for the cities and irrigation. And then, for almost three hundred miles, the river is just bone dry. And all this comes in from what is called the Rio Conchos (filled by subtropical rains) in Mexico.

"Let's paddle forward."

Amazingly, a dust storm blew across the river.

"You get a taste for the country this way," Bones said.

The land had been ocean bottom 100 million years ago. Large plumes of lava eventually worked their way up and erupted as volcanoes on the ocean bed. "Let's stop. Turn around and have a look at this," Bones said. "Big blocks split and faulted and lifted up. The lava worked its way through those faults and cracks and spread out on top of the limestone. What we are seeing here is the lava (a red layer). We are getting into the limestone. Around the bend you will see places where the lava was spread out on top of it. The whole event took 50 or 60 million years, so you had sporadic eruptions and then periods of quiet."

It was twelve miles through this geological paradise to the mouth of Santa Elena.

The land had begun to heave during the time of dinosaurs. The largest known flying creature in the world from that time on was a pterosaur with a fifty-foot wingspan. Its bones were discovered in the park in 1972. No other parts of this hairy reptile with wings, named *Quetzalcoatlus northropi,* after the Aztec god who took the form of a feathered serpent, have appeared anywhere since, but bones of a dozen smaller, similar pterosaurs were found in another part of the park.

Some scientists suggest that pterosaurs became airborne by jumping or falling off cliffs, by dropping from roosting places in trees, or by rising into light winds from the crests of waves. A stronger possibility exists that *Quetzalcoatlus* may have waited like the vulture each morning for the sun to warm the ground and develop strong thermal updrafts.

That afternoon we pitched camp on a sandbar in the foothills of Mesa de Anguila, ready to embark the next morning into the canyon. Guides set up the kitchen and prepared a campfire meal of steak and fresh vegetables. We got by without tents, the climate pleasant and insects few.

This was the first event in the Texas Music Series of outfitter Far Flung Adventures, based in Terlingua. Although margaritas and Texas country singing enhanced the trip for a fleet of participants, rafting one of five river canyons bordering the Big Bend area would, we anticipated, highlight the adventure.

And we were not disappointed. The next day we entered Santa Elena and saw enormous blocks of rock that had peeled off the 1,500-foot black-canyon chasm at the constellation Orion's belt and drifted out into the cosmos and sleep.

For all its hard features, the canyon shelters softness.

Yellow rocknettle, a delicate flower with many stamens, nestles in crannies on flagstone ledges up side canyons. Here, too, was a side canyon, Fern Canyon, with quiet pools and greenness.

A rock wren trilled.

A cliff swallow glided to its mud nest as the river riffled by our camp.

A burro's bell sounded at dawn as a gentle wind blew in.

THE JOURNEY WITH BONES was like a fresh breeze in the fifth year of my incurable illness. I was two manic episodes down an increasingly rough terrain, two hospitalizations toward losing count of them.

In my first encounter on alien soil, paranoia had chugged into the workplace, in the second-floor newsroom of *The Houston Post.* For weeks I had thought that my supervisor, the night managing editor, was trying to fire me. I wrote a memo to his superior, who checked out the assertion. The managing editor replied that I was "as solid as the Rock of Gibraltar."

But my paranoia kept rolling, like an iron wheel downward, toward more serious psychosis. I lost my car in the parking garage of the Galleria, Houston's premier shopping mall. Office bosses' laughter (an hallucination) surrounded me as I hunted the missing vehicle, a white Buick Regal with a T-top. Giving up the hunt, I took a cab to work in a blinding rain, did my job as a general wire editor, and returned late that night when the garage was almost empty. The car had been moved, I feared, and tampered with. I called the *Post's* legal counsel about the brakes and the mirrors, believing my immediate supervisor was now trying to kill me, although I did not say so out loud.

My mind raced.

Oveta Culp Hobby, commander of the Women's Air Corps in World War II and later the first secretary of Health, Education, and Welfare, owned the *Post* at the time and was chairman of its board. I decided that the villain was trying to kill her, too. I had never talked with Mrs. Hobby, but I had corresponded briefly with U.S. Supreme Court Justice Tom Clark, who had known her in their early days. I would fly to Washington to speak with him.

I raced to Houston Intercontinental Airport.

Villains were in adjoining lanes. A whistle sounded as they passed, (an auditory hallucination). I dumped the car in a no-parking zone at the terminal door, bought a ticket, and walked to the waiting area. My actions were errant enough to cause guards to retrieve a phone number of a cousin-in-law from my glove compartment and call him. He came, sat beside me, and tried to talk me out of the trip. Then a guard frightened me. I heard him say that they (I thought killers) would get me in Atlanta. Finally, a contingent of guards surrounded me as the plane was boarded, and they walked me to an outlying station. My parents, in Beaumont, had been called, and we waited. "He's bright," Jim Nickles, the relative, said. "They usually are," a guard said.

It was the middle of the night when my father and mother retrieved me. I quietly got in their car. They had talked to my general physician, and he had referred them to the psychiatric floor at Hermann Hospital. They drove the dark, deserted streets to the medical center, and hesitated, before taking me in.

I search now for an analogy to the river and my interior journey, and none is found, except in the negative. I rafted 155 miles of the Rio Grande to see all five canyons, discovering that the jagged cuts into the river's route are the ultimate beauty, the *piece de resistance,* of that moveable feast.

Jagged cuts to the brain are the antithesis of beauty. The mind—intellect and mood—run ragged for want of a better cliché. Intellect, mood, and fear become bedfellows. Some sufferers find the jags, the mind's explosions, to be exciting highs. I do not. From that night in Hermann Hospital onward, I have never—even in a stretch—found a mental jag comparable to the exhilaration of whitewater rafting.

As with Bone's rafting technique, in this tale we will paddle the natural odyssey forward some and then ease up for the other days of my life and for my psychotic daze.

THE STORY OF THE RIVER rises swiftly today. It is a spring in Houston that matches the springs of sunshine and mild temperatures and the rebirth of plants on the river. I cannot sit here, with patio doors open to the green shoots of crepe myrtle, and not let my mind wander back.

The Lower Canyons took me east of the park in wilds where few humans stray. Genuine back country.

On a seven-day, eighty-three-mile float, the river edge and the arroyos were covered with the profuse blossoms of blackbrush acacia and huisache, shrubs and trees that bees dearly love. In one side canyon, I could see a ladder fashioned from tree limbs and wire leading to a huge honeycomb—men love the bees who love the shrubs.

The canyon landscape resembled a fairy-tale setting. Walls glowed like gold at sunset. At Hot Springs Rapids, class 3–4, thermal springs flowed into a series of pools suitable for warm bathing. Just beyond Lady Finger Bend, turrets rimmed the canyon walls as they would castles, towering above a large expanse of white sand and grass that glistened in the morning sun. Swallows performed a dazzling aerial ballet around their cliff dwellings. And, I swear, I found a tiny people's path among these spangled rock walls—and their stone dance floor.

Slanted slightly, it had boulders for seats and places for romantic interludes between jigs.

But this trip through the Lower Canyons was not merely a leisurely, fantastic idyll—it was also tinged with adventure. The danger was telegraphed to us as we entered Upper Madison Falls, where the jagged remains of a canoe poked up from the rocks and made it clear that this was, indeed, a class 4 rapid. We took it gingerly and still ripped the raft's bottom. But a quick repair let us finish our whitewater joyride through this remote world, where the flora and fauna take odd and beautiful twists of their own. The place is just as much home to the Mexican buckeye, a beautiful form of wheat scented with clusters of purplish-pink flowers, as it is to the javelina, the continent's only native pig.

On a rugged, week-long trek, a good cook adds mightily to the vitality of any exploring party. My guide, Dennis Yount of Big Bend River Tours, fell into the proper category. In fact, as the trip progressed, he achieved the stature of chef. For breakfast he mixed chorizo, a garlic sausage, in scrambled eggs or sliced fresh mushrooms into a ham-and-cheese omelet. He emphasized a fresh larder, serving tender, sweet cauliflower with a T-bone steak. And he touched off one evening meal with an original concoction: baked bananas stuffed with cream cheese and chocolate nuggets.

Ah, how sweet is spring.

CHAPTER 2

POETIC DERIVATIVE

A RELATIVE'S LIFE RESEMBLES MINE in the written word and in mental faults. Either it wasn't known, or the family didn't talk about it at the time I first entered the hospital. From what I learned at a panel discussion of doctors, it would have helped in the diagnosis of my illness.

As it was explained to me, the initial psychosis of a manic depressive and of a schizophrenic look similar. A psychiatrist will have something to go on in differentiating the two in the patient if informed of such illness among his relatives.

I would learn years later that I was first called a schizophrenic, which could account for my not getting treatment for manic depression for a decade. Yes, it might have helped, though the drugs that did weren't around.

But even today my genetic interest focuses on Kenneth. Uncle Kenneth. On the paternal side. Leatherwood.

I participated in his eulogy and did not recognize his closeness. I quoted him:

> "The sadness of farewell is good,
> "It speaks of love divine."

HE WROTE POETRY AS A PASTIME, as did his father (my grandfather). I never bothered to take up the habit, but when the first piece of this memoir was compared to poetry, I became more attentive. Here was linkage that swallowed the duels with demons that we had both inherited, the two-edged sword of our genetic makeup.

As river guide Bones would say when talking about the little isolated mountain ranges below the Rocky Mountains, "They are like little chips off the great block." And so were we.

Maybe all along I did reserve a special place for my uncle. In the shared illness of manic depression, I once in a delusion thought of him as Walt Disney. I was playing a record from a 1958 visit to the Disneyland theme park and imagined Kenneth, not Disney, was moderating the tour from the puff of a steam locomotive out of the station to the adventures of a river jungle. This was a strange twist, because a favorite uncle on the maternal side had flown me to the then-new fantasyland.

Uncle Kenneth's medical history pains me. He did not have the benefit of most psychiatric drugs, not even lithium, for most of his nights, and the terror (I will call it that, for that is what delusions usually are, contrary to some learned thought that we patients are enjoying them)—the terror increased with age. I first became aware of his problem when my dad was called late Christmas Eve to retrieve his brother from a country jailhouse near the Trinity River. It wasn't that he was violent, more that he was "out of his head" and a danger driving. No rural hospital was nearby to treat him, so the small jail became a safe haven—as it would for me in one of my later episodes in Oklahoma.

When my family got Uncle Kenneth out of jail the next day, I took the wheel of his car, and he climbed in beside me. He splashed on a cheap cologne to mask the smell of days on the road without a bath.

I made reference to the fact that he should be in a hospital. "Butch, that doesn't become you," he said, irritated. He had, until then called me "Butch" with fondness.

Uncle Kenneth would not have benefited from the rudimentary drugs available then, even if he would have taken them, which he would not. He damned all drugs and doctors, would not take medicine, and certainly would not have stood for the laboratory tests that go with lithium.

Why was he crisscrossing the state? He was looking for an old girlfriend, he said. I could relate later, having stomped through Phoenix and swamping *The New York Times* switchboard on similar quests. In Kenneth's instance (which took place in the early eighties) the lost love dated back to the Depression. He didn't mention his wife of forty years, left alone and apprehensive that particular Christmas.

In finer moments Uncle Kenneth penned poems that, as I said at his graveside service, revealed his values, his religion, and his reverence toward others. Several were read.

"Enduring," he called this one:

. . . And I met so many people

Who like me were searching too,

And we climbed upon a steeple

Just to watch for folks like you.

Thus my patience was rewarded,

And the end reward I gained;

I no longer was retarded —

My happiness no longer feigned.

I had found a thing enduring;
It would never have an end;
It would have the power of curing:
I had found myself a friend.

He received inspiration from nature:

A trip to Aspen leaves you gasping.
And the ski lift finds you grasping,
Not alone the chair you ride in,
But the God we all abide in;
Grasping that His work tremendous,
Huge, colossal and stupendous,
Dwarf the human mind's conception
of God's glorious reception.
. . . We are micro-organisms;
It is He who made the chasms,
It is He who made it all;
From His grace let us not fall.

Dr. Robert Hirschfeld, the chairman of the Department of Psychiatry at the University of Texas at Galveston, was asked, "Does this illness strike creative people such as writers, entertainers, and musicians?"

His answer, at my federal health discrimination trial against *The Houston Post*, was, "There's an increased frequency of bipolar illness [the modern term for manic depression] in such people."

"Why is that?" Steve Petrou, my attorney, asked. "Why does it target some of those creative people?"

"People who are creative go beyond the bounds of the more normal conformity in terms of thinking and in terms of behavior, and there are some psychiatric illnesses where that happens, and certainly bipolar illness is one of those.

"The problem is when it gets completely out of hand, these people are not productive. . . . Kay Jamison recently wrote about the lives of a number of people [who] had bipolar illness. . . . [M]any of these artists or composers would have very productive periods until it got frankly manic, in which case—or would be depressed, in which case—they were not productive at all."

(Kay R. Jamison's book is *Touched With Fire: Manic-Depressive Illness and the Artistic.)*

Uncle Kenneth suffered severe brain damage when he drove in front of an eighteen-wheel truck while manic. He regained only limited recognition during long years in a nursing home and died in 1998. He had written effusively in a narrative poem of family history and of a rosebush planted by his pioneer grandmother in 1882:

Now in comfort I look westward

As my evening shadows lengthen,

And I venture forth one pleading:

I will walk my way in comfort,

Soothed, serene, and without anguish,

If you promise me but only

I'll be buried in Lampasas,

In the Oak Hill Cemetery,

Where grows the Rose of Life Eternal,

There lives the Rosebush Everlasting.

It was a promise kept.

CHAPTER 3

RIDING ROUGH

IT TOOK MEN OF COURAGE and imagination to settle the rangeland of Texas, particularly the mountainous desert country farther west. Asa Jones was such a man. He chose to put a ranch on the edge of the Chihuahuan Desert, in the Big Bend region.

Faced with thirsty livestock, he ran pipes down the towering bluffs of the Lower Canyons to the river. "When I put those 300 ewes on the place," he was quoted, "there was a coyote for every one of 'em, and a bobcat trailing every coyote."

It's still an isolated, tough place to eke out a living. I was able to get a sense of Asa Jones' life from the back of a horse provided by Lynn Carter, operator of Chisos Remuda, the mountain stable in Big Bend National Park, when I visited in the 1980s. He had me mount one of the unregistered quarter horses. He also had a few paints, all accustomed to the high altitude and rocks. "We pride ourselves in our horses for this type of operation," he said.

THE STABLE NESTLED in a mile-high basin in the Chisos Mountains, most of which was once ranchland. The ranchers first worked the Chisos foothills, but by the late 1920s cattle had overgrazed those grasslands. Shortly after the herds were moved onto the highlands, development of the park began. Forty thousand head of stock were ultimately displaced.

Carter and his crews conducted guided horse trips through the mountains the year round, and on a winter day his son Craig rode with me toward the South Rim, the scenic high point of the park. The trail is a wooded, fourteen-mile loop with a vantage of seeing 107 miles of the Rio Grande, including the yawning mouth of Santa Elena Canyon.

Craig and I talked about his relationship with C. M. "Buck" Newsome, a former U.S. Border Patrol officer who ran the Chisos Remuda after leaving his government job. Newsome had hired Craig's father, and he gave Craig his first pony when the kid was three.

An aspiring country and western singer at the time of the ride, Craig borrowed the title of a book by Newsome, *Shod With Iron,* for the name of a song he had written:

> *Shod with iron and ready to ride,*
> *trying to turn the great Rio Grande tide . . .*
> *He rode a big red horse . . .*
> *He was hired to hold back a nation of poor*
> *who were trying to reach out for a bit more . . .*
> *Now time has taken its toll, and the story's*
> *beginning to unfold; the dust has settled*
> *on the trails he rode, but the memories*
> *and stories will never grow old.*

"About the only time I was nervous singing a song was when I sang that one in front of Buck," Craig said. "He never said much about it. He didn't dislike it, or he would have told me."

Newsome's job with the Border Patrol was to apprehend, process, and send back the illegal aliens who cross the river border into Texas, at times like a tide in the Rio Grande. Said Craig, "You see, if I were one of them, I'd be coming across, too. Living over there you just can't get ahead."

We passed through the Laguna Meadows. This time it was a leisurely trip, but Craig and a park ranger had once traversed the three-and-a-half miles of rough terrain in forty minutes—to fight a fire in the meadows. Our horses crossed the charred area, much of which is still barren, but stands of luxuriant native grasses have returned in spots.

Craig has had other adventures in the park, such as the time park rangers chased a mountain lion after a boy was mauled. "I went up there to take them some food and water," he said. "They happened to tree the cat a little bit after I got there." After the lion was killed, Craig brought it out on his horse.

The two of us reached the South Rim about lunchtime. The view was breathtaking, a panorama stretching for unknowable miles to the south. In his book Newsome reports the distance estimate of Ventura Gumboa, a Mexican national who once worked for him: "I asked Ventura how far we were looking across the river into Mexico. He said, '*Senor, como ocho dias a caballa*'" ('Sir, about eight days horseback').

After eating the chicken Craig had packed for lunch, we took the trail to Boot Springs, skirting ice-encrusted springwater creeks as we rode. In April and May this is a gathering spot for birders who want to see the Colima warblers, which migrate from their wintering grounds in Mexico to nest in the Chisos. The tiny warbler is but one of more than 450 species of birds that have been sighted in the park; no other National Park Service area contains so many. At the Boot camp site, all we encountered were a few lively and fat Mexican bluejays.

Just as the Chisos are as far north as the warblers come, some of the flora and fauna here can be found nowhere else in the United

States. And vice versa. This is the last outpost of the ponderosa pine (in Pine Canyon), Arizona cypress and Douglas fir (in Boot Canyon), and quaking aspens (on 7,835-foot-high Emory Peak).

As we returned to the stables, we caught a glimpse of a white-tailed deer—another oddity in the apparent middle of a desert. Deer roam in these mountains the way they did throughout the lowlands and highlands when a moister climate prevailed 10,000 years ago. When the lower elevations dried into desert country, the deer were marooned up here along with the pinyon pines, junipers, and oaks. That's why, in the fall, a horseback rider can catch a glimpse of a white-tailed deer romping through vivid splashes of red and yellow foliage.

The whole Carter family worked the Chisos Remuda. "As far as the labor situation, I should have had a house full of kids," the elder Carter said. He and his wife Cathey had two, Craig and Lynnene. Craig handled an outpost, the Lajitas Livery, for wagon rides and campfire cookouts. Lynnene lent a hand at headquarters. Mrs. Carter grew up in nearby Marathon and couldn't wait to return to this area after moving away as an adult.

"It's home, it grabs you," she said. "I love it. I really do. I got homesick for the mountains. You can turn around two or three times without bumping into anybody." She reflected a moment and added, "When it rains, you freeze to death in July. If you're out in it and get wet, I guarantee your lips will be blue. It's that cool and nice."

Her advice for park visitors: "You've got to get out and do some riding and hiking and looking, and not just drive through, to really appreciate it and see it."

RIDING OUT OF CHISOS REMUDA wasn't adventurous enough for me, so I contacted Mimi Webb-Miller, a free-spirited U.S. citizen who ranched near San Carlos, Mexico. She'd deserted the big cities of Houston and Dallas for the love of a different way of life.

"We're running horseback trips and truck trips for those who would like to come over into Mexico," she said the first day I saw her. "It's in the frontier zone, so a visa isn't required. We have a ranch about eleven miles from Lajitas. We bring people out to the ranch and take them into San Carlos, which is about seventeen miles in. The horseback trips are very diverse."

I fell for her pitch.

As we jostled inside the Bronco along the backcountry bumpy ranch road, Webb-Miller explained the nature of her trips. She hosted people at the ranch and satisfied their fancy, whether in a ride to an abandoned lead and silver mine or to an old frontier fort, called a presidio. Then there was the view from 10,000-foot mountains.

"I originally came out to run a river," said the young blonde, who was on her way to becoming a legend in the Big Bend. "I'm an outdoor person. I fell in love with the country and came out for my first vacation as a single female alone—and ended up coming out about once a month to break the routine of Houston." She moved to Lajitas and worked in its development and at the Trading Post.

"I think it takes a tough person to live here," she said. "Aesthetically, there's a beauty here like the beauty I dealt with when I dealt with art. Life is very simple. It's basically a matter of existing. But I never seem to have time to do all the stuff I want to do out here. I like to go fishing, and I still haven't been fishing. I enjoy ranch life tremendously. Even though I cook on a woodburning stove and make tortillas, I still enjoy working cattle and being out on the ranch itself."

Webb-Miller grew up in Wichita Falls, Texas, and attended Southern Methodist University in Dallas, majoring in art history. She moved to Houston and started guiding groups through museums and commercial galleries, transporting them in her own Checker cab.

That was another time and another place. The day I visited, Webb-Miller was rolling flour tortillas in the rustic kitchen of her Rancho

El Milagro. Light filtered through a small orchard of quince, figs, and peaches into the unscreened windows. The place had no electricity. At night, she said, she burned kerosene lanterns, and thick block walls combined with the 5,000-foot altitude to keep the room cool. Nor did her home have running water inside. Instead, she and her friend Meno Proano had tapped a spring with pipe and a hose. The spring, and several others, fed a creek that tumbled down a narrow valley. I followed it to a forty-foot waterfall that poured into a pool secluded by dense vegetation.

Back in the kitchen, Proano joined in the cooking after a day of planting oats for feed. He rolled out a goat membrane and filled it with sliced kidney and liver, onions, tomatoes, lime juice, and salt—a traditional Mexican dish called burronate. It then went into the Lily-Darling wood stove in the corner of the kitchen to cook for a later meal. For now we would munch on hot tortillas and feast on the rest of the goat. A cat purred underfoot as mariachi sang over a car radio in the background of our conversation.

The next morning we set out for the ruins of the old lead and silver mine. There were no easy trails here, sometimes no trails at all, and cacti slapped our chaps on the entire route across the desert. Oscar W. Williams, surveyor and Harvard lawyer, wrote a letter about a similar 1902 ride. He noted his horse was always slipping, sliding, and lurching on round pebblestones: "I never saw so many round pebbles, apparently waterworn, anywhere except in the beds of creeks and rivers. Yet here they lay in the high lands as well as the low—on the crests of mountains as well as in the hollows of valleys."

We trotted in the vicinity of the Comanche War Trail. Running across the Trans-Pecos region from the northeast to southwest, it split into two forks in the Big Bend. One fork crossed the Rio Grande near Lajitas and continued into Mexico through San Carlos. The other crossed between Santa Elena and Mariscal canyons. Throughout the mid-1800s, aided by late summer rains that filled water holes, the Comanches penetrated deep into Mexico by way of the Lajitas route, taking livestock, housewares, and captives along with them. Slowed by the pirated herd, they returned with their booty via the other fork, which was farther from soldiers at Presidio. The bones of cattle that died en route still litter a trail a mile wide.

Our ride entered San Carlos Canyon, where we splashed through a boulder-strewn creek, from which an aqueduct (following canyon curves) carries water to townspeople. Ranchers have also constructed small rock huts in the canyon to shade the offspring of their goats. We were more straightforward in finding respite from the grinding sun; we found a cool spot under some ferns that grew on an overhang.

After a lunch of steak and potatoes, we ascended to the rim of a side canyon—a precipice that tested the sure steps of our horses. High in the mountains we came to the ruins of a mining community that Webb-Miller believes once was populated by 5,000 people. The adobe and stone hulls of long-vacant buildings sprawl up the mountainsides. As late as the 1950s men labored here, removing, over time, a million tons of ore (primarily for lead) for American Smelting and Refining Co.

The mine did not exist when Williams, the early surveyor, rode to San Carlos. He had, however, previously discovered another lode native to the area, the storyteller Natividad Lujan. Lujan was born in San Carlos, where he lived most of his life. A grudge forced him to move across the river to Texas. He would at times act as guide for Williams and tell of earlier days by the light of a burning sotol (a desert lily) where they camped. His grandfather had worn the uniform of a Spanish soldier and was sent to serve at the San Carlos presidio, an outpost against the Indians. "Here in San Carlos I was born and raised among wild Indians, many of whom lived temporarily in and about the presidio," Lujan said. "When a tribe was in danger from their enemies, they would . . . make a treaty with our people of San

Carlos, in which they would promise to be good to our people of the town and not to rob or kill any of them, no matter what they might do to other peoples; and we would for our part let them live among us.

"The people of Santa Rosalia used to talk hard about us, because some of these Indians while they lived with us went in a war-party to that place, and killed and robbed many of them. But, Señor, we could not stop them when they started out on the warpath, nor did we know where they were going . . . Thus, many kinds of Indians lived among us. I remember when at one time there were among us Kiowas, Comanches, Apaches, Mescaleros, Apaches, Gilenos, Pananas, and Cionabas."

The observations and collected stories of Williams were published as a book, *Pioneer Surveyor, Frontier Lawyer*, in 1968. S. D. Myres edited it with annotations.

San Carlos, with a population of about 2,500, retains much of the layout and character of Williams's time. Williams had asked for a hotel and restaurant and found none. When I visited, there was one tiny restaurant. Stores carried goods necessary to the home, not the few tourists. A church fronts on a pleasant plaza. The aqueduct provides a means to water plants and to wash the main street, which is almost free of vehicle and sign pollution.

The nearby presidio was built by the Spanish as part of a network to guard the northern frontier of New Spain. Troops first occupied it in October 1773. The ruin sits eleven miles southeast of Lajitas on the east bank of San Carlos Creek. The fortification was located there under a plan that placed presidios at 120-mile intervals from the Gulf of California to the Gulf of Mexico. The plan required sites on unobstructed land with good water and pasture; such restrictions resulted in seventeen forts being more closely spaced.

The adobe walls at San Carlos, which rested on a stone foundation, have melted over time into mounds, but they still outline the presidio's shape. Rows of rooms for subordinate officers, soldiers, and Indian scouts backed up to the quadrangular perimeter wall. A chapel was centered in the northwest side. The main entrance presumably was midway in the southwest wall. Soldiers took their stations in diamond-shaped bastions at the north and south corners. A block of rooms built around a patio and projecting into the central plaza may have housed the captain.

When Webb-Miller and I headed back to Rancho El Milagro (and our dinner of burronate), I had a sense that the day of the horse, the day of the Spanish, and the day of the Indian isn't that far distant into the past.

CHAPTER 4

HOSPITAL DAZE

MORNING BROKE HARD in Hermann Hospital on the first day of the first confinement for going mad. Still mired in delusion, I was allowed to rest from the exhaustive pace outside. But a blaring radio brought my horror inside.

The news of the hour was a massive traffic accident on the Southwest Freeway interchange next to the *Houston Post* building. A truck loaded with chemicals had gone off a ramp, and in a chain reaction cars were smashed up. The poisonous vapor from the chemical would soon denude the lush landscape at the newspaper plant, but there was a more immediate, graver concern, and Hobby, the owner, marshaled the staff to the top floor to escape the deadly onslaught.

It's almost transparent what I thought next. I linked this happening to yesterday's concern for the well-being of myself and Hobby. My mother was still at the hospital and said, "I hope [a cousin] isn't involved." And I concluded that the cousin had sent the truck bomb to avenge my conceived treatment at the *Post*.

THE HOSPITAL CALLED OUT its heavy weapons to combat my evil forces. A psychiatrist was assigned, and he ordered a large daily dose of the drug Prolixin. We didn't talk about delusions, which surprised me, for they were still very much my reality. But then again we didn't talk very much at all. I was, of course, green to the process and didn't know the doctor and his couch had been replaced in part by his pills, pharmacology. Still, as my care under that psychiatrist lengthened, I was known to comment with derision that I couldn't talk to my psychiatrist.

I think my experience—indeed, all of my experiences, from the first to latter episodes—underscore my complaint with a degree of legitimacy. I entered Rusk State Hospital in East Texas and said that I had stopped my medication, Depacote, because I could no longer bear the diarrhea that was its side effect. I added that I had often voiced this concern to my doctor. The facilitator was critical of the doctor. "He wasn't hearing you," she said.

In the Houston hospital's arsenal, however, the real talk came in group therapy, usually in the morning.

Evenings I played chess with a staff member.

After three weeks I was well enough to walk across the street to visit the Hermann Park Zoo.

With my head mostly clear, though questioning some of what I had thought, I was free to go home.

Freer still to drive through the western United States for a rendezvous with other Sierra Club canoeists on the Main Eel River in northern California.

And then work. I was welcomed back with handshakes, and a note from Mrs. Hobby saying, "We missed you."

My troubles with employment and my caregivers would come when I slipped several cogs further into involuntary commitments.

CHAPTER 5

GIRL CRAZY

THE 1980S GOT WORSE AND BETTER at the same time. While I explored Texas unsuspecting of the repetitive, vicious nature of my illness, I found a winning combination in female companionship. Some of it was romance.

Mind you, I was in my 40s. The decades before didn't compare, nor have they compared since.

It was a golden dawn, chocolate on chocolate, diamonds forever.

More often than not, the women were in the Unitarian Church and the Sierra Club, both liberal organizations, both of which contained beliefs that embodied common sense, to borrow from the conservatives. Jesus was the son of God as we are all the sons of God. Women and men are equal and play on the same field. The natural world is our sacred trust. Ultimately, I think we saw the environment and God as one.

We dated vigorously. And although the church's minister spoke against sexual freedom, many of these women, and men, exercised it, it being in the days before AIDS made the front pages. It became my last liberation from teen years without parental sex education, that duty passed along to the church. And the church corrupted the meaning of adultery. All sex outside of marriage did not break the Ten Commandments.

Joy.

MY COMPANION PROTESTED that her friends were spending the summer in Colorado while she vacationed in humid East Texas. I quieted her with a ride on a bicycle built for two in Jefferson, Texas, along with the pursuit of other treasures of a grand scavenger hunt in the region.

The hunt was made possible by two books, *The Best of East Texas* and *The Best of East Texas II*, written by Bob Bowman. Although his imprecise directions could be aggravating, they turned a driving tour into a game on a broad scale.

The treasures were both winners and losers, something akin to those discovered in adventure games played on computers. One of the first and easiest discoveries was the East Texas Oil Museum in Kilgore, Texas. The museum's innovative "muddy" boom-town street provided fun insight into what became in the 1930s the largest oil field in the world. The museum was a tribute to Dallas tycoon H. L. Hunt, who made his fortune in the field, and to J. M. "Dad" Joiner, who persevered to drill the discovery well. That well, the Daisy Bradford No. 3, was still pumping.

Country Tavern near Kilgore was the Marfreless watering hole of East Texas. As at the Houston establishment, no sign told what was behind the doors. The secret was truly the best barbecued ribs around. As the guide says, the dark but respectable Gregg County honky-tonk clung "to the northeast elbow of a highway intersection a few miles west of Kilgore."

Being summer, we headed for the "best swimming hole," called Blue Hole in Angelina County. A turn "less than ten miles out of Zavalla" proved difficult to locate because of the lack of a marker on the U.S. Forest Service road. I don't recall why the directions to cross three wooden bridges and turn right didn't work out, but we ended up stymied by a huge mudhole as did friends who earlier followed the guide. When we finally found the swimming hole, the loud radios of youths on the sandstone cliffs surrounding the two-acre lake forced us to turn the swim into a heads-under-water dunking session.

We could feel we were close to the proverbial treasure chest in Jefferson. We rented bicycles near the Excelsior House, the "best country hotel," and took a leisurely ride through a neighborhood studded with Victorian houses. The Victorian period influenced architecture from 1860 to 1900. One of the best examples from the era in Texas is the House of the Seasons at Jefferson. Although it retains a Greek Revival floor plan of a columnar front gallery, central hall, and balanced rooms, the detail is Victorian. A cupola tops off cornices and round-headed windows. A view of the garden through the cupola's red, green, yellow, and blue glass reminds one of the different seasons. The public could tour the Seasons home and others, including the antebellum Freeman Plantation built in 1850. Slaves worked its 1,000-acre cotton and sugar-cane fields.

"Cotton is where the business was" long after the slaves were gone, said Sam Vaughn, who with his brother Tom owned and operated the T. C. Lindsey & Co. general store at Jonesville, or according to understatement in the guidebook, "a few miles east of Marshall." The store came with a gin.

"The size of a cotton farm (in the first half of this century) depended on the size of the family," Vaughn said. "But the government changed the allotments. A family [that] had a 40-acre cotton allotment and was doing the best they could had it cut to three acres."

The gin processed a record 2,976 bales of cotton in 1937. It closed after ginning four bales in 1973.

Cotton had paid the bills for food and supplies of up to 500 families who shopped at the general store, established on the same spot in the mid-1800s. More tourists than area residents probably bought merchandise there when I visited. The shelves were still packed with everything from cheese to clothes, and display space held tools such as the Kelly plow (forged in northeast Texas and no longer for sale).

The store was built in 1922. Sam Vaughn began working there as a bookkeeper in 1928 and bought it ten years later. His brother Torn joined him in 1947. Tom talked of selling out, but he did not wish to chance closing a store special enough to be a part of Disney movies. In a telephone call he got as excited as his brother about the film role of the store, saying the name was changed to Vainer Store when *The Long Hot Summer* was reshot for television with Jason Robards and Ava Gardner in 1985. The place was more than the "best general store" in East Texas. It *was* the treasure chest.

AT THE POINT WHERE THE RIO GRANDE turns from southeast to northeast is a canyon called Mariscal. This is the decisive turn that gives rise to the name, the Big Bend. River runners simply call it The Bend. Here, in the middle canyon of the park, black rock meets white. Limestone slabs of midnight are followed by intriguing imitations of icebergs. Patterns of reflected light swirl on the opposite wall. Low water furnishes another strange twist to our ten-mile passage through this wonderland. When one of our rafts jammed in the rocky shallows, several vaquera, or Mexican cowboys, came to the rescue. Roping the raft, they pulled it downriver on horseback.

Bones was again my guide this trip. He was appreciative that the woman I shared this outing with could wake up early laughing.

In an afternoon rafting through the canyon we saw goldeneye and bufflehead ducks and yellow-rumped warblers. Leatherstem, a plant used by Indians to stop the flow of blood from wounds, grew in an arroyo. So did a nut-bearing guayacan tree. Beavers had parted Bermuda grass to slide into the river. And man had left his mark on the banks, too. A recluse had abandoned icons in a reed hut. Someone else had once operated a wax factory here; its rusty parts remained. Wax makers added the locally abundant candelilla plant to a mixture of water and sulfuric acid to create their product. When the wax floated to the top of the vat, it was scooped off. It went mostly into chewing gum.

THE MOST IMPORTANT CONSIDERATION when hiking trails beyond the Pecos River boils down to water. People haven't adapted to the desert and abutting country as have two of the most frequently seen creatures on the highways, the roadrunner by day and the jackrabbit by night.

The roadrunner puts the sun to work in energy conservation. It lowers its body temperature in the night chill by as much as seven degrees from a normal 101 degrees. At dawn, the bird suns a patch of back skin by raising its feathers and spreading its wings. The skin acts as a solar panel, increasing the roadrunner's temperature without burning energy. The jackrabbit hops into a depression shaded by a bush and radiates heat skyward from its large ears, thus reducing the use of water by removing body heat. Humans, of course, don't grow big ears, and we don't have a lot of feathers. We depend on the evaporation of perspiration to remove excess body heat from exercise and the sun. The water lost through perspiration needs replenishing. You require maintenance of a water level within narrow limits. It is essential for physical and mental efficiency, and ultimately life.

Robert Huggins, the chief naturalist at Big Bend, advised hikers to drink water even if they weren't thirsty. "Warm temperatures and low humidity can be deceiving," he said. "The reason that 94 degrees at 10 percent humidity feels so comfortable is that perspiration evaporates as quickly as it appears, thus keeping your surface skin temperature cool. This can result in rapid dehydration in an individual who feels comfortable and thinks that he hasn't even worked up a sweat."

And water out here is scarce. Virtually no streams cross the trails as they do in Colorado or California, where a person can dip a refreshing cup of water almost at will. The situation limits the backpacker. The pack must contain a reservoir, a gallon of water for each person for each day of the trip—a rule of thumb averaging variations in individuals, topography, and climate. A gallon weighs 8.3 pounds. For a three-day trip that adds up to 25 pounds of water for each back. You can see the limitation. The weight makes more than a long weekend uncomfortable and almost unthinkable.

Otherwise, backpacking looks as easy as putting one foot in front of the other repetitiously. Usually, it is. But in my first adversity in the sport, I lost a young woman figuratively—and literally—on a trail in Guadalupe Mountains National Park. Worse, she panicked, and we sideswiped disaster.

Later, I would hunt out pages on wilderness survival previously given scant attention in fifteen years of on-and-off backpacking. A surprising number of books about backpacking simply warn against panic. Many ignore the basic procedures that I also ignored which led to trouble. Even the authoritative walker Colin Fletcher admitted to never really giving the matter of survival the thought it seems to deserve.

Fletcher noted that "this kind of 'survival' mostly amounts to 'experience.'" He quoted an adviser on the subject as saying, "What it generally amounts to, anyway, with inexperienced people, is simply not giving in to terror. That's what usually happens: ignorance—then panic . . ." My tale of woe illustrates the point. I share it for emphasis and to warn that, as basic as walking is, in rough terrain with a house on your back, there is more to it.

The Guadalupe Mountains are, collectively, one of the more rugged places in the state. You can climb to the highest point in Texas, Guadalupe Peak (8,751 feet), and gaze on salt flats a mile below. More of the largest known fossil reef appears here than anywhere else. El Capitan, a 2,000-foot cliff, rises dramatically as you approach the park from the south.

Sara (not her real name) and I averaged 1.3 miles an hour in a late-afternoon climb from the car parked at Pine Springs Campground to Pine Top, a primitive campsite up four miles of steep switchbacks. We packed four gallons of water (35 pounds, 4 ounces, including containers) for the 48-hour outing. A two-gallon plastic container of distilled water found at grocery stores fits perfectly in the bottom of a pack. The other water dangled on the outside of both packs in four, quart-and-a-half bottles. For meals, the entrees included lamb curry and rice, sweet and sour pork with rice and shrimp creole (all freeze dried), and barbecued oysters and salmon (canned). By the way, canned goods don't matter so much when you're already packing water for dehydrated food.

My companion had shown commitment to nutrition and readily agreed to draw up the menu. She bagged and labeled each meal. In addition, she got ingredients to mix for gorp (a trail snack combining nuts, sunflower seed kernels, raisins, and coconut) and cereal at a health food store. Frankly, the cereal tasted like twenty-two kinds of birdseed. But there was no denying my companion's fitness.

Sara had not backpacked before, only a trial day hike with full pack before the trip. She outdistanced me on the trail the second day, however, with a drive that approached macho. Thus was born the first mistake. I take it easy, smell the pine-scented air often, and let a less-than-fit body plod along. I ignored rules of the path, which go something like this: Travel at the speed of the slowest, keep each other in sight, and plan your route carefully before setting off. In the thick forests of East Texas, these rules become second nature. You can lose sight of a trailmate at fifty yards there and lose the path in less distance. But in good weather, on a rocky trail along a dry gully arched with trees, with a bright and physically tough companion, I relaxed the guardian role dictated by my experience. It was not a conscious decision, just something felt—the opposite extreme of caution felt with a child. And I lost her. She vanished, and in less than two miles, I reached a junction that pointed the way to fear.

We had spoken of having lunch at the Mescalero campsite, mentioned on trail signs, without consulting a map. The junction marker showed it .9 miles in the opposite direction of Bush Mountain, our next campsite. Translated, that's about 1.5 hours out of the way. And that's the first of three reasons I decided my companion didn't head to Mescalero. Almost no one with a pack 25 percent overweight would travel such an extra distance for lunch. Experience on the shakedown hike and in planning this one also told me she was adamant against backtracking, and going to Mescalero meant later backtracking to the junction. Finally, she wanted to arrive in camp before dark, by about 4, and that was hardly possible by extending the walk. I headed for Bush Mountain. What was outside of reason for me, though, was not for her. As I later learned in certain terms, Mescalero meant lunch to her, and a junction was no red flag urging her to wait.

The second mistake, where water would play its hand, was in the making. My companion reacted like most people alone in wilderness for the first time. She panicked. The couple who "saved" her roughly two hours after she and I parted company found her peeling prickly pear pads for water. Unfortunately, the tough task of getting water from any cactus requires energy (water is used) and questions the value of the extraction of water. My companion still had three cups plus the mobility and daylight to walk back to water at the trailhead. She might be a little thirsty at the end. But, as she explained after the ordeal, "I thought I was going to die." Sara had even reflected on the lack of a will.

Indeed, tragedy might have struck—not because her physical situation was insecure but because inexperience had nurtured panic. She had no way of knowing from past adventures how long she could function efficiently with little water under climactic conditions including mild spring temperatures and high winds. She was unlikely to have read charts showing a healthy person can live a couple of days with a quart of water in even extremely high temperatures if she or he stays in shade and walks at night.

Survival odds diminish with extreme fear. Such fear may block the ability to work and concentrate on the best survival strategy, Bernard Shanks, a former ranger, has said. He adds that it is not surprising that a lack of water outside a protective environment produces a sensation of fear. Panic that is difficult to control with companions becomes nearly impossible when alone. Accidents are likely. Those less prepared will be openly frightened and wander about aimlessly.

Unexpected situations, however, do occur. The classic tale of Hugh Glass, an early Western fur trapper, unfolds with his horrible mauling by a grizzly bear deep in Indian country. One of his two companions was the young and inexperienced Jim Bridger, who became a legendary guide. Glass was unconscious and apparently fatally injured when the other two left with his rifle to protect themselves. He regained his senses and realized he was abandoned. Unable to walk because of his wounds, seething with hatred and a determination to kill his former partners, he crawled to a trading post 200 miles away. Glass lived because of that anger. He later forgave his companions, a gesture not coming my way in the score of years since the ill wind blew.

CHAPTER 6
CHICO'S TOO

WHEN STEVE FROMHOLZ and his wife passed in a raft on the Rio Grande, he boasted about his success in marriage. "I married my best friend," he said.

I appreciate where he was coming from, for I lived with my best friend a half year or less and look back not with regret so much for the brevity but with awe at being served a full glass of wine.

I think Jenny (not her real name) brought pure fun in the door. That's why I welcomed her where no other had come.

I was forty-seven, she thirty-seven. Age never mattered. Oh, maybe she had an extra-playful touch with Chico, my proud Boston terrier, and maybe she had extra spunk as a mate, but she never indicated I was pulling her down.

It became a failing, but for once I didn't mention my mental health. I had changed doctors in order to receive lithium for what he was first to call my illness, manic depression. He said I would most likely not be hospitalized again. I looked to a future with Jenny without worry.

IN OUR GETTING-TO-KNOW-YOU DANCE, she sent a wave of chatty, sometimes witty, letters:

"Carl, I can't get my mind off you today—you're turning into an addiction! But maybe if I write my feelings down, I won't call you so often.

"By the way, are you planning to publish your journal this summer after you get in shape at the Y!! Oh, did I remind you never to let me tell you what to do???

"Hey, you're fun to be with, and to talk to. Thanks for being such a good friend—so soon."

After that I poured the coals on our favorite pursuit, adventure travel. The result was frenetic but not manic, not at the start anyway.

We went first to Kingston Hot Springs, the place upriver where Big Bend residents go to get away from it all. The ranch road out of Marfa was a spectacular drop through the towering white bloom of yuccas to the "hideaway," and for a few dollars we soaked in a hot spring in our room.

The next "event" was also my idea, a loop through the Old South with thirty-seven miles of backpacking from the trailhead of the Appalachian Trail in Georgia. It treated us to a first love, crimson sunsets silhouetting the ranks of small mountains, not at all like the behemoths out West. Water played a sonata—from the waterfall at the trailhead to the small trailside springs for drinking water. Orange and yellow wild azaleas flourished.

After that Jenny took off on her own for a long-planned adventure solo. She would camp for three months in the West as a single woman traveling alone. Bundles of letters arrived as she in free rein and wild abandon pitched her tent from Arkansas to Wyoming.

Her only gruff words had been over that tent. I had put a dirty boot inside, and she fussed about the housekeeping. On her own she didn't have that worry. And on her own she found a cowboy with a horse blanket. Like age, that didn't matter with us. We held tolerance in an open relation most holy.

She didn't mention the cowboy in her letters, nor for a while when she returned. But when he didn't write, she let me know her hurt.

Jenny came home to chaos. I had finished remodeling my condo, which she thought too crowded with furniture. But we took off for New England for the fall foliage with me manic. I shiver at my lunacy. On the north end of the Appalachian Trail, I tried to climb a rock face with a backpack in a blinding snowstorm. In the tavern that night, I joked that we had gone end to end on the trail in the same year.

The delusions were raking my mind. Jenny and I were no longer in unison. I wouldn't, for instance, give her the keys to the rental car in New England. Somehow, we made it back. The outdoors and a similar faith were no longer ties that bound. Sex flew my cage, contrary to a notion that in mania sex is manna.

I don't know if I asked her to leave or she left on her own. I hardly noticed her moving out. She did take me to Huntsville to see my new doctor, who at my insistence wrote a note to my employer saying I could work. I handed it to my supervisor, who said he had done me a disservice.

Then I took off. The trigger was June's (not her real name) return of a bag of toys at the office that I had given her daughter. I thought someone was going to kill her and me, so I ran—all the way to California—in a watershed psychotic collapse.

The truckers on the long haul out Interstate 10 drove marvelous lighted rigs. Lights fueled my mania. I had seen Christmas lights dance in a starry night outside my Fort Worth hotel on a previous trip. This go-around Chico was in the car, and we made it almost nonstop to Los Angeles. When we entered downtown, the smog was terrible, and I called a newsman friend. When he didn't answer, I left a message saying he was failing in his responsibility to clean the air. Then I bought Chico a hot dog at a mall and carried him through hordes of street people back to the car.

We headed toward home, until I decided to check into a tennis resort outside Santa Fe. The pro accepted my challenge, and the lodge a piece of roadside art. Yes, wacky. In town I paced in a park where I thought the new capitol of the nation would be. Then I continued onward to the shambles at home.

Jenny had, of course, moved out, but she did not move on. She stayed my friend through two more psychotic episodes within the year, and for four wobbly years after that. In the course of that time, she moved to Sacramento.

Chico was another matter.

The California bust was his last great adventure. In a later mania, I parked in a dark driveway one night, exhausted. I rolled out on the ground clutching my and Jenny's little friend and then let go. He headed, his dark coat blending in the night, for a drainage ditch. I lost sight, and I lost him.

I don't remember my former housemate having much to say about the loss, probably out of kindness. However, later, when Chica Tres jumped out of a cardboard box full of pups and into my arms for keeps, she reprimanded me. "It's not fair to the animal," she said.

CHAPTER 7
OUT WEST

THE ODYSSEY HAD GAINED STEAM. An adventure travel business was incorporated, following its route, and stories about it appeared in The Houston Post's Sunday magazine. "You reach more readers this way than with a book," my dad said, pleased.

The van travel venture produced, if not a profit, satisfied customers. One wrote me recently, after all these years "We still say thank you, Carl, for the wonderful trip you planned in '87," said Mrs. Andrew Korinda of Boonton, NJ. "I recently read two books about Texas. *The Gates of the Alamo* by Stephen Harrigan and *The Borderland* by Edwin Shrake. I was go glad you had introduced us to so many of the places in both books."

The first tour, in two vans, filled up immediately thanks to a picture of Longhorns publicizing it in *The New York Times*. Some 200 readers phoned for information, including the Korindas, who were on the tour the next year.

The Other Side of Texas business had been the joint brainchild of Nancy Landau, whose reputation in the field would grow as her trips spread worldwide, and yours truly. We were returning from the San Juan Mountains of Colorado, near the headwaters of the

Rio Grande, and we conjured a route through the Hill Country and western Texas.

A travel writer paying his way on that first trip thought we should have limited it to western Texas. He had a point.

Man and beast have roamed the Chihuahuan Desert for centuries.

Normally, they coexist peacefully, but after a mountain lion mauled an eight-year-old boy in the Chisos Mountains, I tracked down Doug Waid, a doctoral student conducting a study on lions in Big Bend National Park for his thesis. News accounts had said it was the first such attack recorded in the park's forty-year history.

"Well, there are a few other instances where lions interacted with people," Waid said as we sipped a beer in his desert headquarters below the mountains. "I know of one case where a lion is reported to have bitten the cuff of the trousers of a ranger at the park, and that lion was dispatched."

The encounter between boy and beast was, of course, more sobering. If the stepfather had not intervened, it could have been a fatal tragedy. Later, the attack lion was tracked and captured with aircraft and dogs. Hair found in the large intestine confirmed its offense.

Waid had done the necropsy on the lion, the equivalent of an autopsy on a human. He raised the specter that that lion was not born and raised in the park. "Looking at the pads on the feet, it did appear to me that this lion hadn't spent that much time in rugged country," he said. "The pads . . . were in excellent condition. A twenty- to twenty-four-month-old lion can't walk around this rough country and have feet that are brand new."

By comparison, the feet of a year-old male he had caught were callused and the pads flattened. He noted the worn feet of other adult lions, but said this one's pads were clean, black, and very full. Also, except for a small hole on one foot where it might have stepped on a thorn, this lion showed no callus buildup or scarring.

"I have no proof that this was not a park lion," Waid said. "Maybe this is a lion that learned how to walk on grass."

Is the theory that someone released his pet in the park more realistic? I asked. "That's a theory. It's a good theory, but that's all it stands as," he emphasized. "I would speculate that there is a good possibility that that's the case."

Why had it attacked? "I have no idea," Waid said. "It certainly wasn't hungry. It had fed on a deer. A quarter mile from the attack site, we found a white-tailed doe about eight years old. The kill . . . was a real mess. This suggests to me that it was done by an inexperienced cat."

In the course of Waid's studies, a mother lion and her male cub had been captured briefly for collars to be attached. He and I had gone into the mountains earlier that afternoon to monitor by radio the different frequencies the collars transmitted. The lions, also known as cougars and panthers, normally are reclusive and stay away from humans. I wondered at our chances for seeing one.

"Well, we saw one yesterday," Waid said, as he and an assistant, Mike Davin, cut off the man-made trail. "We were real clever. We got pictures of her while she was sleeping down in a wash. We watched her for about twenty minutes. Usually, we don't get to see them. They are the same color as everything."

The radio produced a tock, tock, tock. "It sounds like their signal is coming from over the top of the hill," Waid said. "He was in here yesterday, and she left. Now she has come back and is still in the same area. It suggests that they have a kill in here, or it is a very good hunting place, and they are anticipating a kill."

Tock, tock, tock. "I think we will go ahead and move up a little higher. It seems like they are both on that hill. To really get in on them, we will have to go up behind that ridge and drop down."

The terrain was rocky and covered with the spiny desert plant lechuguilla as well as trees and brush. It was indeed hard to believe the cat that attacked the boy could have been in the area long. We moved up intently.

Tock, tock, tock. "Up on the other side of this ridge," Waid said in a hushed voice. "Get on top and do a radio check down. It being a nice warm day, they may be taking advantage of the sun."

The cub's signal came strong and continuous. "It suggests he is stationary—right out in the open where the land or vegetation doesn't interfere with the signal. There's enough relief that it would be broken if he were moving." For all the intensity and suspense, however, we could not see the big cats that day.

THE PARK PRESENTS plenty of space for both lions and man to roam. Its 801,163 acres furnish a habitat for 1,200 kinds of plants, 75 of mammals (most of them nocturnal and not observed by visitors), 55 reptiles and, as mentioned earlier, 450 species of birds. About 350,000 people crowd in with the wildlife annually, although "crowd in" hardly applies where that figures out to two persons an acre spread over the year.

Naturalists hold interpretive programs at amphitheaters in the peak-rimmed, 5,400-foot Chisos Mountains Basin and on river lowlands of the Rio Grande. Overnight facilities include campgrounds near the theaters and Chisos Mountains Lodge, which faces spectacular changes of colors as the sun sets in the break in the peaks called the Window.

Spring arrives early with a slow succession of cacti blooms beginning in late February and lasting throughout the year. "This picture of giant dagger yuccas was taken last spring at Dagger Flat," a volunteer naturalist said one evening during a slide show accompanied by a guitarist. "One of the flower stalks can weigh as much as 70 pounds and have as many as 1,000 flowers. And these flowers are the size of lilies."

A small health resort operated on a Rio Grande river bank here before it was parkland. Beginning in 1909, J. O. Langford welcomed guests to hot baths. The Mexican Revolution interrupted his enterprise, but he returned in 1927 to build a motel and general store. Texans and Mexicans came from as far as one hundred miles to trade and pick up mail. The springs of 105-degree mineral water were advertised as the fountain of youth that Ponce de Leon failed to find. It was thought to cure rheumatism, indigestion, diabetes, alcoholism, and liver troubles. Maggy Smith ran the store after Langford sold out in 1942. She also delivered babies, lent money, and married couples. The store was closed, and the output of the springs is less, but people still come to soak.

REX IVEY, sitting before a mesquite fire in his home, was telling about how he got the Lajitas Trading Post at Lajitas. He hadn't wanted the store, he said, but won it in a wax war. As Ivey told it, a competitor in the buying of candelilla wax tried to force him out of business by raising the price paid Mexicans who brought the wax across the border at Lajitas. The man wanted to monopolize the trade and was willing to pay the same amount as he collected for the wax in New York. This would keep Ivey from making a profit, too, since the Mexicans would sell only for the top market price. The man planned to outlast Ivey.

"It made me mad," Ivey said. "In about a week I went to Chihuahua. I leased 2,000 acres in Mexico across the river from Lajitas and put up iron gates with locks on them. Wax trucks couldn't go to Lajitas then."

The trucks had to travel upriver to Ivey property, where he bought practically all the wax. "When we weighed and paid for it, we weighed it right and paid them (the Mexican producers) right," he said. "The other fellow had been robbing them on scales, and they found that out by trading with us. They told him they thought it would be a whole lot better for his health if he didn't spend any more nights down there at Lajitas. And scared the hell out of the old fellow."

Ivey ran into his competition in Alpine and struck a deal on the street. He would buy eight sections at Lajitas and sell the other man five of them. "He signed it. I kept all the sections on the river and let him have the dry country. He didn't have one drop of water on the river."

The candililla trade was Ivey's then, after 1948, as far as Mexico was concerned. And so was the Lajitas Trading Post. "I paid one Mexican a little over $33,000 in American money," he said, noting a deal struck at Pantera in Big Bend park. "He bought a $1.98 handbag that we sold, put all the money in the bag with his .45, and went back across the river."

Ivey's son Bill, who grew up in Lajitas when it was owned by his father, was leasing the adobe store when we talked. He believed it was built about 1915. "It's kind of a childhood dream, really," Bill Ivey said. "Ever since I could reach the candy counter, I wanted to work in the store. I do enjoy it down here. It's 300 percent more work than I thought it was."

People came across the river then to shop and mingle. Bill, who earned a degree in finance and economics from Texas A&M, recorded credit in an antiquated revolving file. He sold everything from nonprescription drugs to wash tubs and piñatas. "I'm using that degree," he said. "Along with the store, I found I'm not just the storekeeper. I get called on for medical services, veterinarian services, legal services. I'm postmaster half the time. You name it. I do some of it along with the banking. There's no bank. The nearest bank is Presidio."

An oddity penned outside pushed up its own beer tab. Clay Henry, a 130-pound black mountain goat, liked to guzzle longnecks. "He came with the store," Bill said.

Bill leased from Walter Mischer of Houston, who developed Lajitas as a combination small-scale resort and movie set. The little town boasted a flat, virtually treeless nine-hole golf course with thick grass greens on the river bank and a commendable desert museum with dioramas of animal life, an arboretum identifying desert plants, and historical and geological exhibits. New storefronts on a dusty main street housed a drug store, mercantile, hotel, restaurant, and saloon, and accommodated the shooting of western films. Restorations included the Opry House, once a school and now an exhibition center for artists; an inexact likeness of the old church; and the Calvary Post Motel on the foundation of an Army camp.

Lajitas bustled with U.S. troops and cattle traders after the Mexican Revolution exploded in 1911. The soldiers were stationed in response to guerrilla bands on the border who raised concern in Texas when they attacked Ojinaga, Mexico—upstream from at least twenty vulnerable Big Bend ranches. Doroteo Aranga, better known as Francisco (Pancho) Villa, received much of the blame as the bloody raids continued on small Mexican towns and extended to the ranches.

Villa's men may have patronized the Trading Post. It's possible, too, that the rebels moved a half million head of stolen cattle across the Rio Grande in exchange for gold to buy arms and ammunition. They dealt with speculators who saw a cheap avenue into the cattle business. Trades often occurred on a neutral island in the middle of the river at Lajitas, says Virginia Madison in *The Big Bend Country of Texas.*

"Some of the strangest and largest cattle trades in history took place on that island," she writes, "with Texas traders squatted on bootheels opposite mustachioed Mexican revolutionists or bandits, a handkerchief spread between them, its corners weighted with rocks. Thousands of head of cattle waited on the island while the traders stacked gold coins in the handkerchief and drove the best bargains they could. The Mexicans were fighting for a cause, and they were desperate for money. The Texans had the money; their position was protected by guns (the bluffs on the Texas side overlooking the river were lined with nests of machine guns and rifles); and no one doubts that they drove shrewd bargains."

It is doubtful that Gen. John J. (Blackjack) Pershing and his lieutenant, George S. Patton, were stationed at the cavalry post, as some claim, to put down Villa and his gang. The history books say Pershing chased after Villa from El Paso by way of Columbus, N.M., and penetrated deeply southward into Mexico in the Punitive Expedition of 1916. U.S. troops in the Big Bend during the revolutionary unrest did headquarter at Camp Lajitas, a subpost of Camp Marfa. The community had achieved designation as a port of entry substation and as a fourth-class post office. But with peace, it reverted to a collection of families farming irrigated plots along the river and running milk goats in the hills. By 1940 the census was 10.

It was the small population and wildlife that store boss Rex Ivey came west for in the first place, in 1929. "I've been here and on the river ever since," he said. "I liked the country because it is big and open, and then there wasn't anybody living down on the river much. It was a wide-open world." He kept a doctor's appointment in Houston a half-century later, but his heart stayed in the Big Bend. "Too many goddamn idiots that will run over you, in a hurry and don't know you, and don't want to know you," he said of Houston. "Hell, I'm a country boy. And a fellow that's raised out in this big country will get run over and killed in that damn place, and why die in Houston? I'd rather be dead on a mountain than be dead in Houston."

Ivey built a rock house on a hill by the river after he moved to Lajitas. "All down there was solid beavers," he said. "You could hear them playing and jumping in that water all the time . . . I came as a fur buyer. One of the things you could make a little money on was beaver."

The Iveys bought a favorite haunt of mine, the ghost town of Terlingua, in 1984. Thirteen miles east of Lajitas toward the national park, it was once a quicksilver (mercury) mining community. One may slip back to that time while watching a full moon from the porch of the 1908 mining store, or by walking through adobe ruins to the cemetery.

Howard E. Perry, a yachtsman from Chicago and later Portland, Maine, collected millions from this quicksilver mine as an absentee owner during World War I. The liquid metal was extracted from cinnabar, a red ore. It went primarily into the production of blasting caps for explosives. The mine became the second largest producer in the nation behind one in California. As many as 3,000 people lived in adobe huts next to the shafts. Adobe and rock huts sprawled in the hills around a chapel, school, dance hall, theater, a mansion for Perry's rare visits, and the store.

During the mining years, Robert Cartledge, general manager, served as justice of the peace for Precinct 4 in Brewster County. When I first visited Terlingua in 1982, Sadi Jo McKinney upheld tradition and dispensed justice from the general manager's office. Her husband, Billy Pat, wore the badge of constable, and the McKinney family ran the town. "We have about the same problems they have anywhere else," Pat said, slapping at a fly with a swatter. "But we don't have as many of them. We don't have as many people." He estimated 150 residents for the area. During one of our conversations, a woman dressed in shorts and hiking boots entered with a small boy and a complaint. Neighbors' goats were eating her fruit trees.

As was the case when the mine was active, suspects in felonies, such as drug smuggling, ended up in a one-room jail to await transport to Alpine, eighty-two miles to the north. Other than felons have stayed there. Cartledge reportedly pondered the case of a young couple who threatened to elope if he did not marry them. The prospective bride's parents pleaded with him to prevent the elopement. He took action calculated to satisfy both parties: He stopped the eloping couple and locked them together overnight in the jail.

Kenneth B. Ragsdale tells of the past in *Quicksilver, Terlingua and the Chisos Mining Company* and quotes one oldtimer as saying, “We had a good life. We made our fun.”

Residents continued to make their fun into the ’80s. Fromholtz, the Austin singer, with some help from his Terlingua friends, cooked up a little spoof of the Chili Cookoff started there and named it the Cookie Chilloff. The annual winter event featured refrigerated cookies and storytellers. Most dished out tall tales, but not Hallie Stillwell, the owner of a ranch east of the park. Her marvelous stories recounted the truth of bygone days as she remembered it.

“One of my favorite stories,” she said, “is about a car race that happened in Marathon in the early teens. My husband Roy had bought a Hudson Super 6, and he thought it was about the finest car going, and it was. That’s the reason I married him.

“Cecil Adams, one of the other ranchers there, had bought a Buick,” Stillwell said. “So they got into an argument about which car could run the fastest. They were the closest of friends, and there was no bloodshed. They decided to run a race in Marathon and picked a day. They would just make a straight beeline from the west end of town over to a factory—good, straight road by the shipping pens, no stickers or brush.

“They got up early that morning. The favorite bootlegger had come to town with a supply of tequila and sotol. They had to keep this bootlegger going, so they began to imbibe on these good drinks. And they were making bets. Gambling went on all day long.

“It was getting late in the evening. They decided they had better start the race. In the meantime, a medicine show had come to town. The medicine man set up in the road by the stock pens. Well, here came the two automobiles in the race, everybody trailing along behind. They were going so fast they didn’t see the tent with all the medicine. They couldn’t go around so they went through tent and all, scattering medicine and pots and pans (all items for sale).

"The old man came out. He was mad. He was raving. He said, 'I'm going to sue you.' My husband said, 'Just calm down—I'm the sheriff here.' And Adams said, 'And yeah, I'm the county attorney.' They said, 'Here, take a drink of this sotol. You'll feel a little bit better about this.'

"He took a drink. He said, 'I've just got to have some law here.' Ike Gerley said, 'Well, I'm the county judge here, have another drink.' That went on for quite some time.

"The racing crowd decided they would just have to fix all the stuff back. So they put the tent back, and the medicine on the shelves, and hung up the pots and pans. After a little bit, the medicine man said, 'Give me another drink of sotol. Back up and run through her again.'"

TO A TEXAN, the mere idea of something called "The Art Museum of the Pecos" sounds like a contradiction in terms. But it is by no means a joke. This is serious business, conducted by serious folks. But on this sunny afternoon in Marfa, a visit to the museum still leaves me chuckling about the riddle this place will provide anthropologists of the future. The Society of Antiquaries of London surely had the proverbial picnic at Stonehenge compared to what future excavators of this museum at the upper limits of the desert will encounter.

Here, in a field populated by a herd of forty antelope, are clusters of concrete boxes strung out for more than half a mile in mathematical sequence from north to south. If those future anthropologists do their work well, they will discover fifteen such groupings of boxes, all made of preformed concrete, all 2.5 meters high and 5 meters wide. Each grouping is considered a piece of sculpture and contains from two to six boxes. The sculptor was Don Judd.

"Don Judd's work is principally involved with the surface qualities of objects—angles, end relationships—so these pieces change over the course of the day. The light and the shadows on them change," curator Suzan Campbell explained. "George Cisneros [the San Antonio-based composer of experimental New Music] told me he has composed music using Don's work as an inspiration because of the intervals and the rhythms and the patterns. That's one way to look at this kind of work. Look at it more musically."

Even if the anthropologists figure out that this was sculpture for an art museum, not a temple aligned for earth worship, they may still miss the fact that civilization compromised with nature here. Seventeen pieces were planned. "But there is a bump down at that end of the field," Campbell said, "and we didn't want to take the bump down."

Campbell, who was showing me around the institution before its planned 1986 opening, referred to Judd as a minimalist. Since I had read Judd's commentary in *Art in America* magazine, in which he wrote that the label "minimal" is meaningless in all ways, I questioned the use of the word on his home base. "He doesn't like the term," Campbell said, "but he doesn't get to decide, does he, any more than Monet decides he doesn't want to be called an impressionist? What would he want to be called? An artist. But twentieth-century art, in addition to being interested in art, is interested in ideas. This century gave birth to the series of "isms" that we all know and hate so much. But you have to have some kind of vocabulary to talk about it, you have to have a way to categorize art historically."

Judd's most significant work, his trademark, is his boxes. They sit on the ground or floor without the pedestals of traditional sculpture. Wrote Michael Ennis in *Texas Monthly* magazine: "Judd always opened up the boxes by leaving off the top or sides or using Plexiglas. Instead of hiding an inert core, as a traditional bronze or marble sculpture did, the interior volume of the box became an integral part of the piece. The boxes concealed nothing. Here was the absolute culmination of modernism, an art object that represented only what it was—form, volume, color."

So there I was in a field where the antelope play discussing Minimalism with the curator of an art museum. And somehow, in the barren reaches of West Texas, Minimalism didn't seem so out of place.

Campbell explained that the museum actually houses another one hundred of Judd's aluminum boxes in two buildings elsewhere in the area. It would be marvel enough that Judd, a former New Yorker, had selected an abandoned West Texas calvary post and a former warehouse in downtown Marfa to display art work. But he also included exhibits of three other celebrated and influential artists of the last quarter century: John Chamberlain's crushed auto-body sculptures, Dan Flavin's fluorescent light sculptures, and abstract expressionist Barnett Newman's prints.

"The frequent question I am asked is, 'Why Marfa? It's nowhere,'" Campbell said. "Well, New York City is nowhere if you live in Texas, because the hopes of most of these folks ever getting to New York City to do the galleries scene is one in a million. I don't think you should have to be lucky enough or wealthy enough to live in New York City to enjoy original art. Reproductions aren't art. I believe that in the United States we are seeing a dispersion of art throughout the country."

That notwithstanding, Marfa (pop. 2,466) represents a considerable extreme. Road miles between this town and the state's cultural centers of Houston and Dallas number about the same as those between San Francisco and Boise, Salt Lake City and Phoenix, Chicago and Little Rock, New York and Cincinnati.

"This is not a community museum in the strict sense because it is the work of internationally known artists, and the purpose of the museum is collection in depth and support facilities to allow serious scholarship," Campbell said. "We don't draw our audiences locally, necessarily, but we're not against that at all.

"I like to compare it to the McDonald Observatory up at Fort Davis [about an hour's drive away]," Campbell said. "It is a serious installation that has a rather esoteric purpose. Not a lot of people understand astrophysics. But I love to go to the observatory and listen to their talks and be amazed by the size of the telescope. I love to be there even though I don't know anything about it.

"This place, even though it is intended for serious scholarship, should offer something for everyone," she said. "We're never going to be a survey museum where we have one Picasso, and one this and that. Other museums in Texas do that very well, including Dominique de Menil's new museum in Houston. That's an amazing collection. But we have a significant collection of art, and we will have enough interpretation and education that people should be able to get something out of it."

Interestingly, this museum was being funded by the Dia Art Foundation, which is run by Heiner Friedrich of New York and his wife, Philippa de Menil, the daughter of Dominique and John de Menil.

Millennia from now, when the museum has long been a puzzle void of human care, one creature will no doubt survive: the antelope. The species has lived as a native of North America for a million years, grazing in vast numbers alongside bison at the dawn of the continent's exploration. And though their numbers have declined sharply because of overhunting, the antelopes have rebounded through conservation to acceptability as game animals. It is more accurate to call these animals pronghorns since their species, *Antilocapra americana*, differs from the antelope of Africa and Asia and is truly a survivor, outlasting by thousands of years other pronghorn species. It is the only species within its genus, which is the only genus within the family *Antilocapridae*.

Frankly, the museum's pronghorns were the first I had got much of a look at. Others roam widely in the grasslands above the desert floor around Marfa, but they are fast, the fastest animals in the nation. Residents in the area had pointed them out to me, and they had sprinted away at speeds up to forty-five miles an hour. The young are able to outrun a man by the time they are four days old. Curiously, pronghorns refuse—or lack the ability—to jump fences as low as three feet, which is about the height of the one confining them at the museum.

As for esoteric art on the edge of the Chihuahuan Desert, generally speaking there is nothing new under the West Texas sun. To the east, near Del Rio, ancient Indians painted pictographs and chipped petroglyphs into the natural rock shelters that they inhabited. Pecos River culture existed from around 8,000 years ago—near the end of the Pleistocene ice age—to 600 A.D., long before the Comanches and Apaches.

Rock art appears in some form on every continent. It preceded the development of a genuine alphabetic system of writing. The most distinctive, probably the earliest, and surely the longest continued tradition of rock painting in Texas, and perhaps in the New World, centered around the junction of the Pecos River with the Rio Grande, says W. W. Newcomb, Jr. in *Rock Art of Texas Indians.* Newcomb, director of the Texas Memorial Museum in Austin, viewed petro-glyphs and pictographs as irreplaceable and relatively rare human documents that “reveal much about the ways of ancient men . . . illustrate how a vanished, nameless people perceived of themselves and their world, their relation to God and to each other, and their fantasies and fears.”

Seminole Canyon State Historical Park offers a guided walking tour of this Indian art in the Fate Bell Shelter. The rock depictions include many shamans—priests or medicine men—whose followers believed they alone could influence good and evil spirits. Another painting, this one accessible only by water and under a rock overhang near the mouth of Seminole Canyon, gives prominence to a cougar.

The atlatl, a weapon used before the bow and arrow, is frequently depicted on the walls. The weapon consisted of a dart and a two-foot stick for throwing the dart. Upon impact, the main dart shaft would fall away from the hardwood foreshaft and stone point, leaving the victim unable to pull the dart out.

The artwork at Seminole Canyon is colorful, with red dominating. It shows up in 51 percent of the murals, black in 25 percent, according to the pioneer work of the archaeologist A.T. Jackson, *Picture-Writing of Texas Indians.* Orange, yellow, white, and green complete the color range. Minerals most often supplied the paints. Red came from hematite or ocher, and sometimes cinnabar; black from a manganese compound; white from kaolin, gypsum, or barite; yellow from ocher or limonite; and green from copper oxide.

I also took a boat up seventy-eight-mile-long Lake Amistad to visit other sites. Amistad, a beautiful international reservoir often swept by high winds, engulfs the confluences of the Pecos and Devils rivers with the Rio Grande. Jackson notes that a quarter of the state's pictographs appear in Val Verde County, site of Lake Amistad.

Forrest Kirkland, an artist whose copies of rock paintings appear with Newcomb's text, says the effort involved in the Indians' painting of the murals "is proof enough of their serious purpose." The pictures in almost every cave in Val Verde County extend far above the reach of a man standing on the floor, he notes, so a ladder of some kind must have been required. In a few cases they were painted flat on a ceiling more than ten feet high, requiring the use of what we would call scaffolding. Grinding, mixing, and applying the paint took considerable labor since certain figures are nine or more feet tall, solid color on rough surfaces, and finished in three shades.

The shamans "are the focal points of virtually all paintings, dominate most by their size, and frequently overwhelm the viewer by sheer numbers," Newcomb says. He favors the hypothesis that they were part of an early mescal bean cult. The mountain laurel, a beautiful purple-flowering shrub, bears the mescal beans, which are hard red seeds with a narcotic property. Archeologists have not only found the seeds in eight digs, Newcomb says, but mescal cults of more recent Indian tribes also engage in practices characteristic of the pictographs. He theorizes that shamans took the beans during dances to induce visionary experiences, which they later described to onlookers. Newcomb says animals, dances with weapons, pelts, feathers, rattles, and other items important to medicine men in a modern mescal-bean fraternity have their representation in Pecos River pictographs. "It is difficult not to interpret almost every element in the pictographs in these terms," the museum director says. Thus, the red dots associated with shamans in pictographs become mescal beans.

His hypothesis may well explain the fact that many pictographs have been painted over earlier pictographs. Shamans apparently held their rituals where previous supernatural communication of earlier significance occurred, Newcomb feels, and would overlay with their own the earlier illustrations of experiences and gained powers.

The edge of the Chihuauan Desert may be far from the minds of cultured Texans, but it is home to art—and has been for milennia.

CHAPTER 8

GOING TO TRIAL

AFTER A QUARTER CENTURY OF EMPLOYMENT, I lost my job in the turmoil of bipolar disorder. I fought desperately to return to the workplace, filing a health discrimination suit that would go to trial in 1993.

In this precedent to the Americans With Disabilities Act, one of my lawyers, a former investigative reporter in television named Steve Petrou, was trying his first case, endowed with idealistic zeal for this journalist.

A star witness for the defense had been a valued friend socially for years, but loyalty was tattered by my manic conduct in the newsroom, and he had fired me.

Others among the mentally ill were rooting for me to strengthen their case with employers, less than wary of a possible determination that the employer might have been pushed beyond the limits of its patience by an ugly sickness.

THE TRIAL, a sizable undertaking in federal district court, was Carlton E. Leatherwood, Jr. (plaintiff) vs. The Houston Post Co. (defendant). Teams of lawyers would present the case to an eight-person jury in a proceeding presided over by the Honorable Hugh Gibson.

The small maverick Houston law firm of Coane and Associates had drawn up the suit, and my parents helped foot the cost. I do not know the thousands of dollars spent because these parties were always quiet about finances. But I do know that after four years of preparation, lengthened by illnesses on my part, we went to federal court on the strength of a Texas statute.

The case made it on the Galveston docket a few days before Thanksgiving in 1993, and my family settled in a hotel built on a pier jutting into the Gulf of Mexico.

Court was called into session.

A jury of five men and three women was seated.

"The attorneys will be given an opportunity to make an opening statement," Judge Gibson told the jury. "The purpose of the statement is to set forth from each of their standpoints what the issues in this case are, and to provide evidence that they expect will develop in support of their positions."

"Now for the plaintiff, Mr. Steven Petrou."

Petrou strode forward. "Thank you, Your Honor," he said.

"Ladies and gentlemen, this case is about a gentleman who for twenty-two years devoted himself to one newspaper, *The Houston Post.* But the evidence will show that when that newspaper changed ownership, it disowned this loyal journalist and cut him loose simply because he was ill.

"It is a privilege for me today to represent Carlton Leatherwood, Jr. Some of you may have seen his bylines in *The Houston Post*, because in addition to being an editor, which was his main job, he was also a writer. He wrote features for the Sunday magazine of the *Post* on subjects ranging from the environment to museums to the Rio Grande River. He also wrote travel stories, going all the way to Italy to cover some resorts, and you'll find out he wrote more than two dozen editorials.

"Mr. Leatherwood was fired from *The Houston Post* in July 1989. He's coming to you now, a jury of his peers, because he believes he was wrongfully terminated.

"In Texas, an employer, you'll find out, can fire an employee for almost any reason. This is known as an 'employment at will state.' But the legislature and Congress, they have passed laws that say you cannot fire employees for some reasons. You cannot fire employees just because of their race. You can't fire an employee just because of their sex. You can't fire an employee because you feel they're too old. You can't fire because of their national origin. And they have said you cannot fire an employee because of their disability if that employee can reasonably be accommodated. We're going to prove to you, ladies and gentlemen, that Mr. Leatherwood was fired because of a disability, a health disability, and specifically a mental health disability.

"When I say mental health, I hope this doesn't frighten you or conjure up negative images in you, because some of the experts who will testify in this trial will tell you some very well-known people such as actress Patty Duke and golfer Bert Yancy have experienced the very same mental health illness as Carl Leatherwood, and those people have been able to lead productive lives. In fact, Patty Duke was in an NBC movie just two weeks ago called *A Matter of Justice*.

"You will hear evidence that Carl Leatherwood has battled this illness for many, many years, and he'd always been able to get treatment and return to work until July 1989. And before I tell you how *The Post* forced Carl Leatherwood to prematurely end his career, I'll tell you a little more about how it began.

"Mr. Leatherwood was born in a small town in West Texas, and he moved around with his family; they followed the oil patch until they reached Beaumont. He was a high school journalist, and then he became a college journalist. You'll find out he won awards as a writer in high school and in college. And by the mid-1960s, he found himself here in

Galveston as an editor for the *Galveston Daily News*. You'll learn that he was an idealistic journalist who believed that his work allowed him to serve the public by better informing them of the world around them.

"He was lured away from the *Galveston Daily News* and went to *The Houston Post* in 1967. He started out as a copy editor for *The Post*. Later he worked on the wire desk, where he gathered international, national, and local stories, and later he worked on the business desk. As I mentioned earlier, he also throughout his tenure there contributed articles for magazine features and editorials.

"Before Media News and Dean Singleton took over this paper, it was owned for a few years by a Canadian group. And for many years before that, it was owned by the Hobby family, Oveta Culp Hobby. The evidence will be that the previous owners accommodated Carl's illness and rewarded his loyalty with pay raises and praise. You will learn that the old management cared about the welfare of their employees long before there were any laws that protected workers from losing their jobs because of their disability. But you'll find out that the new owners were good at reporting our laws—about our laws against disability discrimination. They were good at reporting but not following them.

"The Texas Commission of Human Rights act was passed to prevent employers from discriminating against employees who are disabled and who have handicaps. Mr. Leatherwood is here asking you, a jury of his peers, to listen to all the evidence and at the end to give him the justice that he was denied."

"FOR THE DEFENSE, the court calls Ms. Cherry Bounds."

"Ladies and gentlemen, good morning," Bounds said as she took Petrou's place before the jury.

"The issue in this case regards handicapped discrimination. As you might have surmised, *The Houston Post* has a difference of opinion with Mr. Leatherwood as to whether or not we discriminated against him because of his disability. We don't believe we discriminated against him because of his disability.

"We believe the evidence will show you that Mr. Leatherwood was with us for more than twenty years, and that during that twenty-year period, the possession and control of *The Houston Post* changed three different times. But the philosophy was still the same, and the philosophy, unfortunately, was of business to make money. And whether or not those changes in management brought about a more businesslike and professional atmosphere than had been experienced under Mrs. Hobby's leadership, so be it.

"The bottom line is *The Post* is in business for several reasons, the number one being to make money, but most importantly they're in business to put out a newspaper. They have an obligation to the public, to you and me, to put that paper out in the most efficient, most effective, and most correct manner.

"Carl Leatherwood was a copy editor. He started with *The Post* as a copy editor in the 1960s. For a period of time his position changed, and you'll hear testimony that his position became a general wire editor. After he was having some problems, his supervisors decided, and they will testify, that it was in the best interest of Carl and the newspaper to move him from that general wire editor position to a business wire editor position. There were reasons for that. The bottom line is they were accommodating Carl's mental health, and they were always accommodating the needs of *The Post.* They needed someone they could rely on to do that job.

"Carl continued to have episodes, and his illness continued to get worse. The employees, his coworkers, his supervisors did everything they could as individuals. Yes, *The Post* is a company, but the company is made up of individual people. Those people know Carl. You'll see them testify. You'll hear them talk about Carl, and you'll hear them say that they like Carl. They enjoyed being around Carl most of the time, but the bottom line is those people, those individuals, including Carl, had a higher obligation to their employer, *The Post*, and that was to see that that newspaper that we get on our front porches every day gets out and gets out accurately.

"A point was reached with Carl where he could not be trusted. One of the greatest attributes of a person as a copy editor or any kind of editing position at a newspaper, and specifically *The Houston Post*, they will testify, is your confidence in their ability to do their job. *The Post's* position is that Carl's ability to do the job finally reached a point that they could no longer accommodate. In the last year or so, he couldn't do the job most of the time.

"Thank you."

"Is the plaintiff ready to proceed?" Gibson inquired.

"Yes, Your Honor, we are," Petrou answered.

"Who will be your first witness?" the judge asked.

"Mr. Leatherwood."

I was sworn in, and Petrou began the questioning:

"Did you do some writing while you were at *The Houston Post*?"

"Yes, I did."

"What kind of writing did you do?"

"I wrote magazine articles, twenty-two magazine articles in about three years."

"Did you also write travel articles?"

"I wrote three prominent travel articles during that time."

"Did you also write editorials?"

"I wrote 20 editorials prior to that."

"Mr. Leatherwood, let me just get an understanding of what you understood your job to be at *The Houston Post*. What did your job consist of?"

"I was a—for 20 years, I was a general wire editor and then a business wire editor. And I was given the freedom to write and photograph during that time."

"Did you express an interest to a management person that you wanted to be a full-time writer?"

Yes. Martha Liebrum, editor of the magazine, knew of my devout interest in writing, thought I would be best traveling about Texas obtaining stories on people, and tried to accomplish this fact with Peter O'Sullivan, editor-in-chief at the time the Canadians owned the paper."

"In your own life, was writing an important part of your job at *The Post*?"

Bounds objected, "He's leading the witness."

"Overrule the objection," the judge said.

"It was an important part, if I may say, for avoiding stress on the job," I said. "For some of these people I know that have been in a job for ten or fifteen years, there is burnout and there is stress, and stress is an ugly component of my illness. And so this relieved that stress, and that was the reason I sought a job other than editing the past twenty years."

Petrou continued his line of questioning. "Did you get some compliments from management on your writing?" he asked.

"Martha, who is one the executives now, said two words that I appreciated very much. They were on a story two newspaper pages long and with pictures partially shot in Galveston. She said: 'Lovely writing.'"

Petrou turned toward the judge. "May I approach the bench, Your Honor?"

"All right."

"Couldn't we look at some samples?" Petrou asked. "I'll not go into the whole thing, just some flavor. This man did more than just edit at *The Post*."

"What year are we talking about?"

"Some were written in 1986, '87. I think the position is he testified that he saw part of his job as writing. He asked to be a permanent writer, and that's the issue of accommodation."

"If you would select a few sample items. I'll consider admitting them."

"There's a sample, Your Honor. It shows his photography and feature writing."

"Was he a photographer also?"

"Yes, he was a photographer also, Your Honor. Then this one here, then two editorials that he wrote."

"That's enough. I'll tell you why I'm going to admit it, if you cannot guess. He claims that his skills included his ability to write. And the issue is, was he discharged because of incompetence or not. The thing of it is that the jury must take into consideration all of his skills in making the determination as to whether they can reasonably accommodate whatever disability he claims he has, and I think it does have that relevancy."

Petrou resumed questioning the plaintiff.

"What is the name of this article, Mr. Leatherwood?"

"The Dudes of Dixie."

"Tell us a little bit about it."

"It's about the first dude ranch in that part of Texas, Central Texas."

"Who was this lady whose picture you have here in the article?"

"Rose Crowell."

"Who was Ms. Crowell?"

"She was the owner. She was the daughter of the owner, who founded it in 1939, and she helped her father."

"Did you interview her for the article?"

"Yes, I did."

"And when was this article published?"

"1986."

"Did you take all the pictures for this article?"

"Yes, I did."

I WELL REMEMBER rounding up ranches in the Hill Country, not Central Texas, as I had testified. It's a time to paddle forward, to take a reflective break from the courtroom. Rose "Billie" Crowell, owner of one of the oldest guest ranches in Texas, sat down in the dining room of the Dixie Dude Ranch to tell about the time the dinner bell rang in midafternoon and horses came running, mounted with Air Force cadets on weekend passes from training bases at nearby San Antonio. The day was Dec. 7, 1941. Japanese planes had bombed Pearl Harbor.

"We had around forty military people here, men mostly," she said. "We had twenty-eight horses at that time, and we would let the boys ride back in the hills. We would try to keep them from killing themselves, but some of them rode like they were flying a plane."

She laughs at the memory. "They were all alerted to report back in the event something happened. Somebody called me over the party line and told me that Pearl Harbor had been attacked. So do you see that big old dinner bell? That was off of a locomotive. We went immediately and rang it. Horses and riders came in here from every direction.

"In no time at all the cadets were in their uniforms and checked out—handed me their money and were on their way back to Lackland and Randolph Air Force bases. During the war we heard from many of those people. Every once in a while we would get a letter back saying address unknown or deceased. Those were sad days, and lots of happy days, too, during the war."

Crowell rose and removed a small framed picture of a young officer from the wall. She spoke softly, pensively. The former guest in uniform had been killed in a plane crash. A cadet in another picture, however, had recently returned to the ranch as a much older man, and she had visited his home in Florida.

As Crowell noted the visits with other guests in their homes from Houston to England and the hundreds of Christmas cards exchanged, I began to understand the real attraction of dude ranches. They are extended families. If you don't have a relative or friend to visit in the Hill Country, they are the next best thing. Crowell agreed and laughed again. "Some of the people that we have had are better than relatives," she said.

"We have one family who has come here every year for forty-six years," she said. "One lady that was a baby in the Galveston flood [1900] has come twice a year all these years. She has grandchildren coming. We have some that have great-grandchildren coming."

The Dixie Dude near Bandera opened to the public with a barbecue for about one-hundred neighbors and friends on July 3, 1937, before electricity arrived in that rural district. Crowell's father, William Wallace Whitley, had bought and worked the land since 1901. His daughter was born on it in 1904.

Today, horses graze serenely beneath the oaks in evening. Insurance requirements no longer permit the carefree horseriding the cadets enjoyed, and guests ride horses single file behind a wrangler. On thirty miles of trails, visitors may spot wild turkeys, redbarked trees called Texas madrones, and sotol. Sotol, more plentiful further west, was once fed to cattle during severe droughts.

"We've always had a jukebox," Crowell said. "A boy broke into one by the pool one night. There were seven of us around that table playing cards, and the children were down at the pool. The father of the boy was a psychiatrist out of Houston. The doctor jumped up right away, put his cards down, and made a beeline for the pool. Another father said, 'I think I'll go down and see how a psychiatrist can handle the situation.'

"The boy came back as a grown man not long ago and said, 'Boy, I was mean, wasn't I?'"

It happens in the best of families.

A SILVER PEUGOET TRAILED DUST under a brilliant autumn sun as the driver headed down a caliche ranch road in the Hill Country. The rough road tamed the speed of his exquisite machine to little more than a horse trot.

If he wanted to savor the Old West, he had no complaint. He was looking at it in his rear-view mirror. In the 1800s push of civilization through Texas to the Pacific, dust was a constant reminder of the rugged and uncomfortable conditions. Men kicked it up as they walked the streets of frontier towns. Their horses and wagons, and the wind, churned it into clouds. And it came to rest in layers on clothes and store goods.

A breed of driver different from the Peugoet pilot had swirled the dust of this ranchland with the hooves of cattle a century ago. And as I, too, churned up earth's powder, I was happy to find another element of realism in the successful conclusion of a search for a touch of the West in Texas. During that hunt for a treasured past, I had heard others ask, "Where can I visit a working ranch?" The answer was the YO Ranch.

And after my first visit, its hospitality expanded to a hotel, the YO Ranch Hilton in Kerrville, thirty-five miles to the east. The hotel's grand opening in 1984 brought together some 2,500 celebrants, including western movie and television actors.

Dust had figured in the finishing touches at the hotel. An argument ensued over the authenticity of the dusty, aged display cases moved into the gift shop. The shop clerk fussed over the situation, said she didn't want that much realism in the place, and won out.

Such concessions to the modern way, however, have not subdued the western flavor of the luxuriously appointed hotel or the diversified working ranch, which also welcomes overnight guests. Five chandeliers, made of more than 350 Chisolm Trail era branding irons, light a massive lobby filled with mounted moose, deer, and bear of trophy class. Leather and longhorn hides cover hand-carved sofas and chairs, some placed near a fireplace. A red metal roof covers the native limestone walls of the sprawling 200-room hotel. At the ranch you may sleep in restored nineteenth-century cabins, which served such needs as stagecoach stop and schoolhouse.

The Charles Schreiner family, owner of the YO Ranch, threw a four-day party for the opening of their new venture. During the event Charlie Three, the patriarch of the Schreiners, led an eight-mile parade of horsemen, longhorns, and wagons. Given the opportunity to act the boastful Texan, he shunned the role. "It's beautiful," he replied with restrained pride when asked what he thought of his hotel.

Across the lobby, the youngest of Charlie Three's four sons talked about his dad's diversification of the YO. "Yeah, he started the longhorns [on a comeback off a government refuge] about 1964," Louis said. "Now there are about 10,000 registered Longhorns in the United States. But then nobody had 'em. They were unwanted."

I asked the breed's purpose.

"They are for the commercial breeder," Louis said. "Calving ease is a desirable characteristic. When a lot of our breeds have their first calves, the rancher has to stay up night and day with them—almost be there to give birth like a doctor would. Longhorns, you just turn them out. We sell our bulls to people to use on their first-calf heifers (Angus, Hereford, etc.). The breeders also want to get a certain percentage of longhorn in their herd to get that characteristic hardiness and fertility."

The Longhorn was the first Old West animal I sighted on the YO Ranch. About 900 of the breed (cows, bulls, and calves) roamed its 50,000 acres. Former Texas Ranger Charles Schreiner began the ranch with longhorns over a century ago, in 1880. "The Texas longhorn made more history than any other breed of cattle the civilized world has known," folklorist J. Frank Dobie wrote in *The Longhorns.* "As an animal in the realm of natural history, he was the peer of bison or grizzly bear. As a social factor, his influence on men was extraordinary. An economic agent in determining the character and occupation of a territory continental in its vastness, he moved elementally with drought, grass, blizzards out of the Arctic, and the wind from the south. However supplanted or however disparaged by evolving standards and generations, he will remain the bedrock on which the history of the cow country of America is founded."

An estimated ten million head moved up the trails of Texas between 1866 and 1890. Capt. Schreiner, himself, drove more than 150,000 to Kansas on the Chisholm Trail. The cattle brought the state financial recovery from the Civil War far ahead of other Confederate states. And it was the Longhorn herd and the addition of exotic game that also brought the YO Ranch recovery from a devastating drought, in the 1950s. Diversification through a Hilton hotel franchise was but another gallop away from the hardship of natural disaster. Conrad Hilton, incidentally, started his chain in Texas, at Cisco.

The Elm Water Hole was the coziest place to get a drink at the Kerrville hotel. Blackbuck antelope and axis deer hides covered stools at the antique bar. The Sam Houston dining room served up those ranch-grown animals at dinner.

The scenic route to the YO Ranch passes the prestigious summer camps on the headwaters of the Guadalupe River. Surface water, however, is another luxury the 100-square-mile YO doesn't possess. Its more than 10,000 animals depend on windmills. One stands sentinel at the entrance. Thirty-two species of exotic game share the spread, but on a winter visit I told foreman Ed Howell I wanted more to see an old-line working ranch. He woke me early the next morning so I could see him run head after head of cattle through a chute. He trapped them momentarily to doctor their ears.

The exotic animals stimulate income from hunting and photography. Tours of their habitat go with ranch visits. Blackbuck antelope, giraffes, zebras, and axis deer are among the imports roaming the hills, which an African chief once compared to his homeland. But the exotics may sometimes produce an incongruous sight for the Texan. I saw an ostrich chase an armadillo one trip. Louis Schreiner said the drought, got so bad in the '50s his dad shipped his cattle to Montana. "He tried to figure out some way to supplement income and came up with exotic game. We had started commercial hunting of white-tailed deer, but that's only six weeks out of the year. So we brought these exotics in, turned them loose, and began hunting them five years later. Now we've got thousands."

The shadow of western superstar John Wayne literally hung over the grand opening celebration of the YO Ranch Hilton. So many of the film stars there remembered their work with him. And then I drove to the Cowboy Artists of America Museum in Kerrville, where I found his bronze statue under a spotlight.

The museum houses the work of professional artists who focus on the cowboy and related subjects. In the galleries around a courtyard you may find the paintings and sculptures of such artists as John Clymer, who produced some eighty covers for the old *Saturday Evening Post*, and Mehl Lawson, who got a degree in animal husbandry and for fifteen years bought, sold, trained, rode, and showed horses. CAA artists follow in the footsteps of Frederic Remington and Charles Marion Russell, whose art, like film, helped secure a romantic thirst for the West.

And with reason. "Of the twenty-nine eventful decades since the Mayflower . . . only one American period produced a unique, enduring symbol of universal recognition . . . America's Everyman is . . . the cowboy," wrote Southwest author Don Dedera.

Griffiths C. Carnes, director of the museum, said, "One of its main purposes is to get the art 'Where the public can enjoy it. We had a lot of people say, where has this art been? I didn't even know it existed.'"

The Cowboy Artists of America association settled on locating its museum in Texas because of support, meaning money, and in Kerrville because of local interest. The locale, of course, has a heritage of many of the elements in western art.

The building was the last public one bearing direct influence by Texas architect O'Neil Ford, credited with setting forth the principles of southwestern regional style. The ten-acre site crossed by limestone ledges and shaded by oaks and cedars is representative of the Hill Country.

Hand-carved oak doors open into the gallery. The ceiling, a series of brick domes, was constructed by craftsmen from Guanajusto and San Miguel de Ajente, Mexico, using rare and ancient skills. The floor was made of mesquite, a very dense wood found in the area as well as other parts of Texas.

Fritz White, a sculptor from Loveland, Colorado, was teaching a class when I visited. The students came from five states. "The CAA artists have all been very successful," Carnes said, "and they wanted to put something back in with young, serious art students. So in setting this museum up, they insisted as part of the agreement that they teach these classes at no charge. They come here at their own expense."

The museum also is accumulating the records on everything ever done by CAA members. "We want to make this for scholars, dealers, and collectors to research and authenticate art," Carnes said. "Heretofore, there has been that time lag. An artist dies, and maybe it is thirty years later before somebody says, 'Hey, he was pretty good,' and starts accumulating all this data. In the meantime, phonies show up, and people get hurt. They are getting hurt, surprisingly enough, with forged contemporary art.

"About a year ago a woman in Dallas called a friend of the museum and said, 'I just got the neatest Melvin Warren print you ever saw for $10.' The other woman said, 'There aren't any Melvin Warren prints for $10.' The caller said, 'I got one.' Come to find out it came from a flea market in Garland. And the guy had stacks of them. They were all done in Hong Kong." With records at the museum, people can authenticate a work.

"The real United States starts west of the Mississippi," Carnes said. "Everything east emulated Europe. What was west of the Mississippi, the things unique to this country, stands us separate and apart from the rest of the world."

The cowboy was a part of the distinctive cattle industry and the fur trade. A statue of a bucking cowboy on the Capitol grounds in Austin refers to Texas as his native home. Dobie backs this up, saying the cowboy was cradled in South Texas, the product of the coming together of the Anglo-American, the herd-owning Spanish caballero, the Spanish vaquero—a mounted worker with cows—and the open range.

In the roundup of ranches, I encountered an anachronism of sound at the Lyndon B. Johnson National Historical Park, where I paid a visit to the working LBJ Ranch of the thirty-sixth president of the United States. Taped remarks of Johnson welcomed visitors to the Hill Country as a tour bus crossed the Pedernales River and passed his one-room school and his grave on the way to the home and fields where he entertained international dignitaries. His widow still lived there. Some 200 head of Hereford cattle roamed the premises.

After the tour I took a short walk to Sauer-Beckman Farmstead for a portrayal of life in the early 1900s. "We raise our own pigs and our own beef," John Matthews, who served as our living history guide, said in a gentle bass voice.

"Yes, sir, we have a smokehouse," Matthews said. "I grew up like this. My folks put up their own meat. In the spring, when the weather starts getting warm, we take a lot of the meat and pack it in lard. I can show you right here. We take the bacon and ham out of the smokehouse, trim it, slice it, and put it in jars and pour lard over it. The lard just keeps the air away from it."

Vegetables from a garden are put up, too, and stored on shelves in a long cabin. I saw cabbage, tomatoes, pole beans, blackeyed peas, and carrots. And canning includes wild grape jelly from an abundance of mustang grapes in this area. The food is prepared on a wood stove in the kitchen of a stone house for park personnel. "The long part is getting the fire going," said guide Denise Abendschein. "Once the stove gets hot enough, it's not bad cooking."

The John Sauers reared their ten children in the house. They built the log cabin first, about 1869, and progressively added the stone house and an attached Victorian one. Today, there are more sounds of the past—a crowing rooster and a creaking windmill.

I MOVE THAT THIS EXHIBIT be admitted," Petrou said, awakening me to further questioning. "Mr. Leatherwood, did you also write editorials?"

"Yes, I did."

"I want to show you what's been premarked as Exhibit 7-G."

"It is an editorial that was considered the best of the day's. At the top of the page it's entitled 'A System Failed.'"

"And what was this editorial about?"

"It was about the way we as a community in Houston treated mental illness and the people that had it."

"Can you read us the first two paragraphs of that editorial, please?"

"In the shadow of downtown, behind the supermarket, the hungry scavenge what the store doesn't want to sell. And as they claim food for themselves, they break bread with the birds, strewing pieces along a parking lot fence. It is a compassionate city.

"Sometimes, however, compassion here rests behind fences, as it did when Eddie Lee Johnson lost his life in an ugly Christmas story. You may remember. Police gunned down the mentally ill young man in self-defense during the 1981 holiday season. This tragic tale is resurrected now because some details deserve reexamination and because it should not die without forging in heart and soul the will to strengthen this community."

"Okay. Mr. Leatherwood, did anybody approve these editorials?"

"Oveta Culp Hobby and George Fuerman, the editorial page editor, approved them for publication."

"Just remind the jury, who was Oveta Culp Hobby again?"

"She was the chairman of the board of The Houston Post [Company]."

"Now let's move on to your illness. Did you call anyone at the *Post* and ask about your job while you were hospitalized in December 1988?"

"I called Ernie Williamson."

"And what was his response when you asked him about your job?"

"Objection, Your Honor," Bounds spoke up, "This is hearsay."

"What's the exception to the rule?" Gibson asked.

"Admission by a party opponent, Your Honor," Petrou answered.

"Proceed."

I continued: "He said, what are you going to do, and I said, well, I need to work another month or two. I had made the statement when I was manic on the night of the 3rd of December that *The Post* was racist and therefore I was resigning."

"Did you mean that?"

"I not only didn't mean it, it had never entered my thoughts in the previous twenty-two years or twenty-one years, and Ernie certainly had not been approached on it or anybody else in management. And so I thought, still weak that, well, maybe I did resign myself. I later approached Ernie and I said, 'What am I being terminated for?' And he says, 'The effects of illness.'"

"I want to go back and talk about the type of treatment you received by the different owners of *The Post* as a result of your health condition.

"First of all, do you still suffer from manic depressive illness or bipolar disorder?"

"Yes, I do."

"In the twenty-two years that you worked for *The Post*, how often did you have to be hospitalized because of your manic depressive condition?"

"Eight episodes."

"After your treatment and after you were stabilized during those eight episodes between 1976 and December of 1988, seven episodes—after each of those seven episodes between 1976 and 1988, were you able to go back and do the work that you did before you were hospitalized?"

"Yes, I was."

"Did you know a writer at *The Post* by the name of DJ Wilson?"

"Yes, I did."

"What did Mr. Wilson cover?"

"He covered the medical beat."

"Did you ever talk to Mr. Wilson about your condition or your behavior?"

"Yes. I apologized for sending him a crazy message. He said, well, it was no crazier than what others at *The Post* had sent him."

"Your mental illness began in '76. In that year you got a raise; isn't that correct?"

"Yes."

"So from 1976 when you were first diagnosed as mentally ill to 1989 when you were terminated, you still kept getting raises all this time; is that correct?"

"That is correct."

"Did your salary more than double from 1976 when you were first diagnosed until you were terminated?"

"Yes, it did."

Bounds took over the questioning of me on the stand: "The reason that you were at *The Post* in the eight hours daily was to edit copy and write headlines and write cutlines for pictures; isn't that correct?"

"Correct."

"So you weren't employed as a column writer or an editorial writer, were you?"

"No."

"If you did that, it was done on your own time; is that correct?"

"Right."

"Your responsibilities as a business wire editor were to sit and review the wire, the stories coming over the various wires; isn't that correct?"

"Right."

"And it was your judgment and decision to choose which of those stories might be of interest or should go in *The Post;* isn't that correct?"

"Right."

"Have you been hospitalized since this June 1989 episode, when you were terminated?"

"Yes, I have."

"You were in fact hospitalized in October of 1989, were you not?"

Petrou: "Objection, Your Honor. At this point I would like to approach the bench."

"All right."

"Okay, Your Honor. I object on the basis that this is irrelevant. It's going into—"

"Why is it irrelevant?"

"After his termination—I think it's going to be prejudicial."

"This is a continuation of an ongoing condition that started back in 1976. If that's your objection, it's overruled. Let's proceed."

Bounds continued: "Mr. Leatherwood, you were in fact hospitalized in October of 1989 as well, were you not?"

"Yes."

"You were hospitalized again in December of 1991, weren't you?"

"Right."

"And again in May 1992?"

"Right."

"And again in December of 1992?"

"December of '92?"

"Yes, sir."

"I don't think so."

"We'll look at some records. You were again hospitalized from April through June of 1993; isn't that correct?"

"Right."

"And you were hospitalized again in October of 1993, were you not?"

"Right."

"Was the 1988 hospitalization voluntary?"

"No, it wasn't."

"It was an involuntary commitment to the hospital, wasn't it?"

"Right."

"Was that the first time that you've ever been involuntarily committed to the hospital?"

"Yes, it was."

"Do you know when that particular episode began in 1988?"

"I know when there were hints of it, and that was in late September, with paranoia."

"So in fact that particular episode began in September and lasted through almost the end of December? Would that be correct?"

"Right."

"And I believe that when you were in the midst of these episodes, your behavior was irrational?"

"Yes."

"Since that episode in 1988, have you been involuntarily committed to the hospital?"

"Yes, several times."

Judge: "We're going to recess for the day."

CHAPTER 9

EXPERT TESTIMONY

"WE HAVE A WITNESS," Steve Petrou announced, "that is being called out of order this morning."

"Call the witness," Judge Gibson said.

"We call Kuyk Logan."

Petrou turned to his witness.

"Did you at one time work for *The Houston Post*?"

"Yes."

"And when did you start at *The Post?*"

"In July of 1969 and was there until the day it was sold on December 1, 1983."

"And who hired you, Mr. Logan, to work at *The Post?*"

"The Hobby family."

"What position did you last hold at the paper?"

"In May of 1976, I was promoted to managing editor, and I stayed as managing editor until I left the paper in December of '83."

NOW, I'D LIKE TO TURN your attention to the plaintiff in this case, Mr. Carl Leatherwood. Have you come to know Mr. Leatherwood?"

"Yes."

"Did you ever supervise Mr. Leatherwood's work?"

"Yes. I was in charge of the whole shooting match. Everything. All reporters, all the editors."

"Were you all working pretty closely together in that newsroom?"

"Very close."

"If somebody made a big disturbance, would you be able to notice it?"

"Yes."

"Can you tell us—describe the performance of Carl Leatherwood as an editor?"

Raymond Kalmans, attorney for the defense, objected to the line of questioning, saying, "The witness testified he left in December of 1983. Mr. Leatherwood was terminated six years later, in 1988."

The court: "I understand. The jury can keep that in mind. Proceed with your question."

Petrou continued: "Tell me about the Carl Leatherwood that you knew while you were the supervisor. What kind of a job did he do?"

"Carl was an extremely accurate, thorough, and dependable editor."

"Did he always do his job?"

"Yes."

"From your experience as a newspaper man, which job is under greater deadline pressure, a feature writer or a wire editor?"

"A wire editor. Because a wire editor is responsible for making decisions on the international and world news that goes into the paper, and this is a decision that sometimes is made just right up to deadline time. There's a tremendous amount of tension and pressure."

"While you were managing editor, did you ever switch employees from one position to another position?"

"Oh, yes, yes."

"As a person in the management of *The Houston Post* under the Hobby family, what was your approach to working with staff members who had health problems?"

"The Hobbys were a benevolent family, and if somebody was sick, their main concern was that they get well and get back to work. We had a loose policy of a sick policy. If somebody was sick, they could be off until they got well."

"Did Mrs. Hobby personally approve some of the raises?"

"Every raise."

"Thank you, Mr. Logan," Gibson said. "The witness is excused. You will resume now with Mr. Leatherwood's testimony."

BOUNDS ADDRESSED THE WITNESS.

"Didn't you show up at *The Post* one day with your dog to report to work?"

"Yes, I did."

"Is spending money a problem?"

"Spending sprees, yes. It is with me and with a lot of manic depressives."

"In fact, each time you have an episode of this manic nature, you spend most, if not all, of your money, don't you?"

"No, ma'am. Not each time."

"How much money did you spend during your manic episode in the fall of 1988?"

"I don't know because I was using credit cards, and I had redecorated my living quarters on those credit cards. Several thousand dollars."

"Could you be a little more specific about what exactly you did?"

"Paint, carpet, flooring."

"For your whole apartment?"

"Yeah."

"And you put that all on credit cards?"

"Yes."

"Mr. Leatherwood, I've handed you what's been marked as Exhibit No. 3. Would you read the cover of that and tell the jury what it is that we're going to be looking at?"

"Medical records on Carlton E. Leatherwood, Jr."

"From whom?"

"From Adriana Nuncio, custodian of medical records for Dr. Archie Blackburn."

"Did you resist the constables when they tried to take you to the hospital in 1988?"

"In my home, I resisted. I did not perpetrate violence. I resisted the constables because I didn't think they could come into my private home and get me. My watch has a little piece on it that they can't fix and my hand came up and cut my lip. It's not a head injury. It is a cut lip."

"Okay. I apologize for the confusion. So we're in agreement then that you did offer resistance to the constables."

"To a degree because I had called 911 to ask if they could come into my home and get me, and I was waiting on the results of that call."

"Would you look down on page 77 where it's underlined 'physical examination.' Would you read that paragraph, please?"

"Patient had resisted the constables who brought him to the hospital. He was initially angry and puzzled. He accepted continued use of lithium carbonate, 1200 milligrams per day, as had been his custom over recent months. Court commitment initially recommended on grounds of likelihood of deterioration to dangerousness if not treated."

"Would you now flip to page 57 in that same record?"

"The date of admission is November 16, 1989."

"This was less than a year after the other report. Down under 'physical exam,' would you read those sentences, please?"

"The initial assessment was remarkable only for superficial abrasion on the forehead. Persisting combativeness requiring restraints and limited the extent of the initial assessment."

"Thank you, Mr. Leatherwood.

"These reports from the doctor regarding your admissions in 1988 specifically, then again in 1989, do tend to indicate a tendency toward violence, don't they?"

"I don't read it as perpetration of violence."

Petrou had a final two questions.

"Is allowing you to be a full-time writer part of the accommodations that you are seeking from *The Post* for your disability?"

"Yes."

"And how would allowing you to be a full-time writer have accommodated your mental condition?"

"It would have been a less-stressful position than wire editor, one, because there are not as many deadlines and, two, a change of pace, change from a burnout situation, can be less stressful."

Petrou: "The plaintiff calls Rebecca Bibens. Ms. Bibens, what was your job when you started out at *The Post*?"

"I was a copy editor, but I have worked in several positions during my eight and a half years at *The Post.* A lot of the time I was a rim editor, which means you just read the stories and write the headlines. Occasionally I would do a little bit of layout. Sometimes I would be a slot person. That's the person who reads the stories after the rimmers edit the stories. You're checking other people's stuff. Sometimes I would work a little bit in the back shop where they put the pages together and just try to make sure everything fits and looks right."

"Did copy editors sometimes make mistakes?"

"Yes."

"What kind of mistakes would they make?"

"Well, grammar mistakes, spelling mistakes. It's not always that they made mistakes, it's that sometimes they didn't catch the mistakes. That was, you know, our job, but when you read so much, you can always, you know, read over something and miss something."

"Did you sometimes edit business copy?"

"Sometimes, yes."

"And when you edited business copy, did you come to know the plaintiff in this case, Mr. Carl Leatherwood, here?"

"Yes."

"When you edited business copy, about how close were you to Mr. Leatherwood?"

"Well, it varied. Sometimes I would be right next to him, and then sometimes I would be a few people away."

"When you were sitting near Carl, were you able to observe him working?"

"Yes."

"How was his conduct on the job?"

"He was always fine, I thought."

"From your observation, was Mr. Leatherwood serious about his work?"

"Yes."

"From your observation, did Mr. Leatherwood meet his deadlines?"

"As far as I know, yes."

"Did Carl Leatherwood seem to care about the quality of his work?"

"Yes."

"Were there occasions when as slot editor you had to review Carl's work?"

"Yes."

"When you reviewed his work, did he make a lot more mistakes than other editors?"

"No, I would not say he made more mistakes than other people."

"Did Carl ever disrupt you from doing your work?"

"No."

"Did he ever cause chaos in the newsroom?"

"Not when I was there, no."

Kalmans came forward for the defense.

"Ms. Bibens, were you working at *The Post* on the day that Mr. Leatherwood brought his dog up into the newsroom?"

"No."

"And isn't it true that Mr. Leatherwood frequently had—didn't—forgot how to work the computer?"

"I don't know."

"Now, didn't he move around a lot? He wasn't just seated at his desk, was he?"

"You mean like did he get out of his seat a lot?"

"Yes."

"Not that I know of."

THE NEXT WITNESS, who had just rushed into the courtroom wearing a white medical coat, was called. Petrou went to work.

"Good afternoon, Dr. [Robert] Hirschfeld. And what do you do for a living?"

"I am the professor and chairman of the Department of Psychiatry at the University of Texas here in Galveston. It's about a thousand-bed university hospital. In effect, it's the oldest university medical center west of the Mississippi."

"And you also teach psychiatry?"

"I teach psychiatry there. I provide psychiatric practice to patients, provide service, and also we train people to become psychiatrists and medical students."

"And how long have you been teaching psychiatry?"

"I would guess twenty years, something like that."

"Do you have an area of specialty in the field of psychiatry?"

"Depression, depressive illnesses, bipolar illness, anxiety disorders."

"Is part of that area manic depressive illness?"

"Well, that's really an old term, manic depressive illness. The more modern term is bipolar illness, in which patients have episodes both of highs, which we call mania, and lows, which are episodes of depression."

"Are you on a national committee regarding bipolar disorders?"

"Yes. I've been very concerned about the rights of patients with psychiatric illnesses and have served as a consultant to several organizations that advocate for the rights of patients and destigmatization. One of them is a group called the National Depressive and Manic Depressive Association. It's a group of about 35,000 members in the United States, patients and family and I'm privileged to serve as the chair of their scientific advisory board."

"Dr. Hirschfeld, can you tell us what is bipolar disorder or what used to be called manic depressive illness?"

"Certainly. It is a medical illness in which people have episodes of highs, that is, where they often feel on top of the world. They feel that there's nothing that they can't do. Sometimes they think of themselves as being very important. They tend to have a real lot of energy. They have much less need for sleep. A lot of times we sleep less than we would like to, but when people are actually manic, they have less need for sleep. They can sleep only three hours a night. They just have a real lot of energy.

"And they often do things that later turn out to be very embarrassing or devastating to themselves and their family. They spend a lot of money. They may go out and be very promiscuous when they're not at all promiscuous kind of people. They may do things that are very risky. They certainly may go out and abuse substances, drink too much, and things like that. So that's what happens when they get high.

"Then they're completely opposite with the lows or the depressions, in which they feel like they're at the bottom of the barrel. They feel that they're just as low as they can be. They feel terrible. Their self-esteem is poor. They have no energy instead of having all this energy. They can't concentrate. They lose their appetite. They lose their interest in things. And it's really striking to see the difference.

"And that's very different from the kind of experience that most of us have when we're disappointed. And we've all had times when something hasn't worked out for us or we've lost our job, or a love relationship hasn't worked out, when we feel pretty badly for a few days. But this is unremitting, and you just can't move, and some people who are very severely depressed don't even get out of bed. They just don't have the energy to do that.

"Are there some patients who are more manic than they are depressed?"

"Almost all combinations that you can imagine."

"And when these people act in this embarrassing manner that you describe, do they know at the time what they're doing?"

"They usually don't, and one of the problems that we have as clinicians is to try to catch the episode early to get the patient's cooperation. Because usually when they get it full blown, the patient has no realization that they're doing something wrong or wild or reckless and are not cooperative."

"Can employers be involved?"

"One of the things I try to do when I work with a patient with bipolar illness is to get as many people involved as possible."

"You mentioned spending sprees. Tell us a little more about that. Why do some people who are in mania go into these spending sprees?"

"It's part of the illness. They just think that there's nothing they can't do and nothing that they can't have, and so they will buy expensive cars, they will buy jewelry, they will take airplane trips around the world. I mean, it can sound very entertaining and sometimes even can be funny until it all comes—you end up having to pay the piper, and people's life savings have been squandered in a week."

"It can happen that quick?"

"Oh, yes. Oh, yes."

"When people are in mania, they sometimes do lose touch with reality; isn't that true?"

Kalmans: "Objection, Your Honor. He's leading."

Petrou: "Your Honor, what's your ruling?"

The court: "What's your question?"

Petrou: "Do some people lose touch with reality?"

The court: "Overrule the objection. This is an expert."

Petrou: "Yes, go ahead, Dr. Hirschfeld."

"In the more severe forms of bipolar illness, people can become what we call psychotic, which means they do lose touch with reality, and they may hallucinate or see things that aren't there, hear voices, believe things that are clearly not true. Not everybody who has bipolar will do that."

"Do some manic patients become irritable?"

"Irritability is very characteristic. And often if someone who is manic is frustrated, if you tell him or her they can't do this or that, they will become frustrated and very irritable and may become quite combative."

"Do some of the people who have mania become disabled from working for periods of time?"

"Bipolar illness tends to be episodic, and people can function at very normal—many people can function at very normal levels between episodes. There are some people who become chronically ill or chronically depressed and can't work at all, but a significant portion of people do very well, especially if they're maintained on maintenance medication between episodes.

"I forgot to ask you at the very beginning when you were introducing this kind of mental illness: about how many people in the United States suffer from this general illness that was called mania or depression?"

"One percent of the population has bipolar disorder, or in the range of 2 million people."

"How can this illness be controlled?"

"Well, the wonder drug is lithium carbonate. There have in the last ten years now been a number of other medications that are also very useful in the treatment of bipolar illness.

"When patients with bipolar illness get depressed, there are a number of antidepressive medications such as Prozac, which has received a lot of press. Also it's very important for patients with bipolar illness to get psychotherapy and psychological management, because as you can imagine, the kinds of things that occur when they're manic really need—can have devastating effects on families, relationships, and jobs. So dealing with that in psychotherapy is very important."

"Okay. Are there times when people with bipolar disease become disabled despite taking medication?"

"There are people who do not respond to one treatment, and they may respond to another treatment, and they may end up not responding to any treatment."

"Can workers who are disabled by bipolar illness or disorder be stabilized and return to their jobs?"

"Often they can. There are certainly people who are unable to work or are completely disabled. Between 80 and 90 percent of the people can do very well. It's that last 10 to 20 percent where the variability is—and this is quite rough, but I would expect that perhaps 5 percent of patients with bipolar illness would be completely disabled. But I would say the majority of the patients can lead productive and satisfying lives.

"I want to read to you a quote by Vincent van Gogh, the Dutch artist, and tell me what it means in today's terms."

Kalmans: "Objection, Your Honor. This doesn't have any bearing on this case."

The court: "Can you come up here? Can't you just ask him questions that go to his expertise? We don't have to worry about quoting van Gogh."

Petrou changed tack:

"How do you compare someone who has mental illness such as bipolar disease with someone who has a physical illness such as heart disease?"

"I don't make the distinction. Both types of illnesses have genetic aspects, biological aspects, psychological aspects, and behavioral aspects."

Kalmans: "Your Honor, we would object to the narrative. There's no pending question at this time."

The court: "Overrule the objection. Proceed."

"Please go on with your explanation," Petrou said.

"For example, with hypertension, high blood pressure, you can reduce your blood pressure by behavioral ways, changing lifestyle. So no one would say that hypertension is not a physical illness and that you can do a lot to treat it in a psychological way."

"Can people who have bipolar disease be accommodated in similar ways that people who have these other physical diseases such as heart conditions?"

Kalmans: "Your Honor, we would object. There's no evidence that this doctor has any knowledge of this particular workplace environment, and we would object to this question."

The court: "Overrule the objection."

"The question was: Can people who have bipolar disease be accommodated perhaps like people who have other physical diseases?"

"Well, my understanding is that this currently is something that would be covered in the Americans With Disabilities Act. Now, maybe that's not specifically answering the question that you asked, but certainly people with psychiatric illnesses, including bipolar illness, can be very productive and can perform responsible jobs."

"Dr. Hirschfeld, can the termination of employment cause the condition of a person with bipolar disorder to deteriorate?"

"Sure. Any very significant distressing event can have a negative affect on any health condition, certainly including a psychiatric one."

"Do you have an opinion as to what employees can do to help people with bipolar disorder lead a productive life?"

"I think that it's important to treat people with any illness as normally as possible, but to be sensitive, with someone who has bipolar illness, to the early signs of an impending episode and to try to warn the person, the family, and perhaps the employer as things begin to deteriorate. I think that's how you would be most helpful.

Petrou: "I appreciate your answers, Doctor. I have no further questions."

CHAPTER 10
RANGE WAR

"**CAN YOU TELL US YOUR FULL NAME?"** Petrou asked the next witness.

"Martha Liebrum."

"And what is your position with *The Post* right now?"

"I'm assistant managing editor. My duties include the features department."

"Were you at one time in charge of *The Houston Post* Sunday magazine?"

"Yes, I was. I was editor of the magazine that lasted from 1974 to 1988. The editor decides what's going into it, assigns stories to writers, edits some material that comes in, selects the presentation, design."

"Was it a good magazine?"

"We thought it was a wonderful magazine."

"Was it well written?"

"We won prizes."

DO YOU RECALL ANY CONTRIBUTIONS from Carl Leatherwood . . . ?"

"Yes."

"Were there a number of contributions from Carl?"

"Yes. In one year he wrote a lot and a little in the year before that and the year after that."

"I'd like to show you some exhibits that we have entered into evidence here. Do you recognize this?"

"Yes, I do. It's a cover story that Carl wrote on going down the Rio Grande in Big Bend."

"Who took that picture?"

"Carl."

"What did you think of this picture?"

"Oh, it was beautiful. He took great photos."

"What did you think of the writing here?"

"I think it's very fine. It was very good."

"Okay. I want to show you another exhibit. Do you know what that is?"

"Yes. It's an article that we ran in the magazine called *Texana*. It was a standing column that appeared almost every week, and *Texana* was about travel in Texas. This happens to be about the Hill Country."

"Who wrote this article?"

"Carl."

"What did you think of this article?"

"It was fine, very fine."

"And do you recognize this article?"

"Yes. It's another article of Carl's. It was published January 1986."

"The reason I'm asking you about it in particular is because—first of all, were you aware that at the time that Carl wrote some of these articles, he was experiencing some mental health conditions?"

"I don't know if I was aware or not, to be honest."

"Did anything that he did whether he had mental health problems or not, did that affect his writing in any way?"

"No."

"I want to ask you if you were aware that, just before this article was published, Carl was in the hospital for about a month?"

"I don't remember, honestly."

"Did you edit Mr. Leatherwood's stories?"

"Yes, I did."

"And did you heavily edit them? Were there—how much did you edit them?"

"Very little, very little. I mean, most feature stories require some editing. Even our best feature writers need some, and he had some but not a lot."

"Were you also in charge of overall features at the time?"

"Uh-huh."

"This weekend section here, is that something that you would have been in charge of?"

"Yes."

"And is this considered a feature here?"

"Yes. It's a cover story on fall."

"Who wrote that cover story?"

"Carl did, in November '86."

"Did you recall telling Carl after you saw the story that this is lovely writing?"

"I'm sure I did."

THE POSTMAN KNEW IT.

"Oh, man, I've been waiting for this all summer," he said, high-stepping across the intersection of Sugar Hill and Tanglewood.

The Boys of October were in the Astrodome that day, but the letter carrier alluded to something else. He could have borrowed a quote used by Mets Manager Davey Johnson, and proclaimed, “This is as good as it gets.”

Autumn was here, in Houston. The message was written on a cool breeze, carried by songbirds, and later delivered with flair.

And this weekend may be the best of the season—the best of times to enjoy the outdoors in Texas. People from the Big Thicket to the Hill Country who keep watch on the trees have forecast a peak of color in fall foliage about now.

Not that that’s all there is. Nature belies the cynics who, narrowly focused on the foliage, say we have no vibrant change of season, True, wild creatures must hustle less to prepare for winter in forests only spotted with brilliant color. The area is, however, the darling in fall of bird lovers and mushroom fanciers on a national scale. And the beaches have special appeal.

A statewide ramble in autumn can open up the biological wonder of Southeast Texas or a park in north Harris County that has built a display appropriate to a blissful Indian summer. Down on the middle coast, a record number of whooping crane chicks are arriving. And out in the Hill Country are the makings of a traditional downhome trip through brightly painted woods.

THE PADDLE SHOT OUT of my hands and away from the canoe. Current widened the gap between the two as an autumn sun set on Village Creek, about 100 miles east of Houston. I now coveted sage Wyatt Moore’s past practice of carrying two paddles when hunting ducks on Caddo Lake in northeast Texas.

He did it mostly for "bushwhacking," what they called his method of duck hunting up there where the season drifts through a little earlier.

Bushwhacking meant he would see a duck, drop his paddle instantly, and go to pumping shot. "I used to carry an extra paddle in the boat," Moore said, "and then if a duck jumped up, I could just forget about the paddle I was paddling with. Later, I would take the paddle in the boat and retrieve the one that fell off in the water."

Over in the Big Thicket, literally up a creek without a paddle, I looked at Chico, a Boston terrier, who had propped his front paws on the port gunnel to stand watch. He had the answer to our predicament. So I dog paddled belly down on the stern to retrieve the paddle.

Village Creek runs through a biological crossroads of international merit, with plant species converging there from all directions. The tangle of vegetation has long been called the Big Thicket. Portions are in a national preserve, though most of this creek is not. At most bends in the creek, white quartz sand invites a picnic or camping.

I paddled toward a sandbar draped with willows, toward a cypress-darkened slough that widens into a pond, toward remembrances of youth. A cypress swamp had existed behind the sandbar. The wind didn't penetrate the tangle there, and the mirrored surface of the water, where an ancient age seemed to hang as real as the Spanish moss, kindled awe.

As I reached my stamping ground, twilight was fading in the western sky, abbreviating the journey, but I embraced an autumnal reward. The crisp air quickened strokes, worked in conjunction with primeval craft and starlight to rejuvenate the soul.

Al Schotz, the director-naturalist of the Big Thicket Museum in Saratoga, stalked seasonal forest colors with me under a blue sky the next day. Transplanted from upstate New York, where the trees put on a splashy show, he found amazing things here.

"During the fall, most of your mushrooms are out," he said. "There are about 2,000 different kinds of mushrooms in the Big Thicket. That's unbelievable. And that's not including molds; that's just including what people would picture a mushroom as being."

We encountered several species of amanita mushrooms, very poisonous fungi, capped in deep orange and white. "The amanitas are most beautiful," my guide said. "They come in almost every color of the rainbow." One half-foot giant deserved the moniker "Big Daddy."

"Because of the humidity and warmer climate, people can find mushrooms on New Year's Day," Schotz said. "They come in all sizes and shapes. One looks like a turkey's tail, and that's what we call our official Thanksgiving mushroom here in the Big Thicket. Anyone interested in mycology—this is the place to be."

He noted earlier that "people have more of a chance to see wildlife during this time of year because of the cool, and the animals are out and about, getting prepared for the winter months." Our steamy summers keep most animals nocturnal then.

A squirrel had built a nest perhaps sixty feet up in the limbs of a tree. "Squirrels are beginning to store up acorns and pecans, and they put them in their special hiding places," he said. "And then they try to come back and find them. Fifty percent of the time they can't find their storage area." In our mild temperatures and without snow on the ground, it doesn't matter so much.

Some creatures do start to slow down. "Snakes seek refuge at about 60 degrees," Schotz said. "Honeybees cease to fly under 54 degrees. When it is below 54, they stay at their hive and they rotate—the ones on the outside will go inside to get warm, and vice versa."

Also coloring the area were red-seeded magnolia cones, purple American beautyberries, goldenrod, dark purple sweet-gum leaves, an orange tint of cypress, redheaded woodpeckers, yellow foliage on white ash and red on swamp maples. "What's different around Southeast Texas, than, say up in Michigan, where the leaves all change at once and are spectacular, is here one tree will change and then another, like a sequence, not all at one time," Schotz said.

INVERSELY, THE CHANGE to a duller color in bird color heightens interest in an autumn phenomenon on the Texas coast of continental importance.

"The thing in animal life to naturalists down here that signifies fall more than anything else is the migration of birds," said Carmine Stahl of Mercer Arboretum and Botanic Gardens, and Jesse Jones Park and Nature Center, both in North Harris County. "The little woodland songbirds come through here and head on to the tropics. One of the world's largest concentrations of wintering waterfowl is out here on the prairies around Katy and Hockley, and in Jefferson and Chambers counties."

Through the course of the year, you can usually see more species of birds within a hundred miles of Houston than anywhere else in the United States, he said. "It's one of the best birding places in the country."

Kay McCracken, a birder of note in Corpus Christi, pays tribute to what we can find in our own backyards. "Your area is really a bit more spectacular than ours in the fall—it has been lately, not always."

In Texas, one begins to see the broad-winged hawk migration over the Piney Woods in August and then around the coast, she said, and it funnels down through the point of Texas into Mexico. The birds number in the thousands. But autumn migrations aren't as concentrated in the bird world as those in the spring. "The birds aren't in any big hurry in the fall, and they take their time," she said. "They may linger in a spot that has food for four or five days. In the spring they refuel every time they stop and keep going to their breeding places."

Though the Houston area has its thrills, for birders like McCracken, the biggest attraction on the coast is near her home, in the Coastal Bend of the state. It is the wintering habitat of the only wild flock of whooping cranes.

The cranes start their 2,600-mile migration from western Canada for the area adjacent to Matagorda Island in September.

This year, the first whooper hit the Texas coast in mid-October, and most will have arrived by the end of November. The population of the rare birds has swelled to an estimated 115 because of abundant water at the breeding grounds in Canada. It is the highest number in the flock since their survival became a conservation cause.

The cranes literally stand head and shoulders above other birds. Measuring fifty inches high, they are the tallest birds in North America. Wings span seven feet from black tip to black tip. The adults sport red faces, the youngsters rust heads.

"We had 96 leave last spring to go north," said Dave Blankinship, whooping crane biologist of the National Audubon Society. "They had a very good reproductive year."

One bird died of natural causes in the spring migration, but about twenty young birds were produced and lived to begin the journey southward. That's a record, too.

"Of course, there's a good chance that some of those birds may get lost from one cause or another during migration," Blankinship said, "but we certainly are looking for well over 100. The increase in the young is primarily due to favorable weather conditions, water conditions on the breeding grounds."

At the time of our conversation, red tide was considered a serious potential threat to the whooping cranes.

"So far there hasn't been any concentrations of red tide up in the area where the cranes winter," Blankinship said. "We know that the organisms and their toxins are concentrated in shellfish like oysters and clams. Clams are a major food item of the whooping cranes.

"Fortunately, when the cranes first arrive here, they feed primarily on crabs, and it is not until later in the year that they really turn to clams as a greater part of their diet. In winter the water level drops, and the clams become more available. But it's a situation where conceivably only one or two clams would be enough to cause a crane some real problems. They will eat a clam if they come across it."

'TIS THE SEASON IN GALVESTON. A monarch butterfly flutters among the sun-drenched hibiscus blooms and palms outside the dining room at The San Luis Hotel. Strollers, both beachcombers and baby carriages, meander unscorched and uncrowded down the beach. Rooms cost less. There are those who fish under a harvest moon. Others dance on a skateboard or a wave or a paddlewheeler. A tour of the seawall in a little surrey is a pleasant thing, if attention to staying above the steep rocky shoulder is not diverted too long by wonderful bodies and sandcastles.

As do the songbirds and butterflies, the snowbirds come and migrate down the coast. Snowbird is not a good analogous term for the people visiting through the winter from the north. The real ones stay home and frolic in the snow.

Probably, the most brilliant leafy display accessible within weekend driving range from Houston can be found around the western Hill Country town of Utopia. The peak of bigtooth maple color will have probably passed by now, but another species vies with it in autumn dress, the Spanish oak on which the golden-cheeked warbler depends for caterpillars to feed its young in summer.

Bee Garrison, whose roots in the hills go back to early settlers, was anticipating "beautiful leaves" near her ranch and recommended sightseeing on roads running from Utopia to Gamer State Park and from Leakey to Vanderpool, "a beautiful drive anytime." People coming over in late November and early December may not see any maples, but the oaks are "so pretty," she said. "The only thing that would ruin it would be if we get a lot of rain and a lot of wind."

Hunters also find wild turkeys and a lot of white-tailed deer for the Thanksgiving table in those hills. It is an old custom.

"We served wild turkey for Thanksgiving when I was growing up," Garrison said. "We grew or found wild everything that we ate back then. Momma used to take venison and fry it up like chicken fried steak, put it down in fifty-five-gallon crocks, a layer of fried meat and a layer of melted lard, until she had the crocks full. Then you would still be having venison steaks long after the hunt. Sometimes they would kill a deer out of season to make jerky, to cure it in the heat of July and August. They would hang it in strips on a tin roof or on a clothesline."

Pecans are another bountiful harvest as smoke begins to rise from the hunters' campfires. Native and cultivated pecan trees grow on the northern edge of the Hill Country around San Saba. "At one time, we were the leading state in the union in native pecans," said John Lipe, horticulturist for the Texas Agricultural Extension Service. "It is said there are 500 miles of waterways in San Saba County. All of the rivers have wide bottoms, and pecans grow native in the bottoms. The estimate is 90,000 acres of native pecans just in that one county alone."

Hal Borland, a naturalist of national eminence, and others within the state have written bizarre accounts of the pioneer harvests. "For many years, only wild pecans came to market," Borland says. "The method of harvesting those wild ones now seems unbelievable.

Nut-gatherers went through the woods, chose the largest, heaviest-bearing pecan trees, and when the nuts were ripe, they cut down the trees. Then they put boys to work picking the nuts from the fallen giants. And that was the end of those pecan trees, forever."

When I first mentioned that story to Lipe, he could not believe it, either. "Sounds like one of those Aggie jokes," he said. "Obviously, it a lot easier to shake the pecans from the tree. To chop the tree down is a lot of work."

AN EARLIER PEOPLE returned home to north Harris County in autumn to apparently gather nuts in a more civilized way. The Akokisa Indians would live on clams and oysters in area saltwaters and then paddle their cypress dugout canoes back up Spring and Cypress Creeks to gather acorns and hickory nuts, hunt, and spend the winter.

The Akokisa traded hides with the Spanish and French from the beginning of European exploration in the 1500s. The tribe's population may have peaked at 3,000 but was decimated by diseases carried by the explorers. When Anglo settlers began trickling over from Louisiana in the 1820s, few of the natives remained.

"We have been developing a typical pioneer homesite of that period at the Jones park," Stahl said. "We have built a log cabin, a smokehouse, and other outbuildings—shed, corn crib, chicken house."

And the small group of Indians around then are not forgotten. A replica of their living quarters has been constructed. It is an oval hut of poles shingled with palmetto fronds, which grow in the state from here to the Big Thicket, and in other isolated stands.

"The fronds shed water very nicely," Stahl said. "Sometimes the Indians added furs for warmth in winter."

The park also contains the largest cypress and magnolia stands in Harris County along almost five miles of paved trails. Foliage color of the other trees may not measure up to the past because of "a bit of an unusual fall this year," Stahl noted. "One reason is that we had a long period of drought this summer . . . that condition caused a great many trees that normally do color up for us to lose their leaves early."

But the dry spell followed by an extended period of rain also produced some forest color unusual for this time of year. Observed Stahl, "We have had more spring-flowering trees blooming this fall than I can ever remember."

ONE HOUSTON PHOTOGRAPHER has chased autumn colors from East to West Texas. "It's flaky," said Blair Pittman, who has pursued the traditional image of fall with more determination than most, and found it. He stayed for two weeks waiting for it in the Guadalupe Mountains. Residents near the mountains on the New Mexico border kept saying that it wasn't right yet, and he had to get back to Houston. "We came back, and they called five days later to say, 'Hey, it's perfect, it's perfect.' I caught a plane and flew back up there. And it was perfect."

"OKAY," PETROU SAID, poised to ask Liebrum more questions. "Do you recall that at one time Carl asked you if he could be a full-time feature writer?"

"I don't honestly remember if he did."

"Is it possible he may have asked you?"

"He may have. We don't have very much turnover in the features department. So whenever there's an opening, a large number of people in the room usually ask. Feature jobs are considered to be good jobs."

"Could Carl have been a full-time feature writer?"

"I doubt it."

"Why is that?"

"Well, general feature writing is different. He has a specialty. His specialty was traveling in the state of Texas. He wrote really well about travel. He wrote nice features about people in the state of Texas, but that's not a job that we were funded for. A general feature writer has to report, interview, cover a wide variety of subjects from abortion to new clothes. I mean, there's just—it's very broad. He had a particular interest that he was good at, reporting at."

"All right, but for some of these features stories, he did interview people, did he not?"

"Uh-huh, yes."

"He could go out and interview people; isn't that right?"

"He certainly could go out and interview the people he interviewed."

"And some of them you thought were wonderful pieces, right?"

"Right."

"Okay. Do you recall ever approaching Mr. Peter O'Sullivan, I think, at the time? Was he the editor in chief?"

"Yes."

"Do you recall approaching him on Carl's behalf and asking whether there could be a spot for Carl as a feature writer?"

"I don't believe that I ever did that. I don't remember that at all."

"If Carl has testified that you did that, would he be mistaken?"

"I believe he would be. I don't remember that at all. This is the first time I've heard that."

"Are there freelance writers?"

"Yes."

"What's the situation today with being a freelance writer? Can you get something published in *The Post* as a freelance writer?"

"A very few articles are bought anymore, and it's true with all newspapers. We have a staff, and we use staff material to fill up pages. We just don't need freelancers as we once did."

"It's hard for someone to make a living being a freelance writer?"

"I think it's hard anytime for anybody to freelance as a writer."

"No matter how good their writing is?"

"Yeah."

"Okay. Do some writers sometimes write at home, at their computers at home?"

"Yes. But a full-time staff person would not work from his home."

"At this point you don't have any full-time staff people working at home, you say. But if somebody was disabled, and had some kind of health problem where he could work at home out of his own computer that did not require him to report to the office, could that person work out of his home?"

"Theoretically."

Bounds took up the questioning.

"Did you ever have occasion to see Mr. Leatherwood bring his dog into the newsroom?"

"One day, yes."

"Was there a disruption?"

"Well, it was a spectacle, I'd say. I guess we'd call it a disruption."

"You were asked a question about whether or not a person as a staff feature writer could work at home. You said that that was theoretically possible. Is that what you said?"

"Because people all have home computers now, we have had writers every so often say I'd like to work at home, you know, da-da-da, I need to keep the kids or whatever; and it works sometimes, and then other times, they have to be in the office."

"Do you think it would be reasonable or practical to have a staff writer full-time working from their home?"

"It's not desirable actually, because we think that the writers need to be there, and they need to feed off each other. They give each other ideas. They discuss their stories. Operating in a vacuum is not the best way to do good feature stories."

"You said that in your opinion Mr. Leatherwood could not be a staff feature writer. Why is that?"

"As I said, he has a specialty, and that's what he's demonstrated, and that's what his interest is, that's what he's good at. We would not hire someone who did not have background with a lot of—showing a lot of range, and he does not show a lot of range."

"People with chronic illnesses, are they being accommodated at *The Post*?"

"We have new ones, you know. Now, with the computers, we have that carpal tunnel syndrome, and that is a problem, yes. It's very accommodating."

"Currently?"

"Currently."

PETROU: "WE CALL DR. ARCHIE BLACKBURN.

"Tell us basically what you do for a living."

"I'm a psychiatrist and am full-time at the VA Hospital and the medical school, Baylor."

"Are you also a medical doctor?"

"Yes."

"Do you know a patient by the name of Carl Leatherwood?"

"Yes, I do."

"When did Mr. Leatherwood become your patient?"

"I first saw him in December of 1988 and saw him until I went back to full-time in the Medical Center in June of '92."

"Do you recall where he was working when you first saw him?"

"He was working at *The Post*."

"Okay. Were you able, from talking to Mr. Leatherwood, to determine how important the job was to him?"

"Well, I did certainly learn that the job was very important to him, and my recollection is that he had been there for twenty-two years, and it was extremely important to him. I guess that I came to know that after he lost the job, which was perhaps six months after I had been seeing him, and his clinical condition, of course, worsened considerably at that point."

"From examining Mr. Leatherwood and reviewing his medical history, do you know if he ever deliberately stopped taking his medication?"

"I actually thought that he did that originally. That's, I guess, my suspiciousness as a clinician. But I came to understand rather confidently that that was not the case. That he would start having his episodes of manic symptomatology first, and then in the course of that sometimes would terminate his medication or just not be taking his medication."

"I want to turn your attention to the fall and winter of 1988, when Mr. Leatherwood first came to see you. Which hospital was he admitted to?"

"This was Memorial Southwest in Houston."

"In this hospitalization, did he come to the hospital voluntarily?"

"On this occasion, he did not."

"Did he later agree to stay in the hospital voluntarily?"

"He did."

"Were you able to stabilize his condition?"

"Yes, we were. We basically restarted the lithium that he had been on, and we also used a small amount of tranquilizing drug."

"Did you release him to go back to work, Dr. Blackburn?"

"Yes, I did. But his return to work was difficult for him in some respects. His mental state had cleared rather remarkably in a short period of time. But my recollection is that, from my office contacts over that period of time, the difficulty for him was associated with the fact that he came to feel rather strongly that he was not going to be allowed to continue in his work, and he was given a new assignment. I don't know the nature of that in terms of details, but he perceived that it was unlikely that he was going to be able to continue to work even though he felt able to go to work."

"And how did this perception of a person with bipolar disorder that he may not be allowed to remain at the job that he's had for twenty-two years, how did that affect him?"

"Well, it was very stressful, very stressful. It had a significant impact on him."

"Do you recognize this exhibit?"

"Yes. This was a letter that I wrote to Mr. Leatherwood's employment. It was to Mr. Williamson, who was the executive editor at *The Post*, and I was simply indicating that the patient was under my care and had been in the hospital, and in my opinion he could return to work."

"Okay. I want to direct your attention to the second paragraph here, where it says 'prior to hospitalization for at least one month, he was seriously disabled by his symptoms.' Does that mean that you felt for at least a month before he even entered the hospital he was having some problems?"

"That was my impression, yes. I would think it was unlikely that he was functioning normally during that period of time before."

"If there are some fellow workers and supervisors that did not know that he was experiencing mental health problems, could they believe that he just wasn't doing his work?"

"That could be true."

"Do you know if around June of 1989, a few months later after that letter, that Mr. Leatherwood was hospitalized again?"

"Yes."

"Okay. I want you to look at another exhibit, a hospital summary. This is for the date 6/19 through 6/24/89. Did he voluntarily come to the hospital this time?"

"My recollection is that this was a voluntary admission. His family and friends and colleagues had been noticing him going through changes and had coerced him into coming would be the right way to say it."

"After his hospital stay, was he stabilized again, and was he able to go back to work?"

"My recommendation was to return to work as soon as possible."

"Here, what is Defendant's Exhibit No. 9?"

"This is a letter with my signature to Mr. Jim Janiga at *The Houston Post*, director of Human Resources. I explained to him that the patient had gone through a change in his mental state, not as severe as before, that he was hospitalized and I had adjusted his medications and that I felt he was ready to return to work."

"And you say there in the first sentence he experienced a hypomanic mood shift? What does that mean?"

"Basically that is something less than manic. An episode is heightened mood, some symptoms but without significant compromise in the ability to carry on ordinary life activities."

"Is it your understanding that he was not allowed to return to work, and as a consequence of being fired, his condition worsened?"

"Yes. It was a major upheaval for him. The stress had an adverse affect."

"Okay. Did his condition reach a point, Dr. Blackburn, where you had to write letters and fill out forms to his long-range disability insurance company and to Social Security informing them about Mr. Leatherwood's worsened condition?"

"I did."

"In your opinion was there a time after he was fired when Carl Leatherwood was disabled from doing the kind of work that he did before he was fired?"

"That would have been my opinion some months of that particular year."

"When you determined that Carl's condition had gotten worse after he was fired, did you determine that he could be disabled forever, from ever working again?"

"I don't think I ever thought that."

"Could he recover from the firing and at some point in the future resume productive work?"

"Certainly."

"Is it possible for people who have mental health illnesses to work in jobs that are not as stressful as the jobs that they used to have?"

"Certainly. It's always better to work than not to work."

Judge Gibson: "We will resume with your testimony, Doctor, tomorrow morning. I hope you enjoy the afternoon off. The weather is with you."

CHAPTER 11
DOCTOR'S HEAT

PETROU BEGAN THE NEXT MORNING with Leatherwood's doctor back on the stand.

"Dr. Blackburn, you wrote Mr. Leatherwood a letter in which you stated that you remained cautiously optimistic that he can be gainfully employed; is that correct?"

"That's correct."

"And can you tell us why you feel that way?"

"That letter was written at a point after he had made some substantial gains during the previous year in terms of schooling, work with the Texas Rehabilitation Commission, and was beginning to focus."

"Dr. Blackburn, if Carl Leatherwood is accommodated for his illness, is there any reason he cannot resume his lifelong occupation of being a journalist?"

"There would be no reason. Perhaps anyway, I'm not sure that any accommodation is required for him to be able to proceed with his life and be gainfully employed again."

"I have no further questions," Petrou said.

The court: "Cross-examination."

Bounds came forward.

"GOOD MORNING, DR. BLACKBURN. I've put in front of you four of defendant's exhibits, which are records from your files regarding Mr. Leatherwood. Now, you testified that you first examined him in December of 1988; is that correct?"

"That's correct."

"I would like for you to turn to page 79 in Exhibit 3, a record of Gayle Goodman, a social worker. Would you please read for me the second paragraph under 'Presenting Problem'?"

"There is a significant discrepancy between the patient's account of the events preceding the commitment and that of the father and Mr. Gary Fortenberry."

"And the next four sentences, please?"

"'The patient denied any emotional difficulties warranting the extreme measure of commitment. He only went so far as to describe himself as eccentric. He expressed bewilderment at the concern and attempt of family and friends to put him in the hospital. He described their efforts as insensitive and repeatedly stated that he wished only to live a peaceful life.'"

"Mr. Leatherwood often referred to people who tried to get him into the hospital as insensitive, didn't he?"

"I don't know."

"You never heard him use that term before?"

"I don't know that he often—that he often referred to people as insensitive. I've heard that at least once or twice, but I can't say often."

"Okay. There's been testimony about Mr. Leatherwood's episode in the fall of 1988. This hospitalization began on December the 8th; is that correct?"

"That's correct. That's when I first saw him."

"At what point does a person become disorganized or delusional or lose their judgment in the midst of an episode?"

"That's an impossible question. Anything can happen, I suppose, at any point. It's not an all or none—psychosis is not like a light switch turning off and on. One's judgment and rationality waxes and wanes."

"Mr. Leatherwood experienced a severe psychosis in 1988, did he not?"

"He did have a severe episode of psychosis, yes, or severe psychotic episode."

"Now, there's been testimony that Mr. Leatherwood went into his employer, *The Houston Post*, and resigned his employment in somewhere around December 1st of 1988, or were you aware of that?"

"I knew that he had tendered a resignation."

"Would you please read for me the last paragraph on that page 79?"

"Okay. 'The patient indicated that he had travelled to the East Coast in October and suddenly went to the Southwest after Thanksgiving. He states that he wished to relocate to Santa Fe, New Mexico. Upon his return to Houston, he tendered his resignation.'"

"Isn't it true, Dr. Blackburn, that you knew that when Mr. Leatherwood returned to work in January of 1989, that that was only on a conditional basis for a couple of months so that Mr. Leatherwood could earn a little bit of money and have an opportunity to look for another job?"

"That is not a strange idea to me. I heard that statement. He was—my understanding is that he was attempting to get himself reinstated, that he was—felt like that his tendering the resignation, which apparently did occur at a point when he was rather irrational, was not either his wish or in his best interest."

"Even though he had decided to relocate and had some complaints about his employer?"

"Well, he also decided a lot of other things that—such as to take a hotel room and continue traveling and accumulated bills in a hotel room when he was not in the city and was doing many things that were irrational in at least part of his illness process."

"Isn't it true that you in fact had a telephone conversation with Ernie Williamson in which he told you that he was going to allow Carl to come back just for a couple of months so that he could earn some money and look for a new job, and you told Mr. Blackburn—I mean, you told Mr. Williamson that you felt that was extremely humane and generous of *The Houston Post*?"

"I had a conversation with Mr. Williamson. The detail of your words, I do not recall. The gist of the conversation in my memory was that Mr. Williamson was supportive of Carlton coming back, was hopeful to get him back, but felt that the powers that be were not going to support that but that he was able at least temporarily to arrange some employment. So part of what you're saying is my recollection, too."

"But if Mr. Williamson were to testify that that's what you told him, you couldn't dispute that, could you?"

"No, I couldn't dispute it. I would say I don't remember all of those details."

"But the bottom line is, you don't remember?"

Petrou: "Objection, Your Honor. The witness has answered that he does remember certain details."

The court: "Overrule the objection."

"Please, turn to page 85. Is this your admission report?"

"That's correct. This would have been my first dictation at the time the patient came into the hospital."

"At the time that you read—I mean, the time that you dictated this report, you had read the five or six pages that had been prepared by the social worker; is that correct?"

"That's not correct. This would have been dictated the day or the day following his admission, and the social worker's detailed history would not have been available to me for probably a week."

"Would you read for me and the Court the two sentences at the beginning of the paragraph about 'Diagnostic Impression'?"

"The effect was mildly volatile. Irritability and, in particular, anger about being hospitalized against his will was manifest."

"Over on page 87. The first line of your proposed treatment plan. Read it, please."

"Hospitalized for observation and protection."

"Who were you protecting with this hospitalization?"

"I was protecting the patient in my estimation."

"Now, at some point you did read the report of Ms. Goodman, the social worker?"

"That's correct."

"Did it present any kind of surprises to you?"

"There was new information in terms of history that I had not acquired. No major surprises."

"Did you find that your conversations with Mr. Leatherwood, his stories regarding events, were different from the report that you read with Ms. Goodman?"

"There were differences."

"Would you turn to page 80. At what point did you make your determination that Mr. Leatherwood had been disabled by this episode for approximately a month before his termination—I mean, before his admittance to the hospital?"

"I don't have any recollection."

"Okay. Would you please read the first sentence in the third paragraph."

"The parents and Mr. Fortenberry's account of these events present a picture of the patient's emotional deterioration since early October."

"So sometime within the first few days of Mr. Leatherwood's hospitalization, you had indication that his episode had actually begun some two months before his admittance; wouldn't that be correct?"

"That's correct."

"Would you, please, read the first two sentences of the next paragraph for the Court?"

"The parents report a confusing situation around Thanksgiving in which the patient invited them to Houston for the holiday and then denied knowledge of the plan when they arrived. He refused to transport them upon their arrival, although he met them for dinner. They reported that he acted inappropriately, was unkempt, and spoke loudly at the restaurant.

"When he suddenly left for the West Coast after Thanksgiving, he called the parents often but refused to tell them of his whereabouts?"

"That's fine. Is it normal for a person who experiences episodes such as Mr. Leatherwood to act inappropriately, to be unkempt, and to speak loudly?"

"It's certainly something that is often reported. These are the type of things that lead one to a diagnosis of manic depressive illness. A manic episode."

"And Mr. Leatherwood himself does exhibit these types of symptoms when he gets into a manic episode, does he not?"

"That's correct."

"Would you please read the second sentence of the fifth paragraph on page 81?"

"According to the parents, they had been in contact with the patient's supervisors at *The Houston Post* in an effort to track the patient's whereabouts."

"So you had an indication on reading those notes *The Post* as well as the—the people from *The Post* as well as the patient's parents as well as Mr. Fortenberry and his girlfriend had all been involved in trying to get Mr. Leatherwood to go to the hospital; is that correct?"

"There's certainly some involvement in their efforts to gather information."

"You testified yesterday that outside stresses often affect a person with bipolar disorder and can cause the reoccurrence of episodes: Is that correct?"

"That's correct."

"Is the condition of personal relationships also an outside stress that can cause recurrence of episodes?"

"Certainly."

"Would you turn to page 83 and read the first two sentences of the third paragraph?"

"The patient's relationship with his parents is not good. He states that he has been unsuccessful in breaking the ties with them."

"Isn't it true that you have seen a pattern in Mr. Leatherwood's experiences in his episodes, and contact with his parents or arguments with his parents have contributed to recurrence of his episodes?"

"That's one of the circumstances that have been associated with the recurrence of his episodes. There are many elements of stress. No one particular stress that I would attribute, I would not say that employment stresses are the only stress this gentleman has had, nor would I say that relationship stresses are the only stresses that have been important in terms of his illness."

"So all of these relationships have equal bearing on his psychological well-being?"

"I would not say equal, necessarily. They all have varying degrees of bearing, yes."

"Were you seeing Mr. Leatherwood on a regular basis from his hospitalization in October through his hospitalization in June of 1989?"

"Approximately monthly, perhaps biweekly initially."

"I said hospitalization in October but I meant December of '88."

"That's what I understood you to mean."

"Would you turn to page 72? The third paragraph under 'History of Present Illness.' Begin with the second sentence."

"Okay. 'The patient remains on a regimen of lithium carbonate, 600 milligrams twice daily. To return to work. He had biweekly office appointments through May 9th. Between that time and an office visit on 6/1/89, a change occurred. Telephone contacts from the patient's girlfriend and employer indicated that emotional behavioral change.

"The girlfriend learned of changes after the patient went on a driving trip with his aged parents. The parents had also been aware of substantial emotional change in the patient."

"Well, how much credence do you put in telephone calls that you receive from family and friends and coworkers of your patients when they call you to discuss the possibilities of emotional changes?"

"All depends on the circumstance and the informants. I try to listen."

"In this particular case, you had telephone calls from his girlfriend and from Mr. Williamson possibly at *The Post* or at least someone at his employer indicating that his mood had changed and his behavior had changed; is that true?"

"Uh-huh, yes."

"Did you not act on any of those phone calls?"

"I would have taken action. I don't remember the specific nature. I think it would have been that the patient was to see me and, in fact, he did see me at some point, at which time I made some adjustment in medication."

"Would that have been the visit on 6/1/89 that you made the—"

"I suspect so. I don't remember the precise details of the timing."

"Do you ever when you get conversation—get calls like this, do you ever take the time to call your patients and check with them if they don't come in?"

"I do on some occasions. That's not a customary practice, but I certainly support the individuals coming in for appointments when something is changing so that we can evaluate our phone conversation or adjust medication. As a last resort, hospitalization would be something that would be considered."

"Would you please read the next little paragraph and then the first three sentences in the paragraph after that."

"The patient had uncharacteristically left the girlfriend at a Hill Country festival. He was appearing preoccupied and easily distracted."

"Continue."

"'At work, hyperactivity and impaired concentration with workers was reported. The patient was reported to be unable to sit down. He was spending more time talking with other people.'"

"Thank you. These things had been reported to you by his girlfriend and by his—people at his employment, correct?"

"That's correct."

"What else are these people supposed to do? If they have contacted you, told you that they've got a problem, how much further are they supposed to go? Are they supposed to bodily restrain Mr. Leatherwood and bring him to your office?"

"I don't have a particular opinion about that. This information is about a hospitalization that occurred as a result of this information and these changes. On this occasion the patient was hospitalized, voluntarily, treatment was modified, and that was good. I would have no complaints about anybody at this time in the picture."

"So the types of accommodation that you're talking about are what these people have been doing; is that correct? They have been noticing behavioral change, trying to get him to go see a doctor, and reporting that?"

"Some people, certainly some people have been doing this very effectively."

"You don't think it's the responsibility of every person who comes into contact with Mr. Leatherwood to do these kinds of things."

"Certainly not."

"Are there certain cases of bipolar disorder such as Mr. Leatherwood's, where he will experience an episode even if he is taking his medication religiously?"

"Yes."

"Now, following Mr. Leatherwood's discharge in June of 1989, you wrote another letter, this time to Mr. Janiga, his employer at *The Post*; is that correct?"

"That's correct. What page?"

"Page 67. In that letter, you simply state in your opinion he can resume his usual work activity immediately; is that correct?"

"That's correct."

"In a February letter, you discussed the continuation of treatment of outpatient therapy. You don't discuss that in this June '89 letter. Why is that?"

"I don't know. I mean there were certainly plans for continuing outpatient treatment, but I didn't include that in the letter because of the—the letter was basically to say that in my opinion, the patient could return to work."

"It was your opinion on June 29, 1989, that Mr. Leatherwood was perfectly capable of returning to work?"

"That's correct."

"This was to return to work in his usual occupation as a copy writer for *The Houston Post*; is that correct?"

"That's correct."

"Had you ever spoken to anyone at *The Post* about what Mr. Leatherwood's job duties and functions on a daily basis were?"

"Not in great detail. That would have been some of, I think, the communication with Mr. Williamson some months before; but I did not pursue that, nor do I have any sufficient understanding of the business to have understood what I was told if someone had told me all of that."

"You didn't think it was important for you to know what his usual work activity consisted of before you released him to return to that activity?"

"That's more or less correct, because I did not see compromise of his mental function being such that he could not perform the jobs that he was accustomed to performing. I felt like he had not performed his work well when he was psychotic. When he was nonpsychotic, he could do his work satisfactorily; that was my sense. So the nature of the job at that point was not something I was concerned about."

"Did you have an occasion to write a letter on August 11 of 1989 regarding Mr. Blackburn's health and his ability to perform his job?"

"Mr. Leatherwood's health and—"

"Ability."

"Yes."

"Ability to perform his job?"

"In August."

"I believe it's on page 66."

"August 11, yes."

"This letter is stated 'To whom it may concern;' correct?"

"That's correct.

"I think that Mr. Leatherwood needed the letter in terms at this point in beginning to look at future employment. This was after he had been terminated. There no doubt may have also been some need from this with respect to his attorney. This was a multipurpose letter to document, basically, the status at that point."

"There's been testimony that Mr. Leatherwood was terminated effective July the 12th in a letter dated July the 25th. This letter was written on August 11th. And in fact, at about that time, Mr. Leatherwood was attempting to get long-term disability benefits as well as Social Security disability benefits; is that correct?"

"That is likely, correct. I don't recollect the precise dates on the nature of the issues with regard to long-term. I know that those were all relevant, but I was not keeping track of the precise nature of those."

"But, in fact, you wrote letters and filled out reports and sent medical documentation to both the long-term disability carrier and the Social Security administration; is that correct?"

"I'm sure that's true."

"That was in an attempt to facilitate Mr. Leatherwood's obtaining benefits from both of those sources?"

"That's correct."

"Now, you wrote the letter on June 29 saying that, in your opinion, he could resume his usual work activity. On August 11, you wrote this letter."

"Uh-huh."

"In paragraph two, the second sentence says, 'Because of these periods of fluctuation in his emotional stability, Mr. Leatherwood may not be able to work with any continuity in his chosen profession or perhaps any other profession.'"

"Uh-huh."

"What had occurred between June 29 and August 11 to change your position and your opinions so dramatically? He had not had another episode, had he?"

Petrou: "Objection. One question at a time if you would, please."

The court: "Overrule the objection. Overrule the objection."

"The change—several changes. It was during that time that the patient was terminated from his employment, and his mood had substantially changed. He was in this period more depressed, he was not in a manic episode, he was not out of control, he did not require hospitalization, but his emotional state was substantially different. His ability in my judgment to pursue some kind of work at that point was substantially less than it had been at the time, both times, after hospital treatment in December '88 and in June '89.

"He chronically responded as people often do when they're in manic episodes. The response—the treatment when they're more depressed—is often slower. But that was just the fact that his clinical condition had changed in my judgment from June until August."

"In that six-month period, how many times had you actually seen Mr. Leatherwood for visits?"

"From June to August, it wasn't six months."

"I mean, six-week period. I apologize."

"I had probably seen him only a couple of times. I don't remember the dates of outpatient appointments, but I would have seen him within several weeks of his hospitalization and then approximately monthly, maybe some extra ones. But I would have had very little contact, but it doesn't take a lot of contact if a person's mood is substantially different and if circumstances are substantially different.

"At this point when I was writing this letter, the patient was fearing destitution. He was unemployed, he did not have plans for employment, he had his bills to pay, et cetera. He was quite concerned, and he was depressed, and that's reflected, I think, in this."

"Had you altered Mr. Leatherwood's medication at any time in that six-week period?"

"I don't remember a change at that point."

"In fact, you did not alter his medication during that period. You did not alter his medication?"

"I said I don't recall altering it during that time."

"He had not been hospitalized during this six-week period either, had he?"

"No."

"And it's your testimony that you probably saw him maybe twice in that six-week period?"

"That would be reasonable. I have no idea."

"Did you have any conversation or telephone conversations or contacts from his parents or his girlfriend or had you had any conversation with anyone from *The Post* in that six-week period?"

"I don't recall any other communication at that time."

"At the bottom of that middle paragraph, you go on to say, 'The manic phases have occurred sporadically in spite of his use of maintenance medication.'"

"Uh-huh."

"'Because of these unpredictable episodes and the necessity of hospitalization, I cannot say that Mr. Leatherwood would be able to perform the material duties of his occupation with a reasonable continuity.'"

"We're talking again about his usual work activity or the material duties of his occupation which you've testified you legally never found out exactly what that was, did you?"

"That's correct. I knew only that they were editorial in nature. And the most important thing from that perspective was that he had performed these duties as far as I understood reasonably well for nineteen or twenty years, and I thought he could do that again."

"Would you read the last paragraph of that letter, please?"

"'From having evaluated and treated Mr. Leatherwood, I know that his education, training, and experience have all been in the newspaper-field as an editor of some type. As this is his current occupation, and as I have already stated, he's disabled with respect to its performance. It follows that he would likely be disabled with respect to similar occupations to which he would be suited by virtue of training and experience.

"So what I've done, I'm prognosticating as far as when the patient is substantially down, he's not manic, he still has the same illness. And we're never very good at prognosticating. As a matter of fact, he has probably done better in terms of his return to ability to function cognitively than I thought he might at this particular time.'"

"In fact, you weren't able to actually prognosticate about his condition from—approximately month to month; is that correct?"

"It has nothing to do with month to month. The fact is, we can never prognosticate that well. In fact, the whole effort of therapy, I guess, is to—when we're pessimistic, to disprove our pessimism with efforts to facilitate the patient functioning better than we think they're able to do."

"Being aware—"

The judge: "I think that this is as good a point as we can find to take a break for a brief mid-morning recess. The jury may retire."

AFTER THE RECESS, Bounds returned to her tough pursuit:

"With regard to your statement, Dr. Blackburn, that the loss of Mr. Leatherwood's job had a significant impact on him—I think you said that yesterday as well as today—isn't it true that most people's job and the loss of that job has a significant impact on them?"

"Yes, that's true."

"You stated that your opinion regarding Mr. Leatherwood's prognosis of never being able to return to work has since changed; is that correct?"

"That's correct."

"When did that change?"

"It changed over a period of approximately a year to a year and a half, during which time he managed to work with educational opportunities, TRC, completed courses in school making some adjustments, some change from one subject to another and made satisfactory grades and continued to maintain his emotional stability during much of that time in spite of having some subsequent setbacks toward the latter time that I was seeing him. But he certainly demonstrated that he was more able to function than he had been in the summer following his termination or during the summer that he was terminated from employment."

"Please look at Exhibit 4, page 7, which is the first volume of the Standard Insurance Records. Do you have that?"

"Okay. This is an insurance form. I completed it on 8/22/89."

"Which was some 11 days after you had written this letter; is that correct?"

"I suppose so."

"And you put on the bottom of that under 'prognosis,' could you read the remarks to the Court, please?"

"'Based on the recurring clinical psychotic episodes, I believe it unlikely that the patient can return to and sustain his usual or similar work.'"

"Now, you told me that it was your opinion in October—I mean, in August that he could not continue his usual work, correct?"

"That's correct."

"But that it was your opinion on June 29 of 1989 that he could continue in his usual work, correct?"

"That's correct."

"Now, at the top of that page under what's marked No. 3, 'Assessment'?"

"Uh-huh."

"It says, 'Date you recommend patient should stop working.' Did you fill in that date?"

"I have June 24th, I believe."

"You filled that in?"

"Which I think was the day of hospitalization, if I'm not mistaken."

"Actually, Mr. Leatherwood was hospitalized from June 19 until June 24 of 1989, correct?"

"Oh, okay."

"So in August, it became your opinion that as of 6/24, which was the date of his discharge, he should quit working; is that correct?"

"I'm not sure. I perhaps didn't read this very well. I don't know, because it's not—my memory is not that I recommended he stop working on that day but that, in fact, he had—was not allowed to go back to work at that date."

"But, in fact, Mr. Leatherwood hadn't been at work since June 1, had he?"

"That sounds correct, yeah, when he went in the hospital. But I think, if my memory serves me correctly, I recommended that he return to work at the end of the hospitalization. And I think I must have been reading this as a typical insurance form that I'm supposed to give the date when the patent last was employed or the last working day. I can't quibble on that. I said 'effort to return to work January through April '89 failed in spite of ongoing treatment.'"

"So is it your testimony that in August of 1989 it was your opinion that he could not—that he should stop working on June 24th?"

"It was my—it was in my knowledge that he had not been working during that period of time. I don't want to, I guess, belabor that, but I don't think that I recommended on 6/24 as I gave that date—I filled it out myself, but I don't think I recommended that he stop working at that time. I think I was filling this out as though he had not been working from June until the date in August when I was completing this form."

"So either you didn't recommend that he quit working on June 24th, or you didn't read the form; is that what you're saying?"

"I read—if I read the form, I read it incorrectly. That would be my speculation. At least I don't think it's consistent with the letter that I wrote in June if I'm not mistaken."

"It certainly is not—"

"From the discharge summary when he left the hospital, I felt he should return to work."

"Well, I think we're in agreement that it is not consistent with the letter that you sent to *The Post* on June 29th, aren't we?"

"That's correct, so I must be inconsistent."

"Following these letters that you wrote in August 1989, did you continue to see Mr. Leatherwood on a monthly basis?"

"That's correct."

"And he, in fact, had another manic episode in the fall of 1989, did he not?"

"That's correct."

"Would you turn to page 63 in Exhibit No. 3? Is this a summary that you wrote or dictated?"

"That's correct. It is a summary that I wrote. It appears not to have the day of admission. I must have been confused at that time, too."

"On the next page, page 64 in the lower left-hand corner, there are some numbers?"

"Dictation numbers which would be close to the time of admission."

"Is that the 'D' that says 11/16/89?"

"That's correct. That would be the time it was dictated, and 'T' is the time it was transcribed."

"So this was dictated by you approximately November the 16th of 1989; is that correct?"

"That's correct. Actually it was—the admission was 11/16, the discharge 12/4."

"Okay, good. Looking at page 63, would you read for the court the first sentence under 'History of Present Illness'?"

"'For the past month, the undersigned had been receiving calls from friends and family of patient suggesting another shift in the patient's mood. He was beginning to be talkative and rambling, restless and preoccupied.'"

"Below that a couple of sentences you say, 'On several office visits, the last on October 30th, the patient maintained reasonable emotional control and confirmed his compliance with usual 1200 milligram lithium carbonate daily.'"

"Uh-huh."

"Did you make any efforts at that time, October 30 or those visits, to change his medication?"

"I would have to review the office visit material to say precisely whether I did or didn't at that time. I don't remember."

"But you did not hospitalize him based on your visits with him at that time?"

"That's correct."

"And at the time that you were having these visits and he was maintaining reasonable emotional control, you were also receiving phone calls from family and friends, were you not?"

"I think the phone calls were subsequent. They were after the hospitalization, but I don't think they were before—I don't know the precise time that was."

"It states here that for the past month, the undersigned had been receiving calls from family and friends. Your last office visit was on October 30, and hospitalization you just said began November 19. So would that have been—"

"I'm not sure whether the calls came before; they came sometime reasonably close to the time. He subsequently was hospitalized two weeks afterwards. So my assumption from this is the end of two weeks. I had additional contacts, reports that didn't coincide exactly with my observations at the time I saw him."

"But you put in here that for the past month, which we've determined would be a month prior to November 16, you were receiving these calls?"

"Okay."

"Are you saying now that that was incorrect and that was only for the previous two weeks?"

"I don't remember. I don't remember that."

"So this document is really the best evidence of what was occurring at that time; is it not?"

"Probably the document, which I think you have my notations of office visits, would be more likely to show whether I recommended hospitalization or whether I had had phone calls from family or friends before that visit. That doesn't trouble me too much. It may have been—either way, I would not necessarily change the treatment on the basis of the input that I had received. I would be confronting the patient with what I was hearing, looking at what—how he was looking, seeing what he was doing. I might recommend medication change, I might recommend some altered strategy. So I don't quibble about whether I know the significance of whether they called before or after."

"Well, the significance that I see is that you're saying here that for the past month which would be sometime beginning in the middle of October, you've been receiving calls from friends and family of the patient, which by my understanding from your testimony and a prior expert's would be his support group."

"Okay."

"What you're telling me is that you saw him and made an assessment and—"

"At that particular—at the time I saw him that he was in reasonable emotional control."

"So you discounted their information or their observations regarding his situation; is that not correct?"

"I don't know that that means I discounted it."

"Well, you obviously decided that you, as the trained professional, knew more than they did, and based upon your personal observation, it was not as serious as they seemed to think it was?"

"I did not call the police—"

"No, I'm not asking you that."

"—lock him up."

The judge: "Pardon me, but don't overlap each other.

"Proceed."

"I'M NOT ASKING YOU if you called the police. I'm asking you if you changed his medication, and you've obviously stated that you didn't feel at that time on October 30 that it was necessary for him to be hospitalized. Is that what you're saying?"

"All I'm—what I've said is that I don't remember if I changed the medication at this time. I did not hospitalize him at that time. I don't remember whether—I wondered whether this might end up in another hospitalization, what was happening, but I didn't hospitalize him at that time. The patient appeared reasonably stable, and I did not remember anything important to put in the summary at that point."

"What does 'reasonable stability' or 'reasonable emotional control' mean to you?"

"That means that the patient is not having obvious delusions, hallucinations, is not hyperactive, is not loud, is not manicky. That's basically what I mean. So everybody in here right now is reasonably, emotionally stable."

"You testified yesterday that it was certainly preferable to get someone such as Mr. Leatherwood with a bipolar disability into the hospital or to notice a manic episode as quickly as possible; isn't that correct?"

"That's correct."

"You also testified that the beginning symptoms of these types of episodes are a mood swing, increased repetition in speech, things like that; is that correct?"

"That's correct."

"And those types of things, the mood swings, are what you were receiving phone calls about; is that correct?"

"That's correct. As I say, I don't know the precise times of all the phone calls and what each phone call was about.

"If, for example, the phone—the hyperactivity was obvious and the dysfunction in other people's eyes was obvious and if I saw the patient and didn't at least discuss—consider with him possible adjustment of medication, that would have been an error on my part. I may have made an error. I may have made a misjudgment, but I don't remember that.

"I'd have to look back at the notation as to what my thoughts were about the medication. But that is—it is true that if the individual is having increased hyperactivity, if there's sleeplessness beginning to occur, this is a telltale sign for me and the patient in the long run to learn—for the—have the patient learn to recognize some of these things so that we can adjust medication on the telephone, for example, with just a call, for example, we need to increase the medication."

"If you are considered to be the learned professional in this particular situation, and two weeks prior to the admission of this patient you did not notice any problem or in your judgment there was not a problem, how can ordinary coworkers or friends and family be expected to spot that sort of thing?"

"I'm not saying that people should spot that. I also was not saying that I didn't spot any problem. He was coming to me on a relatively regular basis because he had ongoing problems. I don't automatically change the medication. I may offer some support, try to understand, try to get the individual to moderate what their activities are which may be self-monitoring, may be reducing some of the stresses."

"Approximately just over halfway down that paragraph toward the right it begins, 'On the day before.'"

"On the day before the night of admission, he was brought home by a neighbor—neighborhood security patrolman who found him lying on the lawn. Subsequently, he asked his cousin to take him to the hospital, which he did. However, while admission was being arranged, he ran away from the hospital."

"Continue."

"Apparently, the family contacted Houston Police Department, and officers located him and brought him to the hospital in handcuffs. Patient was agitated, talking about religious themes, including Mother Teresa and about the universe being saved. He had attempted on several occasions to run away. He was combative with the staff and had to be restrained."

"This is much the same as the situation in which Mr. Leatherwood was brought to the hospital in the fall of 1988, is it not?"

"That's correct."

Petrou: "Your Honor, I want to state an objection for the record here that I believe that after his termination, this intensive questioning about what happened to him and his hospitalizations is irrelevant."

The court: "Overrule the objection."

"Would you turn to the next page, which is page 64? Again, this was written at the time of Mr. Leatherwood's admission in November of 1986, correct? I mean, 1989. It followed the letters that you wrote in August and the forms you filled out in August, correct?"

"Yes."

"About midway down that paragraph, there's a sentence that says, 'The patient had been rather stable until the onset of the present illness episode.' That seems to me to be a bit contradictory to what you just testified to, that in the six-week period between his last hospitalization in June and this in the writing of those letters in August, there had been such a significant change in his emotional state that warranted you completely changing your testimony. Does that not appear to be a bit contradictory to you?"

"Rather stable? I mean 'rather stable' basically means that he wasn't manicky for most of that time. It doesn't mean that he was out of the woods or was not having problems. In fact, what I have indicated that my recollection is that there was more depression, discouragement, deep concern about his situation that—but he was stable. He was coming for appointments, he was taking his medication. And only some several weeks before the hospitalization as you've indicated, I received some calls, began to be aware that he was indeed deteriorating again.

"Now, what you're saying is that in that six-week period between June 29th and August the 11th, you keep saying that he appeared to be very depressed. In your opinion, was Mr. Leatherwood clinically depressed during that period?"

"I'm not saying that he manifested a major depressive episode; I'm not making a diagnosis. I'm simply stating the fact that his mood was that of discouragement and considerable apprehension with respect to his circumstances."

"My problem, Dr. Blackburn, is I have a—it may be semantics. It seems to me that 'rather stable' and 'reasonable emotional stability' is quite different from saying that because of these periods, he can no longer continue with his chosen profession. Do you not see a discrepancy in those two or three statements?"

"Not necessarily. He had been—he was rather stable, but not in a state of high function. There's a—particularly in cyclic disturbances such as bipolar disorder, manic depressive disorder, there is a lot of fluctuation. And when I say stable, I mean there's less fluctuation, but it doesn't necessarily mean that things are operating on a perfectly good level."

"It is your testimony that you did not diagnose Mr. Leatherwood as being clinically depressed in August of 1989?"

"I didn't—"

"But isn't it true that he has really never experienced the low—"

"Has never had—"

"—the clinical depression side of the bipolar disorder?"

"That is correct.'"

"He was low in '89 because he'd lost his job, correct? Is that what you're saying?"

"I was just saying that he was low. I think losing the job is one element of that."

"Most people who lose their jobs do get—have a certain amount of unhappiness, wouldn't that be correct?"

"That's correct. And people who have significant biological mental disorders such as bipolar disorder are more apt in periods of discouragement or loss to have changes in their clinical state. Perhaps to become manic."

"So do we have a responsibility not to allow negative things to happen to people who have bipolar disorders?"

"I would not generalize to that extent."

"In November of 1992, about the time of Mr. Leatherwood's—I mean, November 1989 about the time of Mr. Leatherwood's hospitalization, you wrote another letter, did you not, to a Charles Crane, who was a disability examiner for the Social Security Administration? If you'll look on page 61, you'll find that letter."

"Yes. On November 22nd."

"Would you read for the court the fourth paragraph of that letter?"

"'The degree of psychosis at the beginning of the present admission was more severe than the two previous compensations which I observed. In view of the chronicity, greater than ten years, and the deterioration over the past year, it is my opinion that if the patient is able to return to work at all, it will require at least three to six months more active rehabilitated effort.

"'Although he appeared to be making an adaptation to work from January through April of '89, he has mostly been seriously disabled since about September 1988.'"

"So again, your opinion has changed. Hasn't it?"

"My opinion has not changed. I have different frames of time that I am reviewing the situation."

"In January of 1990, you had an occasion to fill out another one of these forms to Standard Insurance Company. If you'll look in Exhibit No. 4 on page 2."

"Dated January '90."

"And is that your signature at the bottom?"

"It is."

"And this is some two months after that letter you wrote to the disability examiner?"

"Uh-huh."

"Would you please read the paragraph in part B where it says 'Medical Prognosis'?"

"For one-and-a-half years there has been major deterioration with multiple relapses and required hospital care. The patient is not expected to ever be able to return to his prior job situation."

"Do you generally tailor your remarks according to the audience to which you're writing?"

"Certainly do. Try to. Sometimes I fail."

"Then on March, 20, 1990, you wrote another rather lengthy letter. I believe you'll find that at page 50 in Exhibit 3. Who was it written to?"

"This was to the Social Security or TRC examiners."

"What is TRC?"

"Texas Rehabilitation Commission. This was for purposes of ascertaining his status for Social Security."

"Please read the first paragraph titled 'Chief Complaint.'"

"'The patient is discouraged, frustrated, and fearful about reestablishing himself vocationally and socially due to recurring manic episodes which have resulted in hospitalizations, dismissal from work after more than twenty years and financial disarray.'"

"So the recurring manic episodes have resulted in hospitalizations as well as the dismissal and the financial disarray, correct? That's what that says, right?"

"That sounds good."

"Would you turn over to page 54, which is several pages into this formalized letter. Under D, 'Deterioration or Decompensation in Work or Work-like Setting in the Past Year.' Would you read that paragraph, please?"

"'Since about September 1988, the patient manifests declining ability to sustain his usual work. Management changes at work may have contributed. Personal stress related to relationship to parents and girlfriend may have contributed. Three grossly psychotic manic episodes have resulted in three hospitalizations during the past fifteen months. In spite of effort to return to work or perhaps because of the effort to return to work, deterioration and relapse occurred.'"

"It was your opinion at that time that the prognosis for Mr. Leatherwood was to be considered guarded to poor; is that correct?"

"That would be no doubt correct."

"One final document. On May 6, 1991, you had an occasion to write a letter to Michael Jobst, the benefits representative for Standard Insurance Company. Would you please read the first two sentences in the last paragraph on page 46?"

"'In the fall of 1988, progressive hyperactivity and inappropriate interpersonal interactions led to work dysfunction. A trial back at work in the spring of 1989 was experienced as highly stressful.'"

"And, on page 47."

"In my opinion the prognosis is good. Present expectations are for his retraining to include part-time work efforts during the spring 1992. Subsequent to that, a trial of gainful employment may be a realistic goal, though not in the pressured newspaper environment."

"Dr. Blackburn, do you feel like you placed *The Post* in any kind of precarious type of position by providing them with releases to return to work for Mr. Leatherwood and then within weeks changing your opinion as to his ability to perform the job?"

"No, I don't. I changed my opinion after the second hospitalization. That was the—after—actually, I changed my opinion after he was terminated from his employment, and I don't—I did not feel that the clinical situation was that different than it had been six times over ten years when he had gone back to *The Post* and successfully returned to work."

"But all of a sudden you did in August in an effort to achieve disability benefits for Mr. Leatherwood; is that correct?"

"In August after he had become unemployed, his condition was different."

"He needed benefits, didn't he?"

"He did need benefits, that's correct."

"Did you ever give Mr. Leatherwood a release to return to work while you were treating him after June of 1989?"

"I don't recall any situation of doing that."

"In fact you never did, did you?"

"Although there—there would have been no cause for it and no requirement for it in the work that might occur with the vocational rehabilitation thing. The letters that I wrote to TRC are fully in sync with Social Security law, that I don't understand, but there are two arms, I mean, an individual can be disabled, and, at the same time, the TRC works with them to rehabilitate.

"And that's what was occurring, and part of the rehabilitation may be working. We have people working in the veterans hospital while they're hospitalized. We used to call it industrial therapy. Now it's called incentive therapy, because you have to pay people something; it's not enough to work. But work is therapeutic, and so that's not exactly out of sync with what we're trying to do."

"So it was—at some point became your opinion that Mr. Leatherwood could return to work and possibly even in the newspaper industry; is that correct?"

"I would say that now. I only say that on the basis of the fact that somewhere in the midst of time—I don't have this in my mind—he began to do some writing. And some of the writing—I'm not a critic of writing, but he was writing what seemed reasonable. And I figured if he can write reasonably now, then that might be somewhat related to the newspaper work."

"Did you ever notify the long-term disability carrier or the Social Security Administration that Mr. Leatherwood was now able to work, therefore, no longer required the disability benefits?"

"I don't recall doing that. He was continuing to work with TRC during all the time that I saw him until I last saw him in June of '92. So there was no situation where he was at a point of sustaining gainful employment. He was still in a rehabilitation posture with respect to the TRC. So that didn't come up to my knowledge."

"Dr. Blackburn, did you come here pursuant to a subpoena today?"

"That's correct."

"Are you being paid for your time?"

"No, I'm not."

"Are you on a salary with the VA Hospital?"

"I'm on vacation today and yesterday."

"Thank you. I pass the witness, Your Honor."

The court: "Mr. Petrou, redirect."

Petrou was brief:

"Did the stress factors of dealing with his parents and his girlfriend play a major role in his deterioration in December of '88 and in the spring of '89?"

"I think that the issues of the relationships were important but had also been stresses for him over years, and there was no—the most important single change I'm aware of during this period of time during this year or so was the change of his employment. There were always these other problems in the multiple times that he had returned to work before."

"And the defense counsel talked to you about Carl Leatherwood and whether he was violent or not. From examining all of his medical records and from talking to Carl, did you conclude that he was a violent person?"

"No. The only references to violence occurred on the occasions when he was restrained against his will. And on those occasions, he was indeed struggling with the attendants, and that is certainly violence, but it's not the kind of violence that we usually are more concerned with."

"Is it therapeutic if Carlton likes to write and desires to write for him to get a job writing?"

"Certainly."

Judge Gibson: "Thank you, Dr. Blackburn. At long last, the witness is excused."

CHAPTER 12
DOG ADO

"GOOD AFTERNOON," PETROU SAID, turning to the next witness. "Can you give the ladies and gentlemen of the jury your full name, please?"

"Marguerete Johnston, which was my professional name, and Barnes, which is my married name, Marguerete Johnston Barnes."

"Can you tell us what year you were born and how old you are?"

"I certainly can. I was born in 1917, and I'm now 76."

"And how many years did you spend in the newspaper business?"

"From 1939 to 1985."

"So is that over 40 years?"

"Yeah."

"In your career as a journalist and writer, did you come across—did you cross paths with Oveta Culp Hobby?"

"Yes. I was very fortunate."

"Where did you meet Mrs. Hobby?"

WHEN I CAME TO HOUSTON, I had had what I thought was the most glorious job in the whole world as a Washington correspondent. I didn't want to do anything less. So I offered to teach creative writing at the University of Houston, but I soon got lonesome for newspapers because that's what I liked to do. And my former publisher was a very beloved figure in American journalism, and he wrote Mrs. Hobby about me, and she promptly had me to lunch and the next day hired me."

"And can you tell us what was your last job at *The Houston Post*? What did you eventually end up doing at *The Post*?"

"My last job was assistant editor of the editorial page. Now, I have to tell you, I didn't do any editing. I was writing that whole time."

"Did you review some editorials?"

"I read every editorial before it went to press."

"Do you remember while working for *The Post,* running across Carl Leatherwood?"

"Yes, of course, I do."

"And do you remember at one time helping him with one of the very first editorials he ever wrote?"

"That's interesting. I didn't think Carl needed any help."

"But if he testified in this trial that you reviewed his first editorial and made comments about it, would that be accurate?"

"Well, it's very nice of him to say so. I hope I did him some good."

"I would like to show what's been premarked as Plaintiff's Exhibit B."

"Yes, I remember that editorial."

"Who wrote it?"

"Carl."

"What did you think of that editorial?"

"I thought it was excellent."

"Could he become a full-time writer?"

"I don't know why not."

"So he could become, in your opinion, a full-time editorial writer?"

Kalmans: "Objection. He's leading the witness."

The court: "I'm going to overrule the objection."

"I see no reason why he shouldn't. This is a very well-written editorial."

One editorial that was a court exhibit was entitled "Ape and Essence." A Rice University professor had taken the trouble to write, calling the piece "erudite."

THE GHOST OF VICTOR FRANKENSTEIN, the fictional scientist who gave life to a ghoulish creature, resides in northern China as Dr. Ji Yongxiang. Ji has proposed, indeed has already attempted, to produce a near-human ape by fertilizing a chimpanzee with human sperm. He would put this new species to work herding sheep and cows, mining and exploring space and the sea. He also sees the ape-human as a solution to the problem of human rejection of animal organs in transplants.

This futuristic idea leaves itself open to many jabs, but the aspect of reducing noxious labor is as bothersome as any. Consider, for example, the shepherd cast out of the valley and onto the automobile assembly line. Are we really doing him a favor? The job of herding sheep no longer holds esteem as in the biblical time of David. It means hard work and the physical hazards of lightning, bears, hornets, and snakes. Worst of all, it isolates the worker from family and friends and from modern conveniences.

But there is simplicity in the shepherd's life. He eats fresh trout for breakfast and bathes in a tub of water set in the sun. Orange paintbrush and towering pines may decorate the herder's path. He develops a talent with animals—horses, dogs and, of course, sheep—and feels at home with wildlife.

> As a spot-welder in an automobile assembly plant, the transplanted worker would stand on one spot pushing a button on a welding gun 12,000 times a day. Tremendous noise would rule out wool-gathering. On a night shift he still would likely lose much of his contact with family and friends. His redemption would be a good paycheck.
>
> Admittedly, the change in jobs is conjecture. But in applying scientific knowledge to change the face of the workforce, industry must fully consider job satisfaction, the quality of a major part of a worker's life. In the case of the shepherd, standing under brilliant stars flashing in a blue canopy or standing with a flashing welding gun?
>
> If the point is debatable, if the abolition of human need to herd sheep or to perform certain tasks in space has merit, please consider further. The ape-human would likely share our emotions. Frankenstein's monster did. He yearned for the love and sympathy of cottagers he observed in the German countryside. Airs played on a guitar were so entrancingly beautiful he shed tears of sorrow and delight. Should we enslave in any task the human spirit, even if it is breathed by such a creature? No. The spirit is still human, and we fought a war to end its subjection to slavery.

There were lighter contributions to the editorial page; take a kiss:

> **FROM WHAT A TEXAS A&M UNIVERSITY** professor tells us, the custom of kissing must belong to more civilized peoples. Vaughn M. Bryant Jr., the head of that school's Department of Anthropology, says kissing became a national craze in Roman

times, "as commonplace as shaking hands." Among medieval knights, he said, the ability to kiss nicely was a sign of gentility.

But people on the South Seas island of Mangaia only recently learned about kissing. And some, such as West Africans in the mid-1800s, feared it, the professor said. Bryant believes kissing began with a misplaced nose rub in 1000–1200 B.C. in India, where a holy man wrote the world's first how-to manual centuries later. Ah, civilization?

And this editorial about a canoe . . .

A SINGLE JOURNEY WESTWARD from the center of his world ended on a prairie in Minnesota. But writer and naturalist Henry David Thoreau, who traveled mostly in and about Concord, Mass., would have enjoyed Texas in the spring in a canoe. In the spring, more than 570 species of native grasses (out of 1,200 in the United States) and approximately 5,000 different native wildflowers burst anew upon the land. A canoe trip on New England's Concord and Merrimack rivers in 1830 inspired him to develop a natural philosophy. And 80,000 miles of streams, more navigable by canoe than power boat, flow mostly through rural Texas.

For those who wish a Thoreauean experience, many of the state's rivers and creeks will do. From the canyon walls of the Rio Grande at Big Bend to the white sand bars of Village Creek in the Big Thicket, and the white water of the Hill Country in between, the canoe will slice silently into a wondrous environment. This year two canoeists and a small dog chose the Brazos River between Lake Whitney and Waco to welcome spring.

Bluebonnets and Indian paintbrush already lined the route there. On the river, as the current assisted the paddlers with their pea pod of a vehicle, ducks and blue herons took flight. A warm sun penetrated six feet of clear water, where schools of large fish swayed plants and turtles rested on a rock bottom. Springs flowed through thick ferns down a limestone bluff, while trees were greening on the opposite bank.

Read or listen to the rich history of a region, and the mind can see more than the eye. It can feel the presence of the Spanish who named the river, the Anglo-American pioneers in the 1800s who forded Spivey Crossing in wagons and plowed the fields of Smith Bend, the turn-of-the-century campers who left graffiti, and the Indians, whose garbage has become a dig.

This trip the Brazos canoeists basked in the first full calendar day of spring before a norther pushed through their camp. Winter was reluctant to die. But, as Thoreau said, the life that had lain torpid had begun to stretch itself.

"DID YOU KNOW ALSO that Carlton Leatherwood wrote features from time to time?"

"I read them, yes."

"How were his features?"

"Pleasant. An addition to the paper."

"In addition to being a full-time editorial writer, did you feel that he could be a full-time feature writer?"

"Oh, I don't see what we're aiming at, but I knew Carl; he wrote well. At that time I would have said that—"

"That he could be a writer?"

"Sure."

No doubt, she liked the piece on Southeast Texas writer and radio celebrity Gordon Baxter.

WHEN CHRYSLER CHIEF LEE IACOCCA, 61, married a former airline flight attendant twenty-six years his junior, I thought of Gordon Baxter.

Baxter, also in his seventh decade, is a writer and an institution in Beaumont radio—a teller of tales, he calls himself—whose much younger wife Diane flew for Braniff. His musings occasionally appear in the opinion section of *The Post*. The first years of the couple's marriage and of their precocious daughter's young life were spent in a cabin on Village Creek. That creek winds through the Big Thicket, a heavily wooded and ecologically mixed area north of Beaumont. Some of it has been preserved by the National Park Service.

Ever since I read Baxter's book *Village Creek,* I had wanted to canoe by his cabin, maybe meet the man whose love affair with the stream runs a half century. Those fifteen acres in the Thicket have been his Walden, and it is always a pleasure to come in contact with a person close to nature.

Because the Thicket can easily shield a house from view on the creek, I abandoned the idea of canoeing to the cabin and instead drove over. The family has moved into town, to accommodate the accelerated education and people needs of Jenny, but returns to the cabin on weekends.

On the weekend of my visit, Baxter had repaired the leaks in two small pirogues in his home workshop and brought them back to the creek. A pirogue is a boat somewhat canoe-shaped, and some are hollowed out of cypress logs. Baxter built these little eight-foot pirogues out of plywood for the two sons of his first family thirty years ago. After surviving repeated rammings in childhood war games on the water, "they had been kinda dormant over the years," Baxter said. Then "Jenny became a good swimmer, and she cast her eyes on these pirogues like she was seeing them for the first time."

Jenny had dragged one into the water and impressed her dad with not rolling it over. "They are very tender—ten inches wide at the bottom—and she just sailed out," Baxter said. "She had picked up a big old awkward one-bladed paddle and still handled it OK." Today, Jenny pushed off in the repaired boat with a double-bladed paddle and without the problem of leaks, and her joy shone.

Her dad discovered the joy of canoeing to and from this sandbar in his teens. He and a pal built a canvas boat in the 1930s and drove up to a Village Creek bridge from Port Arthur in a Model A.

"We would come up and launch into the creek and float down the creek, and this was about as far as you could go without getting tired and thirsty," Baxter said. "I would pull up on this sandbar and lie under that line of willows and just lust for the place."

In intervening years the sandbar, white quartz crystal stretching some 100 yards, and its attached woodland, have become a realized dream of Baxter's youth.

Baxter suggested Jenny and I climb into an aluminum canoe with him to paddle around the sandbar and up a baygall on the property. A baygall is a swampy piece of land in the Thicket with a variety of trees, notably red bay, common bald cypress, and

May hawthorn. Once you see one, you feel swampland has gotten a bad rap—in truth it possesses an awesome, tranquil beauty. We didn't, however, make it to this one by canoe. "I thought the creek was high enough that we could canoe into the baygall, and it ain't," the creek romantic said. "It's always changing. I didn't know this [a ridge of sand] was here. It wasn't here last year. This is this year's surprise."

We sat and talked under the willows on the bank of the little eddy.

"That big blue bird that you saw, that's the great blue heron." Baxter said. "We may be looking at her daughter, but a blue heron has been here as long as I've been here to notice the creatures. She lives back somewhere in the baygall and feeds from these sandbars."

The heron, to Baxter, is the Spirit of the Holy Ghost Thicket. "Archer Fullingim (the late publisher of the *Kountze News*) named this place the Holy Ghost Thicket because he said if you stay back in here long enough you begin to speak in tongues," Baxter explained. "Archer was one of the prime movers to save the Big Thicket, he and Sen. Ralph Yarborough. The people who lived here didn't want it to be a park. When the word got out that the world's record magnolia tree was in the Big Thicket in Hardin County, a group of them went out at night and cut the thing down. The ivory-billed woodpecker was a favorite target of characters who wandered through the woods carrying something to shoot. They got them all down to where they were about extinct, and Archer began to publicize the fact. 'Save the ivory-billed woodpecker' became his cry. One day one of his neighbors came in carrying his rifle in one hand and a dead ivory-billed woodpecker in the other and dropped it on Archer's desk. He said, 'Is that what you've been looking for?'

It was the first one Archer had ever seen, and it was the last one, and it was dead."

"I believe the creek will heal you," Baxter said. The clouds riding the warm, moist air from the Gulf of Mexico closed together on the last rays of morning sunshine. "I've always suspected that there is such a combination of pollutants in the creek that it will shine the aluminum on your outboard motor and also heal minor cuts and wounds. I also vow that the creek heals my mind. I've walked the sandbar in all the ups and downs of my life, in the victories and the tragedies. I've walked the sandbar and cried out, 'Oh Lord, what do you want of me?' The sandbar is the place for that; it is my sand-floored cathedral . . . after a while you begin to know which way to go."

Jenny was between us, listening attentively. We knew that for sure later when she asked what "speaking in tongues" was. Her father had sung and danced on the sandbar to pacify her as a baby. "She had the croup and the colic, and oh, she had a terrible time," Baxter said. "I would take Jenny in my arms—stiff, crying, and flailing her arms—in the middle of the night, and I would take her down the front steps of the cabin and out on the sandbar. We would walk in the moonlight, and I would hold her ear up against my heart so she could hear my heart beating. I walked in a slow, steady, rhythmic pace, singing. If Jenny grows up and can remember all the old rabble songs, all of the barroom songs, all of the early day, foot-stomping, Baptist-come-to-Jesus revival songs . . . I sang everything I knew to her, and she would grow warm and limp and quit crying . . . Diane said it was self-defense that she would stop crying.

Later that afternoon, stopping near Kirbyville to buy juice of the fruit of the May hawthorn, I wished I had asked the Baxters for the recipe for mayhaw jelly. Local residents call the trees mayhaws, and Fullingim had given them his recipe. He had sent his jelly to the White House until he and President Lyndon Johnson got crossed up on politics, my host explained.

I didn't ask for the mayhaw recipe because I was mindful of Thicket mores as set down in Baxter's purchase of his sandbar property. He had mentioned to the owners he wanted to buy it, and ten years later, they sold it to him. He asked them why they waited so long. "We wanted to wait a little and find out what kind of feller you are," they answered.

How long, Bax and Diane, for a recipe that will curl up your toes on the chair rungs and make your eyes water and your nose run and you will know that there is indeed a God in heaven in all his mystery?

"DID YOU EVER OBSERVE Carl Leatherwood making big disruptions in the newsroom?"

"No."

"Did you ever see him bring his dog into the newsroom?"

"No. Others brought their dogs."

"Pardon me?"

"I'll—if you want to bring a dog to the newsroom, I don't think there were any rules against it."

"Okay."

Kalmans: "Objection, Your Honor. That's obviously not responsive to any question."

The court: "All right."

Johnston: "Sorry."

"After you left *The Post*, did you continue writing?"

"Oh, yes."

"And are you an author now?"

"Yes."

"What is your book called?"

"*Houston, the Unknown City: 1836 to 1946*."

"Thank you for coming."

Kalmans stepped closer to the stand:

"Ms. Johnston, when did you leave the employment of *The Houston Post*?"

"January 1, 1985."

"All right. You have no personal knowledge of anything that went on at *The Post* after that date, do you?"

"No, none."

"Pass the witness."

JUDGE GIBSON: "The defense will call its first witness."

Bounds: "Your Honor, at this time we call Dr. Richard Pesikoff."

Bruce Coane, a lawyer for the plaintiff: "Your Honor, may we take this witness on *voir dire*?"

Gibson: "Why would you want to take him on *voir dire*?"

Coane: "Your Honor, this witness is being called as an expert witness. He does not have any information about relevant facts. It's our position that he is not a qualified expert to testify in this case. His expertise has nothing to do with the issues."

Gibson: "What is his expertise?"

Bounds: "Psychiatry with an expertise in manic and all emotional disorders."

Coane: "His resume as presented to us shows he's an expert in child psychiatry. It has nothing to do with this case."

Gibson: "I overrule the objection. I overrule your request to *voir dire*."

"Would you state your occupation, please?" Bounds asked.

"I'm an associate clinical professor of psychiatry at Baylor College of Medicine. I'm in the private practice of adult and child psychiatry, serving about half adults and about half children and adolescents. I'm also a psychoanalyst."

"Okay. Have you ever done an actual examination of Carlton Leatherwood?"

"No, ma'am. I have not met him."

"Have you reviewed any record regarding Carlton Leatherwood?"

"Extensively."

"In what capacity are you here today, Dr. Pesikoff?"

"I was retained to review the records and give a medical opinion of everything I have read."

"How familiar are you with the disorder of manic depressive disorder?"

"Well, very much so."

"You have patients that have been diagnosed with that disorder?"

"Yes, I do. Many."

"Have there been any significant changes in the treatment of manic depressive disorder?"

"In the last few years, because we've had a number of patients who did not respond well to lithium, we've added some of the other drugs which were mainly for seizure disorders. Depakote and Tegretol are two that we use now with a lot more freedom. We try to mix them sometimes to get better results."

"And what does Depakote do?"

"Well, I don't think any of us truly knows what any of these drugs actually do. As a net result, they are given in order to stop the kind of up-and-down, up-and-down manic depressive episodes that these patients suffer with—the mechanism isn't real clear as to exactly how that happens because there isn't any naturally found lithium or Depakote in people's bodies."

"After having reviewed all these records, do you have an opinion about the general diagnosis of Carl Leatherwood?"

"Yes, I do."

"What is your opinion with regard to the general diagnosis of Carl Leatherwood?"

"I would agree with the diagnosis that I read in Dr. Ranjit Chacko's report from Methodist Hospital this last month. I think he has a bipolar illness. I think it's severe. It's been present for about seventeen years now, to the best of my figuring. It's been a terrible illness for him. I do think bipolar manic depressive illness is a proper diagnosis."

"You say that you think he has a severe case of this bipolar disorder. Has it always been severe?"

"I think it's been getting worse and worse. He started out, typically, like many patients do in their thirties, with his first episode. He's had thirteen, I counted thirteen, hospitalizations up until this October. I may have missed one. That's a lot of hospitalizations in seventeen years. That's a pretty severe illness when you're in and out.

"And during that entire period, Mr. Leatherwood has had different degrees of contact with doctors. It's not like he hasn't gone for help. I mean, he's certainly tried to get help. And in spite of that, his illness is so malignant and so significant that it has continued—keeps breaking through. He has periods when he's okay, even some periods when he had a couple of years he was all right. Then he goes down and down and down. It has an unfortunate downward course, and it's not been possible—I've read all his records—for us to stop that in the state of medical science today."

"Based upon your expertise, do you have an opinion about the general course of treatment that's been given to Carl Leatherwood?"

"I think it's been—he went through a series of different diagnoses. I don't think he got on to lithium until the '80s. I think that was fortunate. At least it appeared to be a fortunate breakthrough for him, but even that hasn't really helped. I think his illness has continued to be a severe illness that's been downwardly focused. Maybe his symptoms have changed, according to the chart, but there's certainly little doubt in my mind that it's a manic depressive illness at this point."

"Is there some point in Mr. Leatherwood's course of this illness that you believe he has started his downward approach that you're talking about or has it always been downward?"

"The first, I guess, twelve years, thirteen years, he had eight or nine hospitalizations. It's always been a severe illness for him. And as I read his symptoms, he had these terribly psychotic episodes where he would become very confused, lose his contact with reality, and need to be in a hospital for a period of time, and that has continued up until the present."'

"Is that unusual for that type of course to be taken for this type of illness?"

"Unfortunately, that's not unusual at all."

"But there are people who have bipolar disorder who don't have this spiraling down; is that correct?"

"Thank goodness. Most of the patients that we have who are manic depressives have, let's say, a mild or a medium severity of this disorder. And they may have one or two hospitalizations where we really do pick up on it and they may go years without any problems. There are a lot of factors which influence whether or not you're going to be a pretty good patient. Some of it's biological. Some has to do with your support system, you know, your husband, wife, kids, things like that, the kind of job you do, and so forth. But most patients, if they take their medicine, if they're complying patients, if their illness doesn't interfere with their ability to know they need their medicine, have a milder course than Mr. Leatherwood has had."

"But in your opinion, Mr. Leatherwood is not in this category of mild?"

"No, he's not. He's not for a number of reasons. He's had too many episodes, very severe illnesses. And one of the worst things about his illness is that when he starts getting ill, he believes he doesn't need his medicine. Of course, at that point, he stops his lithium. You can read his records. He comes into the hospital with almost no lithium in his blood system, which tells you he's stopped his medicine. Of course, then it just gets worse and worse."

"Specifically, I'd like to turn your attention to the fall of 1988. Are you familiar with the hospitalization that Mr. Leatherwood had in December of 1988?"

"Yes, I am."

"He was hospitalized in the middle of December 1988; is that correct? Is that your understanding?"

"Yes, it is."

"Do you have an opinion about when this episode actually began?"

"From the best I can read, it was building up for a couple of months before—September–October. That's what is referenced in the various notes in the chart."

"Is there any significance to the fact that Carl Leatherwood was involuntarily hospitalized for the first time in this particular episode in 1988?"

"It speaks to what I'm saying. The fact that the illness is getting worse, his ability to see himself is deteriorating. He's already, at that point, out of contact with reality. You can't reason with him. You can't just say, Carl, you're not doing well; you've got to go in the hospital. He can't hear you. My patients tell me when they are in that state,

'Dr. Pesikoff, I can't hear you. I can't reason with you. You don't make any sense to me. I don't see anything wrong with me.'

"So you would, therefore, need to go to the authorities, down to probate court, get a court order, and have the patient picked up and involuntarily confined. That would be indicative of a worsening of his illness and a loss of insight into his illness."

"In your opinion, was this episode more severe than the previous episodes he had?"

"It seemed to be more so, yes."

"Based upon that, would this episode have been perceived by other people around Mr. Leatherwood?"

"Absolutely."

"At what point in an episode such as this does a patient lose their ability to reason or have judgment?"

"In severe versions of manic depressive illness, the window of opportunity, to use a familiar phrase, for a number of my severe patients, is one to two days. And they call me—they say, 'I was up all night, I'm pacing, we've got to do something.' That's that one or two days. I get their husband or wife—I'm just thinking of a lady in particular—down to my office. We get a lithium blood test that day, and we start to pump in more medication and try to avoid—I'm not always successful in keeping this kind of patient out of the hospital."

"If the patient is not able of their own accord to notice that there's a beginning of a problem or if they don't have someone around like a husband or a wife who lives with them and notices those sorts of things, what is the possibility that you're going to catch them within that window?"

"Negligible. I can't even catch them with husbands and wives overseeing them. And if you have nobody watching you, that day or two or three, that window just passes by without anything happening and then you're in the midst of that bizarre psychotic period."

"What if a person is employed? Could their coworkers be expected to notice that window?"

"I think that's asking an awful lot. I can't even pick it up sometimes. It can flash by. It can happen over a weekend. There's no way. Yes, on occasion, I think you might say something to a fellow employee if they were acting weirdly, yes; but, I mean, as a routine, by the time you try to convince them to go somewhere, that's a very, very unrealistic proposition."

"Mr. Leatherwood returned to work in January of 1989. In Defendant's Exhibit No. 3, there are several pages of Dr. Blackburn's notes following that hospitalization that December. On page 40, could you tell us what you find?"

"1/14/89 shows that he's taking lithium carbonate, 300 milligrams, two tablets twice a day. That's 600 milligrams twice a day for a total of 1200 milligrams. That would be a reasonable dosage of medication."

"Do those notes indicate any problems that Mr. Leatherwood is having?"

"Personally, there's something about parents—some kind of interpersonal conflict between girlfriend and his parents and Mr. Leatherwood."

"Throughout these notes, there is again a note dated January 28th where there was a session. February 11th of '89, there was a session. February 25th of '89, there was a session. March 11th. Do you notice in these notes of Dr. Blackburn's anything of particular concern for you with regard to Mr. Leatherwood's condition?"

"Yes. You can watch the quality of the notes change as you get to March 11th. I highlighted my series of notes in the middle. It says paranoia recurs, suspicious that some of the stories had been formulated. So Dr. Blackburn in March of that year is writing in his records that once again he's picking up that paranoia in Mr. Leatherwood. And, of course, paranoia is one of Mr. Leatherwood's major psychotic symptoms when he's ill. He's very paranoid. And so it's already there in the March office notes of his physician."

"Based upon your review of his hospitalizations and his conditions this time, do you have an opinion about Mr. Leatherwood's condition during this period of time?"

"I think he's continued to be ill. He has never recovered fully from this severe episode, and by March of 1989, he once again is back in a paranoid state. So it's one long, continuous downward illness, with a drop of some recovery, and then it's down again and he's falling again."

"In looking at these records, is it your opinion that Mr. Leatherwood in the past had been able to recover a relatively acceptable degree of stability?"

"I guess it depends on what kind of job you're talking about. My understanding is that because of his illness, *The Post* created a position for him in the '80s so that he could remain with the corporation, so that, while he couldn't go back after a few of these hospitalizations, they did try to keep him, and they made a new job to fit him. But by '89 after years of this illness, it doesn't appear that he could maintain himself, even for a couple of months now without again becoming psychotic."

"Mr. Leatherwood was hospitalized again in June of 1989; is that correct?"

"Yes, it is."

"Do you have an opinion as to when this episode that resulted in the hospitalization in June of '89 began?"

"In December of '88, probably in September or October of '88. It sounds like one long, downward spiral, like a stock that's dropping, then has some little upticks and then drops again. I think he was in the course of a malignant portion of his illness, a tragic kind of illness, and they stopped it for a while in December; but, unfortunately, his health doesn't always respond the way we want it to, and it resumed its downward spiral soon after the hospitalization of December of '88."

"Dr. Blackburn's records reflect a change in Mr. Leatherwood's medication on June 3rd. Could you tell us what the purpose of that change in medication may have been?"

"Dr. Blackburn must have been picking up what we're seeing because he wanted to use one of the major tranquilizers. He was adding Mellaril, which is like Thorazine, Prolixin. And in his notes, he writes, hypomanic episode, meaning that the man is on the cusp already now of a major manic episode."

"How does a manic depressive disorder affect a patient's judgment?"

"Terribly. Terribly. I mean, it's a horrible illness. When you are psychotic, your judgment is centered around your bizarre thinking. So in the midst of the full-blown episode, you don't have any kind of judgment to be a doctor, a lawyer or anybody, a newspaper man.

"During the periods when you're shy of that full-blown illness but you're in a hypomanic state, your judgment is impaired. You rush things. Your speech is pressured. You have trouble sitting still. You have trouble concentrating. You're agitated. You're very irritable. You don't sleep at night."

"Dr. Blackburn wrote a letter on June 29th releasing Mr. Leatherwood to return to his normal duties immediately. Have you read that letter?"

"Yes, I have."

"Do you have an opinion as to whether or not Mr. Leatherwood should have been returned to work in June of 1989? If so, could you please tell the court what it is?"

"I think this is a well-meaning letter, but it is a very misleading letter. I don't think Mr. Leatherwood was anywhere capable of working. I don't know Dr. Blackburn's motivation for writing it other than trying to be nice maybe to his patient; but, A, the man did not have a hypomanic mood shift. He had a manic episode. You don't hospitalize hypomanic disorders—at the price hospitals charge for full-blown manic episodes. This man in no way has recovered from his illness.

"There's nothing in the notes that indicate anything that tells me that he is able to go back to work. Usually what you do with patients who've had severe illnesses is you give them a chance to recuperate. I don't care whether it's a broken leg, a hysterectomy, or psychotic episode, you know. You give people a week or two or three to go home and try to collect themselves."

"Following the writing of this letter on June 29th, Dr. Blackburn wrote a letter on August 11th. I believe you have it.

"That letter, according to Dr. Blackburn's testimony, was written to aid Mr. Leatherwood in obtaining various benefits. That letter indicates, I believe, about the middle of the second paragraph that Mr. Leatherwood is not in his opinion able to continue with his regular occupation. Is that a correct paraphrase of the letter?"

"Yes. He writes, 'Because of these unpredictable episodes and the necessity of hospitalization, I cannot say that Mr. Leatherwood would be able to perform the material duties of his occupation with a reasonable continuity.'"

"Do you think that's a major shift in opinion from the June 29 letter?"

"This is my opinion of Mr. Leatherwood. I agree with his opinion. It's a 180-degree change in direction from everything else that's been written by his physician. I mean, he writes he is disabled with respect to his performance. I agree with Dr. Blackburn. I think the man was disabled for a long time."

"Do you find anything in Carl Leatherwood's medical records to establish any basis for this 180-degree change by Dr. Blackburn in a period of six weeks?"

"No."

"And in November, Mr. Leatherwood was hospitalized again; is that correct?"

"November 1989; that is correct."

"Dr. Blackburn has, in his records prior to that hospitalization, a statement that he had received numerous phone calls over a period of about a month from friends and family and others regarding Mr. Leatherwood's condition. Is that unusual to receive those types of phone calls?"

"No, it's not unusual. If you have a couple of friends or wife or kids who are current with you, you may get calls from concerned people telling you that their friend or their spouse is ill. I mean, that certainly happens in my practice."

"If you'd received calls from people such as this, but then you had had a visit with your patient and you did not observe any obvious delusions or hyperactivity or loud behavior, would you dismiss the calls and decide that you were the more competent person to decide about their emotional stability?"

"I think that's naïve. I think you see them maybe fifteen minutes or half an hour every month, and these people either work with them or live with them and know them and see them all the time in a noncontrolled environment. I don't think you can ignore—what I do is I ask them to come in. I also have them call my nurse, usually, every single day when in the middle of one of these episodes. I usually believe the people who are calling because there's no reason for them to lie to me. Why would they call a psychiatrist and lie to them? These people who are ill slide right out from your hands like mercury. You really have to hold on tight. It's a real challenging piece of work for a physician to do. And if it's looking more and more to me like we're going to end up having to hospitalize this patient, maybe get them in a little bit sooner so they don't end up in one of these severe psychotic episodes."

"If, as in the case of Mr. Leatherwood, the course of treatment is a little bit less controlled than you tend to treat your patients, can the people around them be expected to control Mr. Leatherwood?"

"Don't be misled, even by the fact that I ride tight rein on my patients, I can't always control them. I have patients who I do my very best to control who end up in the hospital. I think the illness is stronger than me, my nurse."

"November 22, 1989, Dr. Blackburn wrote another letter, this time to the Social Security Administration. In that letter, he writes that Mr. Leatherwood has been mostly seriously disabled since September of 1988. Do you agree with this assessment?"

"Yes, I really believe that that is the truth. I think he did in fact write the truth, that the man had been severely disabled since the fall of the previous year, yes. It goes on to say, you know, he was restless, hyperactive, sleepless at times, psychotic, delusional—I think that's all true."

"Based upon your understanding of his job and your understanding of Mr. Leatherwood's condition in 1989, did his condition impair his ability to perform that job?"

"Absolutely."

"Pass the witness, Your Honor."

Witness: "I could get a little water?"

Judge: "Yes."

Coane stepped forward: "Would you like to proceed, Doctor, or would you want to wait for the water?"

"I think we can go on."

"Okay. Doctor, so in your opinion—well, let me ask you this: Is it your understanding that Carl wants to return to work?"

"That's been his position, as best I understand it, that he's wanted to work, yes."

"Okay. And despite his desire to work, it's your opinion that Carl Leatherwood cannot return to work; is that right?"

"Are you talking about at *The Houston Post*?"

"Let's start with *The Post*. Yes, at *The Post*."

"Yes, that's correct."

"Have you read any of his writing?"

"I've read all his works. All the ones that were in the addendum to the deposition."

"Did you find in reviewing those articles that there was any evidence in there that he was delusional or paranoid or manic?"

"No."

"So in the periods where he's not delusional, paranoid, or manic, you would agree that he can probably perform his job?"

Bounds: "Objection, Your Honor. What he's discussing is writing articles on his free time, not what his job was at *The Post*."

Judge: "Let the witness do the responding."

"Given the circumstances that you're describing of writing ad-lib articles, I guess, casually with no pressure, no time limits, yes, I think he can probably still write. I hope he can."

"Doctor, at some point in this lawsuit, I was given a copy of your *curriculum vitae*. Just so we're clear on this, you don't claim to be an expert in the newspaper business; is that correct?"

"That's correct."

"If you had to name one area of expertise in your practice of psychiatry, what would that be?"

"Would be very difficult because I have about three or four areas where I specialize."

"Right. And child psychiatry is one of them?"

"Oh, absolutely. Child psychiatry, adult psychiatry. I'm a board certified adult psychiatrist. I'm a general psychiatrist. I was chief of one of the hospitals for three years. I write on issues of custody in the law. There are a number of areas."

"If you'll glance at your *curriculum vitae* that you have in front of you there, would you agree that the bulk of your major educational and research interests are in child psychiatry, at least according to your *curriculum vitae?*"

"I get tapped at Baylor to teach that because there are much fewer child psychiatrists, and I often do the TV and public relations work for Baylor because we don't have a lot of child-adolescent psychiatrists, so a lot of my presentations are on child and adolescent. But the six years I spent at the Psychoanalytic Institute, Houston-Galveston Institute, was all adult.

"Let's look at the major educational and research interests on your *curriculum vitae*. You listed five of them. Would you read them to the jury, please?"

"Adolescence and drug abuse, children and divorce, psychiatry and the law, psychological growth and development in childhood and adolescence, and sleeping disorders in children."

"Thank you. Also on your *curriculum vitae* here, I count about eight pages of publication, speeches, and lectures that you've given. And would you agree that most, if not all of these, have dealt with child or family psychiatry?"

"Yes, I would."

"You don't have any complaints with Dr. Blackburn's treatment of Mr. Leatherwood, do you?"

"I think I would have kept a tighter rein on Mr. Leatherwood in terms of some of those phone calls that came in. I think I probably would have tried to verify those. I would have probably asked the patient to keep in closer contact with me, rather than every three weeks since he's had such a severe history. And, of course, I am very confused by the variety of the notes and letters that Dr. Blackburn wrote. Otherwise, he had the medications, I think, the ones I would have used. I would agree with most of the other treatment."

"You used the word earlier, when Ms. Bounds was questioning you, 'disability.' Are you referring to manic depression as being a disability, or bipolar disorder, whatever y'all call it now?"

"Sure. I would call any mental or emotional illness a disability, be disabling, as I think it was here."

"Okay. From your understanding of the case, from 1976 until at least that episode in 1988 that led to his hospitalization, Mr. Leatherwood was able to perform the duties of his job unless he was having an episode; is that right?"

"That's my understanding, yes."

"Okay. So throughout that time, just to make sure we're clear on this, throughout the time of 1976 to 1988, it's your understanding that Mr. Leatherwood had a disability of manic depression, correct?"

"It wasn't really diagnosed that way in the earlier papers. To be fair to those doctors, they didn't call it manic depression. I don't want to change history. They called it schizophrenia, then they called it schizoaffective disorder, then it evolved to manic depressive. If I could change your words and say that he had a major psychiatric illness, diagnosis shifting, but, yes, I would agree to that kind of phraseology."

"Okay. Did you ever notice in Dr. Blackburn's notes any comments about work or employment being therapeutic for Mr. Leatherwood?"

"I think he made reference to the fact that that was one area that Mr. Leatherwood actually was drawn to and it was one of his areas of strength, something he derived satisfaction from."

"Would your reading also indicate that the termination was a very distressful thing for Mr. Leatherwood?"

"I certainly agree that to have to be let go from a job is always very distressful, yes."

"Is it particularly distressful for someone in Mr. Leatherwood's mental condition, as you understand it?"

Bounds: "Objection, Your Honor. He's—"

The court: "Overrule the objection."

"I think he's a more sensitive person because he has this illness, and I would agree with that."

"Do you think that some day—in your opinion, do you think some day he could return to a job as a newspaper writer at a major newspaper?"

"I have a crystal ball in my office which I turn to in moments like this. No, I don't really think so. But I think a less-stressful job, something that used his intellect and his writing skills, maybe he could do something with it. I would hope so."

"Sir, you're being paid to testify here today?"

"No. I'm being paid for my time and that is all that I have to sell, and I sell my time and my expertise."

"What do you sell your time for?"

"I get $300 an hour when I do this kind of work."

"Your diagnosis of Mr. Leatherwood is bipolar illness, chronic-severe with multiple episodes. Is it really ever possible for anyone with that diagnosis to work in any type of job?"

"Sometimes, yes. It's not easy. The general course of those severe versions makes it really hard to do that. You know, if you had a job where you could do it at your own pace and didn't have any time lines and the conditions were ideal, some of the time he might be able to work, yes. I don't want to say that he couldn't work at something sometimes."

"Are you saying that even today he has never recovered from that severe episode of 1988?"

"The answer is I think he's had up and down, up and down—what has occurred has been going down. I think he's probably lucid now, although that's a guess. Dr. Chacko, his present doctor, is a good doctor. I know him. He's getting good care. I'm glad he is at Methodist with Dr. Chacko. He's on a different medical regimen. He's on valproic acid and lithium now, which is a good mixture. And it looks good. I mean, I can only tell you that for the moment at least—that doesn't tell me—it's three weeks since he was in the hospital, so I'm not good enough about prognosticating. And I'm hopeful that maybe we've gotten a handle on it, but, I mean, that's my medical school talking. I wouldn't stress a job or anything like that right this minute, but he looks lucid to me."

"Do you have any reason to doubt that he enjoys the job of a writer and editor?"

"I think he loves writing. He wouldn't have worked for a newspaper all these years if he didn't love that."

"Do different writing jobs at *The Post* have different deadline requirements?"

"That's my understanding. I've worked with a number of reporters who've done investigative kinds of work, and they'll take months to put together stories. And then you have people who write about hurricanes and that's real on-the-spot stuff. The answer is yes."

Bounds returned to take up the questioning:

"Dr. Blackburn, have the effects of Mr. Leatherwood's mental illness—"

"Dr. Pesikoff."

"Sorry. I'm so busy listening to everybody talk about—Dr. Pesikoff, I will represent to you that Dr. Blackburn has testified that the reason for the difference between the two letters that you have a problem with, that being the June 29th letter and the August 11th letter from 1989, was his recognition of a severe depression in Carl Leatherwood. Did you find any evidence in Dr. Blackburn's records of such a depression?"

"There's no mention in the notes of any severe depression."

"Is that something that you think a prudent doctor would have written in the notes if it had occurred?"

"I think if he had thought of it, he would have written it down, yes."

"Dr. Pesikoff, do you have an opinion as to whether or not Dr. Blackburn did Mr. Leatherwood and *The Post* a good service?"

"I think he made it very confusing for *The Houston Post* and Mr. Leatherwood by writing different letters at different times containing different information so that it confused *The Post*, it confused Mr. Leatherwood, and made it impossible for anybody to get an accurate picture of his illness."

The court: "The witness is excused."

CHAPTER 13

VERDICT

KALMANS: "We have one more witness, Your Honor."

The witness took the stand.

"Would you state your name for the record, please?" Kalmans asked.

"Ernest J. Williamson."

"Mr. Williamson, by whom are you employed?"

"*The Houston Post*."

"How long have you been there?"

"Since 1971."

"What was your first position with *The Houston Post*?"

"I started as a copy editor."

"And at that time, did you come to meet Mr. Leatherwood?"

"Yes, sir."

"What position did you assume when *The Toronto Sun* purchased the paper?"

"That happened in 1983, and I became managing editor."

"What job do you presently hold with *The Houston Post*?"

"I'm now executive editor; I was named to that position in 1988."

"What are your responsibilities as executive editor?"

"I'M RESPONSIBLE for the whole shooting match. The city desk editor works for you. The photo department editor works for you. The business department works for you. The librarian works for you. In addition, I assumed a lot more budgetary responsibilities, a lot more decisions on personnel, administrative things, but the big new responsibility was managing the budget."

"Mr. Williamson, did you have over the years or develop over the years any kind of a personal relationship with Carl Leatherwood?"

"Oh, yes. We became very good friends early on."

"Did you have any out-of-the-office relationship with Mr. Leatherwood?"

"Yeah. We had some really interesting experiences. We went sailing quite a bit on Carl's boat. I remember spending a great day on a Hobby Cat out in Galveston. That was the best of the sailing trips, I think. We had a rather ill-fated trip in a canoe down Buffalo Bayou. I say that because I don't remember being in the canoe. I remember carrying it a lot. The only water we saw—I think we tipped it over. And I was sick for about six months after that, and Carl used to tease me about it.

"And we played a lot of tennis together. Even invited me over for dinner, my family, once. One time my father came in from California—it was during the holidays—and I think I had two tickets to go see the high school playoff game and I couldn't go, so Carl was gracious enough to take my dad. And my dad still talks about it because there was a guy named Earl Campbell running around for Tyler High School."

"Did you have occasion to come to know Mr. Leatherwood's father over the years?"

"Yes, sir. I don't know the exact date, but I think the first time I met him, he came and watched Carl and me play tennis."

"And over the course of years, have you had occasion to talk with him periodically?"

"Yes, sir."

"I want to direct your attention to the year 1980, Mr. Williamson, and ask if you had occasion to play any part in the move of Mr. Leatherwood to the business wire?"

"Yes, sir."

"And why was that?"

"We thought it would be a less-stressful job for him."

"Why did you feel that way?"

"Basically, the pace on the business desk isn't as frantic as the pace on the main copy desk. There are fewer stories to choose from. There's not as many pages to fill. The workload isn't nearly as great. And it was a lot easier to supervise because there were only two or three people doing that."

"Now, over the course of years that you and Mr. Leatherwood worked together, you then became aware of the mental illness that he had?"

"I knew he had problems coping on the job, yes."

"And how did you learn of those?"

"I knew there were times he was hospitalized."

"Did you have occasion—to periodically receive messages on your computer about Mr. Leatherwood's performance?"

"Yes, sir."

"And what types of messages or concerns did you receive?"

"Well, the ones I remember most were the ones in the fall of 1988. The nature of them—there were all kinds of complaints and problems. He seemed to be having trouble doing even the basic skills. Often a story will come over and somebody will say, here, cut this story to ten inches and write this kind of headline, and Carl would give the story back, and there were no cuts made on it. He wasn't able to focus on that, apparently.

"During that time, he was doing maybe one or two stories a night when the rest of the editors were doing eight to ten. He was spending a lot of time talking to other editors. Some people said he was being—almost amounted to harassment. The people in the computer room said he was repeatedly calling them to say that his computer wasn't working right, and they would repeatedly come up and check it, and it appeared to be working fine.

"There was a period when he called the Associated Press in Dallas and said that there was a virus in their computer system and none of the stories were working properly. That turned out not to be true. It was pretty much one thing after another."

"As the years passed and Mr. Leatherwood's problems continued, did you periodically have occasions to become involved in assisting to get him to the doctor or to the hospital?"

"Yes. Between Edith and me, we would frequently call his parents."

"Over the years, did the degree of difficulty change in your being able to get him to go to the doctor?"

"Yes. It seemed particularly—by the fall of '88, it was almost—I guess we first noticed that aspect of it in '85. But in the fall of '88, it was almost impossible. People first started reporting symptoms or telling us about it in the beginning of October, and by the middle of October, Edith was almost working full time trying to get Carl to go to the doctor. And there were repeated complaints. I had talked to him and tried to get him to go to the doctor. We called his parents.

"Early in November, we gave him some time off to go see a doctor. He wanted to go see a doctor in California because he thought the doctor could help him. His dad was going to go with him. So we thought he went; then a couple of days later he was still in town and said he didn't have the money to go.

"He was trying to see a Dr. Hauser. Edith and I spent a week trying to get ahold of Dr. Hauser. He was working in Huntsville and here both, so he was almost impossible to get ahold of.

"So, yeah, we spent a lot of time trying to get Carl help. The nature of the change, too, he didn't seem—he was much more belligerent, much more antagonistic. He didn't seem to understand what we were saying. He had no idea that he was having problems."

"In late November, Mr. Williamson, did you have occasion to receive a telephone call from Mr. Leatherwood's father wherein the subject matter of a guardianship was discussed?"

"Yes, sir. Carl wouldn't go to the doctor. There was a period when we lost track of where he was. We expected him back on Monday, but we got a call on Monday saying he's in Arizona with his dog, and we didn't know whether that was true or not. His father later said he didn't think that was true. At that point during one conversation, the father said he was seeking guardianship and if I ran across Carl or if he showed up, would I please call him."

"In early December, did you have occasion to meet with Mr. Leatherwood in your office?"

"Yes. Late in the afternoon, I think it was either the 2nd or 3rd, I was in my office with Pat Roberson, my administrative assistant, and Carl accosted us in the office, and he had a very agitated look about him. He was obviously unshaven, his hair was a mess, he was dishevelled. He was clearly out of control. He said he was resigning from *The Post*, that *The Post* was racist, that it was sexist, that I myself was racist and sexist, and he was resigning and handed me his I.D. card. I got him out of the newsroom so he wouldn't make a scene, and called his father, and the next thing I knew—it was a couple of days later—Carl was in the hospital."

"I want to direct your attention now to on or about December 24, 1988. Did you have occasion to receive a telephone call from Mr. Leatherwood?"

"Yes. It was on or about that date, a call from Carl saying that he was in the hospital, that he wanted to come back to work. I told him that there wasn't much point in coming back to work over the holidays and that I would see him on January 2nd, which was a Monday."

"Did he come in then on January 2nd?"

"Yes."

"Do you recall your conversation with him at that time?"

"Yes. Yeah, I remember this one very well because it was something I thought about for a couple of weeks, and it was pretty agonizing. I told him that I was going to accept the resignation, but that I knew he had financial problems and I knew he was going to have trouble getting back on his feet, so I told him I would make the resignation effective around March 1st. It was just to give him time to earn some paychecks."

"Following that conversation, did you have occasion to call Dr. Blackburn?"

"Yes. Right after the conversation with Carl, I called Dr. Blackburn because I wanted to inform him what had happened so he could arrange whatever support might be necessary for Carl and to keep him apprised of what was going on. I remember quite clearly that after I told Dr. Blackburn what I had done, he said that was a very humane, compassionate thing for myself to do and for *The Post.* And I guess the reason I remember it so well is because Carl was such a good friend and we'd worked together so long that, while I knew I was doing the right thing for *The Post* and it had to be done, it was quite agonizing for me. I felt reassured and reaffirmed by what the doctor had said."

"Did you tell Dr. Blackburn that people above you wanted Carl fired?"

"Absolutely not. The only pressure I felt was the pressure on me from the people below me."

"How did the employees in the newsroom as a whole feel about Mr. Leatherwood?"

Petrou: "Objection, Your Honor, hearsay."

The court: "Insofar as you could determine that from their attitude and their spoken words."

"It was pretty obvious from talking to them, everybody liked Carl. Everybody felt sorry for Carl. And in the early days in the '70s and '80s, there was almost a protective cocoon around Carl. By '88, everybody was worried and frustrated, and exasperated and tired, and there was no doubt something had to happen."

"Mr. Leatherwood didn't leave *The Post* on March 1?"

"No. We decided we'd keep Carl in employment, but we decided that we would change his job."

"And why did you make a decision to change his job?"

"We looked for one that was the least possible stressful job we could find. And we felt because the people that he had worked with on the business desk were so—had been so burdened with doing his work and had been exasperated dealing with it, that we couldn't put him back there because that would be really stressful. So we gave him a copy editing job. But then in May, to quote other employees, things had got out of hand, that Carl was unable to do any work, so I sent him home on the night of the 31st of May."

"I want to direct your attention to June 1, 1989, and ask if on that date you experienced any problems with Mr. Leatherwood?"

"Yeah. Carl came in—he was obviously in an agitated state. Dick McCann, the news editor, said he wasn't doing the job. I brought Carl into my office and showed him some of the things he had done, and he was very belligerent, wouldn't accept that he had made any errors. I was really unable to talk to him. He was very antagonistic, so I sent him home again."

"You have in front of you Defendant's Exhibit No. 20?"

"Yes, sir."

"And what is that?"

"It's a note from Eileen O'Grady, assistant business editor."

"And did you receive that from her?"

"Yeah. She had told me about this incident right about this time. I told her would she please get me a note on it, and this is the note."

"Would you read the exhibit out loud?"

"During the week of May 30, 1989, I had a conversation with Carl Leatherwood in the newsroom. We talked about exercise routines for a few moments and I noticed he was very animated. As he started to leave, he told me he was 'walking five miles a day to keep in shape for Jane.'

"Do you know who Jane is?"

"Yes. Jane Baird, business writer."

"Did you have any contact from her during this period of time about Mr. Leatherwood?"

"Yes, sir."

"What was that?"

Petrou: "Objection, hearsay, Your Honor."

The court: "Overrule the objection. Do you want to come up?"

"I had mentioned to you once before that the reports that were generated by the coworkers that came to management were relevant to their reasons for discharging him. It does not fall under the hearsay rule or the public records rule, and that's why I'm ruling—I don't care whether you agree with me or not. I want you to understand it."

Kalmans continued the questions: "Would you tell us about the conversation that you had with Ms. Baird?"

"Jane felt she was being harassed by Carl so much so that she was taking the phone off the hook at home. There was also a period when Carl was bringing gifts in for her children, and there was one episode that upset Jane in which Carl was standing outside her home and looking in her window."

"I want to direct your attention to on or about June 16, 1989, and ask if you had occasion to have a conversation with a Kate Thomas about Mr. Leatherwood?"

"Yeah. Kate came into the office that day, was worried and exasperated and frustrated and mad at me because Carl was walking aimlessly and disheveled on Westpark, the overpass right by *The Post*, and she was worried Carl was going to come into the building. And she was also concerned nobody was taking care of him and he wasn't getting help, so she was totally frustrated as were we all."

"Did you report that conversation to Mr. Jim Janiga [the human resources head]?"

"Yes."

"Did you have occasion to subsequently learn that Mr. Leatherwood had been hospitalized on June 19th?"

"Yes."

"Did you and Janiga meet after Carl got out of the hospital?"

"Yes. And finally Jim asked me what I wanted to do. I felt I had no choice but to terminate Carl."

"Why, Mr. Williamson, did you reach that decision?"

"One, he was unable to perform his job duties on a consistent and regular basis. The previous nine months, he wasn't at 100 percent of his capabilities—four-and-a-half months out of that period. He was making a lot of errors in copy, and he was becoming a tremendous burden on everybody he worked with.

"In my opinion as executive news editor, Carl's presence at *The Post* put the paper at risk. From Day 1 in my journalism career in covering high school sports in California to the University of Missouri to my years at *The Post*, I've learned that newspapers are kind of a special business. They're in many ways a public trust. People look at us to see how they're going to live their lives and make decisions on how they're going to live their lives. They turn to the business section to see how their stocks are doing. They turn to the sports section to see what time the Rockets are playing so they can watch it on TV or go to the game. They look in the news section to see how their congressman voted on NAFTA.

"As executive editor, I felt it was my duty to ensure and is at all times to ensure that we're giving the best information we can and that it's accurate and reliable. In Carl's situation, I had someone—I had a friend and somebody I had worked with for twenty years who had impaired judgment, by his own admission. Not only did he have impaired judgment, but he didn't know that he had impaired judgment when he had it, and it was getting so that we couldn't tell him he had it. I felt it was my responsibility to the people that read *The Post*, to the people that work at *The Post*, and to the people that own *The Post*, to let Carl go; and it was a very painful decision for me and still is."

"Mr. Williamson, do you feel that you could have done any more than you did to attempt to accommodate Mr. Leatherwood?"

"No, sir."

Petrou came forward:

"Mr. Williamson, you said you did all you could to accommodate Mr. Leatherwood; is that correct?"

"Yes, sir."

"There's one thing you didn't do, isn't there? You didn't ask him if he could be a writer, did you?"

"I didn't feel he had that capability."

"I'd like you to take a look at Plaintiff's Exhibit No. 7-B and read it, please."

"'The system failed'? Is that what I'm supposed to read?"

"Just get a feel for it, if you would."

"Okay."

"What do you think of it?"

"Fine."

"Is it good writing?"

"Yes."

"Okay. Were you aware that Carl Leatherwood wrote that?"

"Doesn't surprise me."

"It doesn't surprise you?"

"No."

"It is good writing?"

"Yes."

"Okay. I shall give you a more recent example, 'Grand Times on the River.' And who wrote that story?"

"Carl Leatherwood."

"And what do you think of the writing?"

"It's good."

"Now, I want to show you something even more recent. What's the name of the publication?"

"*The Leader.*"

"What's the name of the story?"

"'North Houston's Day Lily Lady.'"

"Isn't it written September '93, I believe?

"Yes."

"Who wrote that story?"

"Carl Leatherwood."

"Who took the picture on the front page there?"

"Carl Leatherwood."

"What do you think of that story?"

"It's fine for what it is."

"Did you detect any errors or bad writing in it?"

"No. It's fine for what it is, actually."

"You know Carl Leatherwood wrote that story just a couple of months ago?"

"Right."

"Mr. Williamson, is feature writing more or less stressful than editing?"

"On a daily newspaper, it can be as stressful."

"But, generally speaking, have you done feature writing yourself?"

"Yes."

"Okay. Are there the same daily deadlines for a feature writer as—do you have to turn out a feature story every day?"

"Not every day, no."

"Okay."

"But certainly more than freelancing once every couple of years."

"But you knew at the time that Carl Leatherwood was not like everybody else, right?"

"Yes."

"And he had some real serious problems, didn't he?"

"Yes, sir."

"And he would have episodes and not make sense some of the time?"

"Correct."

"And you have, I believe, 1,100 full-time employees at *The Houston Post*?"

"I have 180 myself in editorial. That's more than enough."

"Did the thought ever cross your mind, perhaps we should give Carl a chance to write a little bit?"

"No, sir. I think we're off-base here a little bit. Those articles you showed me were freelance pieces done on Carl's time when he was capable of doing it, with no deadline pressure, when it was convenient for Carl to do that. I put out a daily newspaper."

"As a way of accommodating people who perhaps have a certain disability, have you thought of allowing a person like Carl Leatherwood perhaps to work on a computer out of his own home?"

"No."

"And why is that?"

"Because it gets back, sir, to the fundamental principle of why we're in the business. I have a responsibility to make sure that the editors and the reporters that work for me are capable of making judgments. And a writer who goes out on a story and is doing interviews and collecting information and is writing a story has to be aware of what's going on and be able to make the judgments just like an editor does, as a matter of fact more so, because he knows what the situation is. The difference between judgment required of an editor and reporter—they've both got to exercise judgment."

"Right. I mean, is there any evidence that Carl doesn't know how to interview people?"

"There would be no evidence if he was outside the office that I'd know he was having a good day or a bad day."

"What about with your other reporters? If they're outside the office, would you know if they're having a good day or bad day?"

"Well, yeah. Yes."

"The other reporters, though, don't they send you their stories from wherever they are, Washington, D.C., or Austin, Texas? Don't they send it via computer or modem and it appears in *The Houston Post*?"

"Yes."

"Do you get a chance to review their work?"

"Yes."

"So the distance itself is not a problem, is it?"

"No."

"Even though Carl has had episodes since 1976, would you be surprised to learn that, according to a memo of one of his supervisors, Carl did not miss a single day's work for eight years, and four of those years were after 1976?"

"No."

"What was Mr. Leatherwood's copy like until 1976?"

"It was okay."

"Did you ever observe it yourself when it was not okay?"

"Yes."

"When was that?"

"I saw a lot of it in 1988. Some in 1985."

"I know it was a tough decision for you to fire Mr. Leatherwood. You told us about that. Do you think, however, the firing violates any policy stated in your handbook?"

"No, sir."

"I'd like you to look at page 7 of Defendant's Exhibit No. 1. Please read it for the Court."

"It is our policy to provide equal employment opportunities for all employees and prospective employees without regard to race, religion, color, age, sex, disability, or national origin."

"Dr. Blackburn said that he felt that you wanted to keep him on the job but the higher-ups above you did not share that feeling; is that correct? In other words, you really wanted Carl to stay with *The Houston Post* but somebody higher up kept you—"

"That's absolutely wrong. The only pressure I felt was I knew it was going to be tough. I knew Carl was going to have trouble. The torment I had was I knew he had to go and people below me, Carl's colleagues, were exasperated with the situation and frustrated with the situation and we had to do something. There was nobody above me who told me what to do."

ON THE SIXTH DAY OF THE TRIAL, the jury retired. The next day, November 23, 1993, the Galveston paper reported the verdict in a story by Carol Christian:

> **HOUSTON POST LOSES DISCRIMINATION CASE**
>
> *The Houston Post* on Monday was found guilty of discriminating against one of its former employees, Carlton Leatherwood Jr., who had previously worked at *The Galveston Daily News.*
>
> An eight-person jury debated about three hours before finding in favor of Leatherwood, who was *Daily News* city editor in 1966 and 1967. Leatherwood, who has manic-depressive illness, filed the suit against the *Post* for firing him in 1989 in violation of the Texas Disabilities Act.
>
> "It's satisfying that we could take a mental-illness discrimination case and have a victory of any kind," Leatherwood, 52, said Monday after the verdict.
>
> "There are few mentally ill people who can afford to go to court to begin with so they often end up in the street or in very low-paying jobs."
>
> U.S. District Judge Hugh Gibson, who heard the case after it was transferred from Houston, will determine the amount of money the *Post* will be required to pay Leatherwood.

> Bruce Coane, one of Leatherwood's attorneys, said Monday that both sides had agreed upon $170,000 for back pay.
>
> Additional claims have been made for attorney fees and future pay, as well as reinstatement, Coane said.
>
> The judge will not make the monetary award for at least 15 days, Coane said. First, the *Post* has 10 days in which to file a motion for the jury's verdict to be thrown out, and then Leatherwood has five days to respond to the motion.
>
> Leatherwood, who had worked at the *Post* for 22 years as a copy editor and business wire editor, said he thought the *Post* would appeal. Neither the newspaper's representatives nor its attorneys could be reached Monday for comment.
>
> In closing arguments Monday at the U.S. Courthouse, Leatherwood's attorney Steve Petrou said the *Post* had not done everything it could to accommodate Leatherwood's illness.
>
> He said the accommodation best suited for Leatherwood's illness would have been writing feature stories and editorials, tasks he had done in the past. "Not a single person who has taken the stand, including (Executive Editor) Ernie Williamson, has found anything wrong with his writing," said Petrou.

The judge would soon overturn the verdict, and the Fifth Circuit Court of Appeals would uphold the judge's decision. By that time, *The Post* had folded, and Coane advised that even if I prevailed in the Supreme Court, I would not necessarily collect an award. The case had ended, and so had my newspaper career. As Petrou summed it up, a federal judge had said I was too sick to work. At the time, I was both disappointed and in disagreement with the ruling, but I came to realize that the defense doctor, with more hindsight, had best recognized how severe my condition was, how downward its trajectory.

CHAPTER 14

CHASM

WITH THE LOSS AT TRIAL, the last vestige of daily bread, of social sustenance as I had availed myself for a quarter century, disappeared. I had tumbled into a chasm. To survive, I was dependent on Social Security Disability and the kindness of aging parents.

It was not a bad life, but neither was it challenging, or imaginative, or inspirational. It was more a relief, that I wasn't out hungry and walking the streets. That's why to utter complaint evokes the feeling of whining. Let it go whimsically; the height of amusement was watching lizards sun on the patio.

To the so-called friend who joked about my job situation, I say it was no joke. Going without work nigh on twelve years, and maybe more after this writing, was a blight on my condition. If the scene under such stringent economic circumstance had ever approached serious romance, it is not too extreme to imagine the partner pulling up short because of a guy too sick to work. Too, your occupation defines you. What is one of the first questions at a party?

My doing without a car for seven years further aggravated the social and work situation. But I resorted to the bus both out of financial necessity and out of fear that I was a danger to myself and others if I drove when manic. First, my uncle had driven into the eighteen-wheeler, and, second, I had spun off a highway once.

Whereas dating had been routine, I managed only a few dates in this state, one to dinner and the movies, where my health problem came up. My guest had experienced the onerous malady in her family and understandably did not answer the call for another movie.

That, however, starts to sound like complaining. It should be clearly stated that my daily life was just an abridgment and also included three vacations, down, of course, from the annual, or greater, foray. I remember a letter writer complaining to a newspaper columnist about only one trip to Oklahoma in so many years, and the newsman rebuked her, saying some don't get any. So, I want it known I'm not an ingrate.

Gary Fortenberry, a friend from the '60s, twice invited me, paid my train fare, to his Pacific Northwest home, so that I could share it and the outdoors with his wife Gail and their daughter Erin. I'm deeply grateful.

The other trip? I paid from a settlement in a pedestrian-car accident for a Sierra Club camping trip in Yellowstone National Park. I suppose I must not pass on without noting the irony of trying to avoid an accident in a car and to then get hit on a sidewalk.

CHAPTER 15
TELEPHONE BLITZ

THE TELEPHONE HAS TRIPPED ME UP.

I occupied a pay phone on the psychiatric wing of Bexar County Hospital in San Antonio and called an old Scouts buddy who was now a general in the Air Force. How I saluted him I do not know. Whatever it was, it was not conducive to conversation, at least not memorable. I remember him flashing his most compassionate and authoritative voice and saying, "God Bless You," before hanging up.

Outside mania, he rarely surfaced, so it wasn't obsession. But if not on this occasion, then on others, when a jet was overhead, I imagined him in it, protecting me.

Before this admission, the buildings all around me were juxtaposed by a nearby ranch owner who could rearrange them with a toy laser.

And then I slept in a muddy field.

Deputies found me.

It is possible that, in this series of delusions, I flew from Austin with Chica in a first-class seat so that I could make a Harris County hearing. I called from the air that I would be late. I know that Harris County deputies drove down to San Antonio later to retrieve me.

I must say here that all officers, including those in Houston, Harris County, San Antonio, and Bexar County, have provided exceptional treatment in seeing to my welfare. I am indebted.

THE GENERAL WAS IN GOOD COMPANY getting a call from me when mania struck. But how I do the hat trick of producing his and others numbers I do not know. In the hospital I did not have pen and paper to write what the operators gave out. My goodness, at home I couldn't punch the buttons without looking at the number two or three times.

My ability, too, to find numbers when I am sick has been uncanny. Once, at my parents' home for a Thanksgiving dinner, I got the notion to call a person whom I met a score of years earlier on a 1963 fishing trip to the Middle Fork of the Salmon River with Uncle Ed Thomasson. The girl was fourteen when we talked about integration in her dad's café, the Pheasant Café, in Richfield, Idaho.

She wrote a reply to my letter on stationary emblazoned with her name, Billie, in blue in the shape of a skirt, smart teen writing material. I kept it, and that is what set off my search for her during the holiday. It was postmarked at her mother's home in a small town near Boise. Lo and behold, by checking directory assistance, I learned that her mother still lived there. Excited, I called in the middle of their dinner. Billie was there.

I called back, but small wonder, she didn't seem to remember me. I told her about the letter. She wanted a copy. So I tried to send it to her home in rural Idaho by fax, on her phone line. Further communications did not patch the blunder in mania.

Another call was to Queen Julianne at The Hague. It was made from a pay phone at a restaurant on the spur of the moment to wish her happy birthday around May Day. I recalled the piece of trivia from my visit there ten or fifteen years earlier, in 1974. When I called, I woke somebody in the middle of night with my greeting. It could have been the queen herself, since my touch becomes magical in illness.

The calls have been costly in terms of the closest relationships.

There was an especially supportive friend in Boston whom I had known ever since she and her family trailed me in a raft on a later Middle Fork journey. I visited them, and they rode in my van on the first Other Side of Texas tour, bringing their friends for my interpretation of the state.

She was an authority on Indians, having sent me the last set of her early books, and she encouraged me as a writer.

Then her husband languished with cancer, eventually dying. He was a pioneer in computers for the Navy.

His death changed her. We rarely wrote.

I called during an episode. The only words I remember, that I thought were said, were hers: "You should be in the street." I can't imagine what provoked that, or the return of an unopened letter I wrote from Rusk.

It was a tremendous loss to sever communications after twenty years. Why, these people had driven me to Walden Pond and invited me to Beaver Creek, Colorado, to ski with them and their daughter. They had hosted dinners for me and their local friends. Some in our party had skinny-dipped on a hike up the Presidential Range in New Hampshire. We were personal.

My feeding frenzies with a telephone have cast a net of uncertainty over others as well.

I was never sure if I got through to Jackie (not her real name) at *The New York Times* more than once. She worked on the copy desk at *The Post* circa '70 and made us proud with her rise at *The Times*, as an editor listed in the mast. But I didn't contact her now except when manic.

That was the pattern with Eileen (not her real name), too. She was the one girlfriend that my parents thought I should marry. We skied and played tennis evenly matched, but passion was absent. We went our separate ways—until I started phoning her during episodes. She took the calls good-naturedly, and in our last conversation said she was selling rings, not that I would be a good customer.

A royal telephone blitz focused on international operators. Never before having called abroad from home, I seemed to have a battalion of operators at my command. I fantasized that a newspaper office friend was herself Princess Di and I Prince Charles. We were a big society item on both sides of the Atlantic and at the same time wore reporters' hats as we covered a story breaking world-wide. It doesn't make a lot of sense, and never did. But the waking dream cost me a $650 phone bill.

AT&T wanted its money when I came back to earth.

CHAPTER 16
IN DEATH'S SHADOW

IT WAS NEAR TWO YEARS that I watched life slip away from the homestead like dying embers in the night. My father was first to go, at eighty-five, from complications of Parkinson's disease. We moved him to a nursing home after many restless nights, and in October 1997 we buried him in his hometown, among the pink granite and limestone of the Hill Country.

My mother's time for interment in the family plot was months later. She, too, spent her last days in a Beaumont nursing home, suffering the pain of ovarian cancer, and was eighty-five.

AS AN ONLY CHILD, I called her Mama. She had not wanted the end for either to come like this, in a nursing home. She fretted when my dad was admitted ahead of her and when he asked, "Is this our home now?" But then, as in her own case, she relied on the wisdom of doctors, who said good care would be difficult at home. Oh, she didn't let go. She drove to his "home" each morning and stayed the whole day, straightening over him the sheets he tossed off and feeding him. It was the type of care a thin staff could not devote much time to. And she would faithfully ask that the attendants put my dad in a wheelchair for a daily push through the halls, and when I was along, to the patient garden. This care for her husband of sixty-one years was a proud achievement. "I'm glad I lived long enough," she said.

This is not to say she lived in a serene state. When her memory faltered after Daddy's funeral, I took her to a geriatric psychiatrist who, based on a brief examination, said she had dementia, a deterioration of the brain. He recommended assisted living. She balked. Seeking further guidance, I wrote details of her conduct to my psychiatrist, asking what to do. He urged a locked-up unit for life, saying I could find a judge to order it. I balked. There was plenty of light in her yet.

Yes, there was the verbal abuse. She would, for example, thrash me daily for not using the car visor that blocked my vision. No amount of explaining quieted her. But to the doctor and a friend who associated this with dementia, I replied, "If that's dementia, she's had it all her life."

In August 1998 her primary physician gave me a choice to make for my mother, chemotherapy or a hysterectomy with chemotherapy. I elected the operation, but local surgeons would not perform it because of the high risk. So I took her to Houston to see an acclaimed doctor who examined her and said he would operate. However, her doctor back home researched things further and said the operation would "destroy" her. I took that to mean insurmountable pain.

Chemotherapy was started on the glowing recommendation of a specialist, and it left her so dazed with nausea and temperature fluctuations that the primary physician stopped the treatment immediately. There were these irrefutable aftershocks: She was permanently weakened, and death was imminent.

Thus began her nursing-home residency. She was free to come and go as she pleased, although we never tried an overnight excursion after the trip to Houston, where pampered care in a luxury hotel with gourmet room service was lost to the occasion. We instead made short forays, not all pleasant. When lunch was Italian, and I ordered

Italian soup, she reprimanded me repeatedly. "But I wanted soup," I protested. Warmer, like the fall afternoon, was the kind suggestion of a nurse that I take her for ice cream. We both enjoyed the soft cones.

We watched the Astros playoffs in her room long after others were asleep. I made a point of it, and she maintained interest despite knowing her time at the plate was about up. She had asked, "How long do I have to live?"

"About six months," I said.

"You shouldn't have told me," she said.

We celebrated Christmas as she weakened. The Novaks, her best friends, brought a ham dinner, and we took her home for the final time. It was a traditional setting, except I took her in the bedroom to see a snow scene on the computer, and she couldn't see. She would soon close her eyes to her failing sight.

There were tears. One of the nurses reported she had them all crying when she expressed sadness that she had but me to be with her in death. "Some don't have one," the nurse told her. The only tears I saw were the last time I brought her pal Chica, a Boston terrier, to the nursing home. The little dog jumped on her bed. I thought she was hurting her legs. But my mother shook me off, and she was crying. She hadn't had a pet as a child, and Chica, in a string of dogs I owned, came closest to being hers.

One day Barbara McNeill, who was a Gordon when I knew her growing up in First Christian Church, invited me out for a welcome break. A registered nurse, she had labored to abort her mother's fatal complication in a hospital room across the hall from my mother's.

Barbara and her husband Alan, a lawyer, took coffee drinking as seriously as I did, and on a sunny and mild January day, we sipped away in their home. Shortly a phone call came for help in driving a herd of cattle from one pasture to another. I asked Barbara why the move. She explained, "It's a male thing."

The task was done, and shortly thereafter Alan ventured that they should name the newborn in the herd, a rambunctious red male, Carlton, after me. With a namesake, I recommended they run a tab at the feed store on me.

Soon after, my mother perked up a bit when told about the calf, having been a farm girl. Successive days later, she would ask, "How's the little calf?"

Death came in the night, when I wasn't there. The nurse said her blue feet forecast her end, but at 10 p.m. I went for sleep, leaving a sitter on watch. At 2 a.m. I got a call reporting her heavy breathing, a sign before she would go. I hurried. "She's gone," the nurse said as I entered. The sitter volunteered that "she went in her sleep."

My mother had worried that no one would come to her services. She was a homemaker and, sparingly, a community volunteer. Most of her friends were dead. Yet fifty showed up at her visitation, and another twenty at a graveside rite in a remote corner of the state. A casket spray with eight dozen red roses was placed by her son.

CHAPTER 17

HOME

"AND NOW HE IS HOME," I intoned over the freshly dug grave of my father.

"To this favored place where he swam as a boy, planting bare feet and swinging out into natural pools of spring-fed creeks and rivers.

"To the live oaks and cedar breaks he tramped for deer.

"He is home in late October, when there is a hard clarity to the air, a softer glow of the sun on pink Texas granite of a billion years, and limestone ledges.

"He is back home with family, in their spiritual home of Lampasas. His brothers are or will be buried here, and his parents and grandparents."

AND THEN MY WORDS gave way to his words in a memoir he wrote, *The Little Red Flag,* about his first job in this community he loved, a rite of passage into adulthood.

"When in a group of people and the conversation was about sports, I have attempted to tell about the little red flag. I only wanted to tell about its usage in golf in the middle and late years of the twenties.

These persons would only look at me in disbelief or make some remark to cause me to feel that I wasn't telling a true story.

"The golf course consisted of nine holes built about two miles from town on the rolling grass plains dotted here and there with live oak trees and some brush thickets. The drainage of this course was in the middle, which we called washed-out gullies. Most of the land of this nature around Lampasas was used to graze sheep, because native grass and weeds grew abundantly.

"After thirty-five years each hole is a distinct picture in my mind. As the saying goes, 'I ran my legs off' on this golf course for about three years using the little red flag. I was only a boy on his first job and was closely associated with men for the first time, most of whom operated businesses in this small town of a population of 2,000. By this close association I knew how each would play each hole.

"The first hole was a par four, about 315 yards. The fairways on this hole and all other holes were mowed with a weed mowing machine which left about four to six inches of grass and weeds. The rough was sometimes mowed to about eight or twelve inches, but most of the time was higher than that. A short slice to the right on this first hole would mean a lost ball in a thicket of grass and bushes. The approach shot to the green could easily go outside by rolling under a barbed wire fence just back of the green. All greens were made out of sand and treated with oil. All were enclosed with a mound of dirt about ten inches high.

"The number-two hole was about 535 yards and par five. There was a barbed wire fence all the way down the right hand side and was out of bounds when you hit the ball over it. The number-three hole was about 170 yards and par three, but in order to make a correct shot, you had to shoot over a corner that consisted of two barbed wire fences coming together and forming a space to hit across of about 50 yards, which was out of bounds.

"All caddies hated the barbed wire because that meant torn clothes and flesh, lost balls, and an unhappy golfer.

"The number six hole was about 440 yards and par four. On the left hand side of the fairway about 150 yards out were very tall live oak trees. It was reported that a golfer hit a ball that knocked a crow out of the very top and killed it. On the right of this hole was a very thick thicket of oak trees of all sizes. Back of the green was a very large mesquite tree.

"The number seven hole was about 350 yards and par four. On the right side of the fairway, it was very rocky, and there was an oak thicket. This fairway and the number eight fairway joined each other, and the gullies and drainage I spoke of a while ago was part of these two fairways. The number nine hole was about 390 yards and par four. There was a row of large oak trees that crossed nearly all of this fairway about 175 yards away, and most all of the golfers tried to shoot to the left because the number two fairway joined the number nine. But there was a lot of balls that hit in the top of the large oak.

"I know you are wondering how a little red flag could cause me to remember each of these holes. I was told one day that I could make some money if I went out to the golf course and learned how to caddie. This I did, but it was a very hard and trying experience. The definition in Webster's dictionary of a caddie is, 'a lad who carries golf clubs.' This definition is incorrect as far as this golf course in its use of a caddie. First I learned that every caddie had about fifteen little red flags of his own. Next I learned that every twosome, threesome, or foursome had a preference for a certain caddie. Since I was only fourteen, most of the caddies were older and more experienced. I then learned that there were a lot more caddies than needed.

"No one wanted a beginner because a beginner lost balls, since there was definitely an art in seeing balls in the air, listening for them to hit the ground, and seeing them on their first bounce before the weeds and grass could hide them from sight. Furthermore, it appeared, to succeed, one had to conquer competition and personalities. As I learned later, this was done by patience, mastery, and determination to be good at your first job.

"So I went home and told my mother I needed fifteen little red flags. I had seen flags of different sizes and attached to the wire of a clothes hanger in some crude fashion. I told her that some of the boys had cut strips of red cheesecloth and attached them to the wire by bending it close together. I know now what was going through her mind. *If you are going to have a flag, make it look like one.* She bought enough red cotton cloth to make fifteen red flags of a size of three by four inches. She hemmed them all the way around but left a wider hem to slide the wire through on one end. Then I bent a small loop at the top of the flag and closed it tight with part of the flag covering the loop. Then to make sure it wouldn't slip off, she sewed it some more with needle and red thread around this loop. Then I took them down to Payne's Bicycle Shop and they made a sharp point on the other end so that it would stick in the ground easy.

"The next day I left for the golf course a proud little boy. Our pastor and neighbor, the Rev. Lawrence Williams, gave me a ride, as would become his custom, and that put me one up on many other caddies. But I was later disappointed on that and many days to come, for I couldn't land a job.

"Finally, I caught on. I paired up with an older, more-experienced caddie to learn the basic steps. Such was the practice that most foursomes had two caddies if they were not good players or if they did not have enough confidence in just one caddie.

"But here is the part no one believes and which proves *Webster* wrong.

"You would stand out in front of a twosome, threesome, or foursome about 175 yards on all holes of par four and par five for the first shot. As each one would hit their ball, you were supposed to watch it and run stick a flag by it. The player could seldom see the ball in the fairway and never could see it or seldom find it in the rough if the red flag wasn't by the ball. If it were a par three hole, you stood close to the green. On the second shot of a par four and par five hole you stood within twenty-five yards of the green. You were supposed to flag every ball before the next golfer shot and retrieve if at all possible all balls over the barbed-wire fence. This was quite a task and was done by only the best of caddies.

"As I got better and more confident in myself, I would go down and ask Dr. Fariss, a dentist, for a job that day so I would at least have one to caddie for, and most of the time he would tell the others he had a caddie already hired for them, also. This is the way I got ahead of the other caddies before the players reached the golf course.

"Dr. Fariss usually played with Dr. Dickinson, another dentist, and Dr. Willerson, an MD. Their average score for nine holes was between forty-three and fifty, but sometimes Dr. Fariss would break forty since his drives were pretty accurate and went about 225 yards.

"The more you caddied for the same players, the easier it was, because you knew just about how high the ball would get off of the ground and which way it would go. I practiced running by a ball, and holding the flag on the end of the small loop, I could stick it close to the ball by throwing it instead of stooping down. Of course, I would miss quite often and then have to return and stick the flag up.

"Wooden tees were used in the fairways since the ground and grass were not in condition to hit from. These tees were usually pushed in a small slit in a piece of rubber cut from a tire inner tube so that you could retrieve them easily and not lose them.

"Thanks, however, to the little red flag, I earned 25 cents a player and a lesson about determination."

CHAPTER 18

THE STORYTELLER

MY GRANDFATHER, MY FATHER'S FATHER, was a wellspring of storytelling. He visited from his San Angelo home by train in my last years at home in the '50s, and my dad had the foresight to record these true tales from a life that stretched from 1873 to 1969, or ninety-five years.

In these reminiscences, Granddaddy (P. E. Leatherwood—he went by his initials) told of "the best sport I ever enjoyed" He said:

WE MOVED OUT ON PATTERSON CREEK, thirteen miles north of Lampasas. The country was open, didn't have many wire fences. And let it come a rainy time or a time we couldn't work, we'd get out on the horses with a greyhound. It would take right in after a jackrabbit, and all the other dogs in the community would join in, too. And these common dogs acted as shortstop. They'd see the greyhound bringing the rabbit around in a circle and cut across and confuse the rabbit. Then the greyhound would pick him up.

"So one day I was out hunting with my uncles, and we jumped a rabbit and took after it. Their horses ran away with them and went over the hill, and the greyhound routed the rabbit back toward me.

So I got right in behind them and rode standing up in my stirrups, whipping the horse on both shoulders with my old hat and yelling at the top of my voice.

"And the greyhound was just nipping at that rabbit at every jump, and finally it caught it.

"We couldn't catch more than two, and we would catch the second one and quit because the greyhound was run down."

Had I been keen on genealogy in my youth, I would have appreciated more, and harvested more, from this fertile mind.

Said he, "My grandmother and grandfather Leatherwood came from South Carolina. My mother's mother was Grandma Jones. She was a school girl with my grandmother Leatherwood—my two grandmothers were schoolchildren together. They came from South Carolina to Alabama, and then the Leatherwoods lived over in Mississippi awhile and went back to Alabama. Then they came to Texas.

"My grandfather moved up near Liberty Hill and bought a tract of land to farm. My father had just become of age and helped him grub out the farm; then he went back to marry my mother. When he got back to Alabama, my grandmother Jones felt like it was a breaking up of them for mother to leave them. So he said, 'All of you get ready and go to Texas with us.' They came to Texas and settled in Bastrop County, where I was born August 21, 1873."

His father died when he was six months old, and his mother, grandmother, and two uncles moved up near Liberty Hill near his grandfather Leatherwood before all moved to Lampasas. His mother died when he was eight, leaving him an orphan in the care of his maternal grandmother.

He attended boarding school at sixteen.

"It was a co-ed school, and the boys had a long row of rooms called the Sheep Shed, and the girls had a dormitory, a two-story building with a big dining room. The boys and girls got their meals together. And we had a teacher at each long table.

"One morning for breakfast we were served oatmeal. One of the boys kept picking at the bowl of oatmeal, and the teacher said, 'Is something the matter with your oatmeal?' And the boy said, 'Look here what it is.'

"It was a whole mouse cooked in it."

The patriarch of the Leatherwoods told of his personal work history, which spanned the Depression. He began work at seventeen and before long, after returning from a fishing trip, landed his job for the next twenty-five years, which was bookkeeper at Barnes and Manuel, a hardware store in Lampasas.

"I resigned to take the postmastership of Lampasas," he said.

He held the postmaster position from 1920 to 1922. There are family accounts that this job ended with difficulties. But a combing of newspapers and postal records do not support this.

Maybe my mother knew something more. She and her father-in-law indulged in the social grace of coffee in the kitchen long after my dad, an early riser, and I had gone to bed. With each visit she ushered him into our household with much honor and special thanksgiving.

He eventually worked for Standard Hide and Fur Co. in Dallas, leaving his wife Lou and five children in Lampasas for another ten years, a place they recalled with fondness. However, "The Depression came on, and the fur and wool business closed up, so we went to San Angelo to live in 1932, and I had a hard time getting started again. I took most any little job I could get."

Finally drifting into stability, he retired at eighty-one after eleven years at Findlater Hardware Co. in San Angelo. His good health and nimbleness of mind permitted him to do income tax returns for clients into his 90s. How alert was he at the end? He could recite in order of service the full names of all the presidents of the United States.

It was not until his death bed that I learned of our kindred spirit. Granddaddy told of turn-of-the-century camping trips by wagon to Fall Creek Falls on the Colorado River of Texas. The campers included school teachers and other professionals from Lampasas; a cook tent separated the tents of men and women.

It was obvious he had a vision for me. His gifts included a leather briefcase and a handsomely bound world atlas, both of which I held onto despite the coming of attaché cases and changes in national boundaries.

The Leatherwoods were united through marriage with the George W. Porters of Troy, Texas, when my parents exchanged vows on September 5, 1936. The honeymooners spent that Labor Day weekend at the Hotel Wooten in Abilene.

My mother kept the menu for their Sunday dinner. I don't know the choices made, but whatever they were, it was a splendid feast that might have included fresh Galveston shrimp, chicken okra soup (my mother loved okra), broiled fresh Alaskan salmon with cucumber slaw, three vegetables, lettuce and tomato salad, fresh Elberta peach tart and buttermilk—all for 75 cents.

There were also five children in the Porter family. All the children in both families would marry, but eight would have an only child. The generation of my aunts and uncles experienced both the Depression and World War II—and begot three more generations.

The patriarch of the Porter family, George, was diagnosed with heart disease in 1928, and the farm chores fell to Mida, the wife, and the children. None of the offspring stayed to tend the land when they became adults, moving into teaching, oil, and homemaking.

Of this family's genealogy, there is this proud belief that Mida Nelson was descended from Thomas Nelson, a signer of the Declaration of Independence.

CHAPTER 19

SUPPORT

TO NAVIGATE THROUGH THE STORM that churned my waters, I have acquired an umbrella of professional and lay support reaching beyond the usual confines of what is called a support group, a gathering of people to discuss their illness.

To use the generic, the broader group includes doctors, accountants, lawyers, parents, relatives, and friends—and a support group.

When I was sinking at the office, Bob Cooper, a certified public accountant, threw the first lifeline. He had, through a breakfast meeting of professionals, become aware of a small law firm that fought for workers' rights, and he gave me a clipping on that firm.

I sought counsel and they, Coane and Associates, took my case. Early on, Bruce Coane, the chief, described himself as a workaholic, but our course proved him above all else patient. At least six manic episodes requiring hospitalization—in a period of four years—intervened between his accepting the case and our going to trial. More than once the court set a trial date, and I got sick and couldn't appear. Finally, the judge said to make a tape for my appearance, if my mania coincided with the trial date again.

THE LEGAL EFFORT PRODUCED a positive side effect. Asked to participate in the preparation of my case, I regained self-esteem and felt I belonged in society. My lawyers always accepted my calls and welcomed me to their offices, where I was invited to sit in on depositions of witnesses. Come each Christmas, Coane boosted spirits further with an office party, featuring live music.

We finally went to trial and, as has been told, lost.

But I needed lawyers on other occasions. First, I applied for Social Security Disability. No doubt my filling out the paperwork at the Social Security office while manic helped. And with Coane's effort I was approved on the initial request, an unusual happening.

My luck got worse, but legally not bad. I was run over on the sidewalk. The driver hit a large crack in the concrete near my home and whacked me from behind, throwing me on the hood. I was out for several hours and in therapy for a shattered pelvis for weeks. The driver's insurance paid a minimum, but the city balked on its responsibility.

Meanwhile, I had another manic episode, and in the midst of litigation, I changed lawyers, from the Coane firm to Steve Petrou, the lawyer who led my discrimination case in court, but who was now independent. My action cannot be explained with any complaint against Coane. They would not accept my phone calls while I was at Rusk, which is reasonable, and that may have precipitated my abandoning ship.

Petrou took the city on, and in mediation won a settlement.

And later, when my mother became terminally ill with cancer, he was called upon again to draw up a will that established a trust for me. It was feared that if the money went directly to me, I could lose it all in a manic spending spree.

Judy Nickles, a paternal cousin five years my junior and a special-education teacher who'd been widowed in a plane crash, was asked to act as trustee and accepted, although the position paid nothing and she was going against the advice of her lawyer. A third lawyer had a hand in the will. Being in my mother's hometown, Alan McNeill would handle the probate, and when he took a look at the will, he recommended a codicil to clarify a passage.

We also bobbled with professionals with the taxes of the trust. A nationwide accounting firm figured our taxes the first year. But the second year, Cooper, my CPA, took another look and said because distribution of interest income was made to me, I, not the trust, should pay the taxes. Since the trust had a higher tax rate than me, amended returns would mean a refund of several hundred dollars.

Beyond the professional support, my parents all along buoyed my finances, seeing to it that I did not fall below my basic standard of living.

A staunch supporter from the beginning of my employment troubles was Kay York, the founder of the Depressive, Manic Depressive Association in Houston. She encouraged me in the lawsuit, and I learned many practical things about my illness in the support group—things doctors don't have time to tell you in twenty- or thirty-minute appointments with them. It probably was where I acquired the courage to talk openly about my health, where I learned how the words of circumstance sounded.

These people and others in this book have effaced stigma, have emboldened me.

CHAPTER 20
RISPERDAL

NO RESTRAINT, I'm rising out of the chasm.

On Risperdal.

Huffin' and puffin' from the roundhouse.

Let's celebrate.

It is the longest period without a psychotic episode in the twenty-five year history of my manic depressive illness.

For five years, since getting on this extraordinary drug at Rusk State Hospital in March 1997, I have been free of demons and am now removing the monkey from my back in society and the workplace.

The world may come crashing down yet, as it did in 1988, when this ugly force evicted me from the office and a wonderful friend from my home, but my doctor and I are shoveling coal to the engine until it does.

THIS DOCTOR is Dr. Ranjit Chacko at Baylor College of Medicine in Houston. And he is fending off the detractors as soon as I present them. For a brief spell I saw a county doctor in order to obtain this expensive medicine without cost. But she cut my dosage by 25 percent, and I rushed back to Chacko. He said her action was "playing with fire."

"It's working," he said, looking up from his desk, on a recent visit.

Later, my neurologist noted that my right hand was shaking at rest, a Parkinson's motion. He wanted me to drop the Risperdal at once, saying it was the contributor. I reported to Chacko, who explained that it was a minimal Parkinson's effect and that the drug to replace mine had not been tested on manic depressive patients.

"I won't do it, I won't do it," he said when asked if I should change.

He has seen my manic behavior whereas others who try to manipulate the drugs have not. He knows how serious and deep my psychosis can be. I think I can speak for him, too, and say how grateful we are for something that works. The others just don't know.

But Chacko didn't start us down the road to giddiness over our success, though it is to his credit to have maintained drug and dosage since not long after I began taking it at Rusk. A doctor there, whose name should be chiseled on a building or something—yet remains anonymous—prescribed it about midway through my hospitalization for one of my worst episodes.

I had walked the streets for a month, writing nineteen bad checks, including one for a tomato. In my final act this time, I had thrown a drink from a glass into the face of someone who I thought was attacking me at the Four Seasons Hotel. I was thrown down and restrained until police came and took me to Ben Taub Hospital.

I asked for transfer to Rusk. Its old buildings remind me of a college campus. To some its program may sound like pampering, a little soft—but we aren't criminals. And some who live at or near street level may need a massage. The older woman who picked up butts was memorable. She was so smooth on the dance floor. (There were two dances weekly at the recreation building my first go-round.)

I'm getting away from the doctor whose meritorious service has ignited my flight to old strengths. However, it's the whole setting that provides good treatment, so let me continue a tad in this vein. I've been to Rusk twice, and it had more classroom work the last time. First time, we had horticulture classes down at the park where the magnolias and fig trees grow. At the fishing lodge, the supervisor served up peach cobbler. Just a small lake, but pleasant.

Oh, I got aggressive once in the cafeteria. I couldn't get a fork to eat the messy soft taco that they served as finger food. Disgusted, I dumped the attendant's loaded tray at his feet. For this, I was hauled before one of the doctors to explain, and he ordered me a bologna sandwich "without a fork," the attendant explained.

One makes some friends during a five-week stay. There was a woman who had an extensive hangup about espionage—certain countries she couldn't visit, all that. Still, the company at smoke breaks was good.

Surprisingly, I talked to the doctor trimming my toenails longer than I did the psychiatrist. Yet, the latter came up with this miracle. It was something to sip coffee over at the cantina, decorated at holidays.

Meanwhile, the big rub with Risperdal is money. After a disagreement with the county, Janssen, the manufacturer, supplied my needs because my income was under $15,000 a year. With the distribution of interest income from a trust set up in my mother's will, I no longer qualified. But the income is still small, and if my drug bill continues at $5,400 annually in the United States, that's $108,000 over the next twenty years. That will erode substantially the principal in the trust.

CHAPTER 21
MARRIAGE VOW

OUR FAMILY VISITED OUR PLOT at Oak Hill Cemetery in Lampasas after the tombstones for the three of us were in place. My parents thought there was room for a fourth, and I told my mother I might marry. Surprising to a degree, she seemed to find pleasure in that, rather than regrets the union might occur after her death.

"You might marry," she would say later.

The stumbling block to marriage for a good many years after I left home was my determination to avoid the closest of relationships with women. For all I knew they were all as unreasonable as my mother. It would remain for a psychiatrist years later to label her invectives emotional abuse.

One incident in her later years conveys the tone of the lifelong strife with my mother. After moving home and after seeing more and more meals served out of cans, I suggested that I take over cooking duties. To that she staunchly replied, "I'm not going to give up control of the kitchen."

Nor did it help for my mother to find unforgivable fault with each and every woman I dated—with one exception. That exception I found unattractive because we had no spark—no romance—between us. With the most favored of the others, mental illness had, of course, intervened. From my mother's perspective, it appears that she would approve of her child's marriage only after she would, by act of God, have to let him go.

AT THE GRAVESITE, my mother extended a promissory note that marriage was, finally, okay. And there was the promissory note on the part of the son that he entertained seriously the idea of marriage, even in the sixth decade of life.

At this late stage, for better or for worse, I have a growing sense that it is an institution of companionship, hang the children, that should not pass me by. I am convinced that—let my mother be the guide on this—that in the end we need to hold on to each other the most.

I missed the boat the first time, where 90 percent of us will wed at least once by the age of fifty, and I don't want to miss it again at sixty.

Whether I marry depends on the contemplation of an altered landscape. First, I now know women to pursue where none could be found in the social chasm at the onset of aging and financial woes. Second, e-mail has enhanced communication. Even those only slightly interested will drop a line on the 'net, and serious chats aren't rare.

My friendship with Mary (not her real name) was reborn on the Internet after a forty-year hiatus. Her e-mail address had shown up in a high school classmate listing.

"Hi, Mary, hope to see you at the reunion. Your name has come up more than once lately. First, my mother died, and I learned a little later of your mother's death. Sorry to hear it. Then, in going through papers my mother saved, I discovered two letters you wrote during a summer I spent in Arizona."

Mary replied:

"I can't tell you how good it is to hear from you. Thx for taking the time to let me know about the letters. Sorry to hear about your mother, too. If you're moving back to Houston, give me a ring. We've lived here for five years. I guess I won't say "we" much longer. Two weeks ago, my husband of thirty-eight years left me and wants a divorce."

My ears perked up.

About that time I was also online with Denise (not her real name), one of my more faithful correspondents. Though she lived in Austin, she followed Houston Rockets basketball. To my query, she replied, "Yes, I saw the fight . . . about twenty times. You know how they do the replays over and over from all different angles. Shag started it, but Charles shouldn't have bounced the ball off his head."

At fifty-three, I liked her bounce. And we went back a ways. Two years earlier, she was down on her luck in a Houston suburb. Her husband had left her, she had lost her job, and she had dropped out of a doctorate program in public health. I dropped her a Christmas card; she called. I drove out. Despite it all, despite the emptiness of a 3,000-square-foot house taken over mostly by cats and dogs, we savored the moment with coffee before a fresh Christmas tree.

Her mother rescued her from her financial plight.

And Denise rescued my spirit.

She always had, with a gangly brood of twenty-three cats and six dogs, four of them greyhounds.

She also has a history of husbands, the history part of which she attributes to depression, serial marriages that she doesn't tell about on the first date. But she still was a great source of cheer and general spirit raising. After all, she came to see me at Rusk State Hospital, where visits are rare. I told her then (she thought I was manic) that her men were like chewing gum—she chews them up and, once satisfied, spits them out.

But forget gum. Relationships are more like sand, shifting, always shifting.

Mary and I attended many theatrical events for a year. Then her husband came back.

Denise found a former classmate through e-mail, and they were an item for a year. Then he told her goodbye on the 'net.

But, lo and behold, now enters Jill (not her real name), a former classmate and a family friend with whom I talk freely. She is seeking a divorce after forty years of marriage. My ears perk up once again.

CHAPTER 22

FAMILY

ACORNS FELL in unusual abundance that year. And what the squirrels left, the little dog Chica collected in a loose pile on the patio's orange and blue tiles. It was Thanksgiving, and she had brought her offering to the table (well, to a table leaf placed at a suitable height).

When she was young and I was comparing her wistfully to the old Boston terrier, Chico, a handyman gently and wisely said, "Give her a chance." Well, she added seven years, and I guess I hadn't been paying attention—but, all of a sudden, she was smarter. On a walk, I'd say "Back," and she would turn back for the barn.

The table leaf for Chica helped round out the place settings for family as I regrouped from the throes of death and an emptiness born out of my own dereliction with relations. I had noted to an old acquaintance in another city the lack of siblings, parents, children, and in-laws at my table, and she had answered the e-mail:

"I certainly know what you mean about family. I am the only one left to speak of in my family. My brother is a lost cause—never know where he is, and I am really better off if I don't know. He would only want money! Of course, since my mother was a single parent since I was six, there are no connections there. Anyway, I do not know what

I would do without my two sons and darling daughter-in-law, whom I am very fond of."

ROSE CROWELL, the top hand at the Dixie Dude ranch, had wisely schooled me, "Some are better than family."

And to contemplate whom Chica and I sit with leaves no room to bemoan a bare cupboard, but is for us to partake a rich broth.

In the first instance, I was fortunate to have a friend of thirty-five years and his wife sell a Los Angeles newspaper at the inception of my greater freedom. It gave the couple, James and Codette Vowell, greater freedom to play. And they kept up the highly energized image of California.

When I visited, the week stacked up something like the nursery rhyme about household chores. Wednesday was tennis on a lighted court atop a nine-story building. I went along for the ride, but must confess that I spent my time on the rooftop watching far better players, if only because they knew how to keep the balls out of the traffic below. Thursday was exercise with a trainer, in which I did participate. Friday was the start of weekend skiing from the Vowell's A-frame on nearby Big Bear Mountain. I had not skied for fifteen years, but love the sport and stayed up on the bunny and beginner slopes. Minus the black- and blue-diamond runs, it was still a thrill.

A few years earlier, over on the mountain at Whitefish, Montana, I had encountered a pair of Canadians, who had taken up the sport at sixty and were intermediate skiiers. That told me it could be done. James wasn't much younger, fifty-seven, and kept up with the feistier Codette, forty-five. Well, most of the time. Together, they were separated only by age—gentle dispositions, enthusiasm for an infinite variety of activity.

We adjourned from the ski slopes to an intimate Valentine's Day dinner that Monday. A special guest, Erin Fortenberry, nineteen, joined us. She was trying to make her way in film and was the daughter of Gary and Gail Fortenberry, who live near Seattle. The Fortenberrys were also old friends, he by a few months on James. The daughter carried the same black hair of her father at a slightly earlier age and the same incisive reasoning.

Gary had broken into backpacking, whitewater canoeing, and skiing with me, possessing a trusting mother. For years he told with relish about our misadventures, remembering them long after I had forgotten. Well, not quite. I still remember telling him that we should slalom a line of trees in the Guadalupe River, and we didn't make it. We wrapped a fabric Foldboat around one of those trees, and the outing got worse because of a storm.

But Gary still hasn't forgotten, and he and Gail have been paying me back, with train trips to their home overlooking the San Juan Islands, sailing and mountain camping.

This year they were warming up in a Volkswagen camper van for a long haul through Europe and Asia, taking me through frigid North Cascades National Park, letting me savor the multitude of snowy peaks. And the tall timber was so magnificent I vowed to return for more again and again.

There was a practical side. I could buy prescription drugs cheaper in Canada.

Back home, Dorothy and Sonny Novak of suburban Spring extended a family tradition, welcoming the Leatherwood entourage on Christmas Day and keeping in touch throughout the year. She had been "the daughter I should have had" for my mother.

As my mother neared her end, Dorothy comforted her, talked in terms I could not. "Carlton will be all right?" the cancer patient, but above all mother, asked. I can only guess the answer, for I have not been lonely since.

Meanwhile, the Vowells came to Texas just to join me in a game of golf one weekend, over at Horseshoe Bay in the Hill Country. The traps there do yawn, but James and Codette stayed stony-faced and finished each hole despite burying a few balls in the sand. I won't deny it—I picked up out of frustration several times. But it was on this trip that Codette said at dinner, "Carl, do you want to go to Paris and Crete with us? I haven't checked with James, but . . . ." I didn't hesitate to accept. "Those are the places I've always wanted to go back to," I said.

So we went, and one of the supreme treats was the full moon over a harbor. I said to the girl who brought me cognac and pistachios atop my hotel in Iraklion, the capital of Crete, "See, see, the moon has come up." And she with wry wit and good English said, "Finally."

We played golf on Crete, but before we got to the course, we walked Samarian Gorge. When remembering the friendly Greeks, I also think about my friend James, who, after my legs gave out on the hiking trail, offered a helping hand all the way to the sea, to the blue, blue sea . . . finally.

CHAPTER 23

DRUG RUN

GREEN TILES OF ALFALFA lay below the plane window as my flight approached the Phoenix airport. I was on a drug run to the Mexican border. My friends and I had chuckled half-heartedly about the mission. They understood that the object was to obtain prescription medicine at a reduced price. But it was unsettling to associate the flight with illegal drugs and to find humor in a prescription-drug bill that amounted to $450 a month.

Beyond its businesslike purpose, the trip was also imbued with desert dust from decades past—a layer of nostalgia for an uncle and aunt now gone, whose home had been a second home, and for a landscape still dry, a contrast to my coastal home.

My cousin Tom Thomasson picked me up at Sky Harbor airport. It was good to see him. We drew closer when his mother, Aunt Ida, became the last of our parents to die. I flew out for her funeral, representing my immediate family as mandated by my mother. Tom returned the visit, coming to Houston a few months later. A reluctant traveler until then, he sealed the bond with zeal and enthusiasm, with pleasure.

AS WE UNDERTOOK the land link of our drug mission, I told him about blinking to make sure that the private plane paralleling our commercial one to touchdown was real. My first thought was that Uncle Ed, a pilot who introduced me to adventure, was at the small plane's controls, shepherding us in. Tom said he had recurring thoughts about his dad, too, when he saw a plane.

The highway heading west cut through low mountain ridges and saguaro, the cactus with many bent arms that looks like some funny rubber man. As they disappeared in our mirror, ocotillo took over the desert floor, extending its slender but festive red blooms to the sky.

Tom and I discussed our upcoming purchase at the border. I wanted a year's supply of Risperdal 2 mg. It would stay fresh that long, my psychiatrist said. "Check the color, packaging," he suggested. I was also working on a sample box of a new medicine, lansoprazole 30 mg, for a stomach irritation. These two prescriptions together were $395 of my monthly drug bill in the United States.

Tom checked on supply and legal limits in advance with the pharmacist. He learned that we could legally buy a three-month supply. However, there was a practice of crossing the border twice, an hour apart, with each person carrying the limit. That would get me my annual supply. "No, we'll do it legal," I told my cousin, "and we'll double-check the regulations with the Border Patrol before we cross."

Tom readily agreed with this plan.

It lessened my anxiety. I had heard enough about imprisonment for firearms violations after shells were found in a pickup. And I had been stopped and searched for no apparent reason when crossing back to Laredo on foot several years before.

When we reached Algodones, Mexico, our destination outside Yuma, Arizona, we parked on the U.S. side of the border in a large lot with cars bearing the plates of many states. The U.S. Border Patrol station was across the street. I walked over to an agent and asked how much medicine I could bring in. "Three months supply with a prescription," he said.

With a prescription. That was key. And I had the keys.

We entered the village.

It had more than one drug store, but Tom led me to the one he had traded with and the one with which he had arranged for the supply of Risperdal. We made our way down the narrow streets, passing many stalls with cheap arts and crafts before getting there. At the store, we found the pharmaceuticals neatly displayed and the pharmacist knowledgeable. "That's the generic [for the stomach capsule]," she said, writing out a bill that priced each of the Big Two medicines at $100 less per month. We had a net saving even after travel expenses were deducted.

Tom and I left the drug store, and I relaxed with a beer at Caliente, a bar and racing forum, while he played the horses. The establishment had a prominent street sign but was tucked away, down a shoulder-width alley. His dad Ed would have been comfortable here, relaxing with a beer in a small town in Mexico. Indeed, we had relaxed together on fishing trips in the Sea of Cortez, which forms a shoreline with Baja California, the Mexican state we were in.

Maybe Tom and I were being a little eccentric, maybe less than prudent, but we were doing it his way. After all, he flaunted prescription-glasses care and bought "off the rack" at a drug store whatever seemed to fit his eyes. I found the practice of buying drugs this way a little less of a comfortable fit. I was foregoing U.S. packaging, but I also knew that U.S. standards weren't necessarily the benchmark of quality, that to believe so was arrogant. A wool sweater bought in Paris had lasted a quarter of century, and a medical exam for a torn ligament in Greece was accurate—the injury to the foot was flesh, not bone.

Tom and I headed back to the saguaros, stopping for a date shake along the way. Before he put me on the plane, we drove out to the abandoned hangar and office of Thomasson Dusting Service, an aerial applicator of pesticides on crops. The desert slowly wears at the facility, in the shadow of Picacho Peak.

Not far away, facing the peak from an oasis, Uncle Ed and Aunt Ida rest. The headstone notes she was in Eastern Star and he flew as a captain for the Army in World War II. "He just loved to fly," his son said when we paid homage.

CHAPTER 24

THOMASSONS

HIS PASSION WAS PLANES.

As a crop duster in south central Arizona, he would roar down on the rows of cotton so low that the tail wheel of his biplane occasionally would tap a concrete irrigation ditch.

As a sportsman, he piloted single- and twin-engine planes on fishing trips from Baja California to Salmon, Idaho.

As a trendy aviator, he helped bring helicopters to agriculture and dam construction.

Uncle Ed Thomasson did all these things, while letting me join in, immersed in an aura of wealth beyond my means.

After tending to business, which included a hangar of ten planes, a shop, and offices, he usually went up in a Steerman, a biplane painted with the Thomasson Dusting Service colors, blue and white. It held the powdered pesticide in a tank behind the propeller, and an open cockpit followed.

The pilots, including Ed, were at their respective fields by dawn, checking the wind. It was as much a foe as heat, which later in the day caused the chemical to rise rather than fall on the cotton.

I WORKED AS A FLAGMAN to pay my way through college. All of us put in seven days a week from dark to dark, with a break in the middle of the day. Ed and I adjourned to his mother's house at Picacho for home cooking and napped on the floor in early afternoon.

The pilots loaded more pesticide, and the flagmen went back to pacing sixteen rows for the Steerman and twelve for the smaller Pipers, which sprayed the cotton. Sometimes a power line would cross the end of a field. The pilot might fly under it, and the flagman would either speed to his next post or hit the ground. Our contact with the chemicals has worried me much of my life, but my general physician doubts they have had any effect on my health.

Being a relative to the boss begot privilege.

One summer I joined Ed and Don, one of the three permanent pilots, on an excursion to the Middle Fork of the Salmon River in Idaho. Aunt Ida, my mother's sister, stayed behind to tend the books and deal with farmers and personnel. Tom, their son, was like many teenagers and did not share the family interests.

The river ran through the Sawtooth Mountains, which had not yet gained their designation as the first wilderness area in the nation. It was primitive, as attested to by the crude landing strip, dirt with a hump in the middle. We set down there without mishap, along with another Cessna 182 from Washington state. After setting up camp, the rest of the party fished for salmon while I explored. I had never encountered so much wildness. Walking downstream, I discovered whitewater with salmon leaping up it, heading back to their spawning grounds. And nearby, a fleet of rafts produced new excitement, giving rise to the thought that I could one day return and run these rapids.

When I returned to camp, the others showed me their success, huge fish that another party on mountain bikes had helped land. But I had no feel for the sport, no joy in filling the belly of the plane with something so magnificent in the wild. When we winged home, I did talk of shipping a small one to my college for a dinner with fellow students.

The next major fishing trip with my uncle was to Baja California. We launched two boats and two planes across the Sea of Cortez from Bahia Kino, Mexico. The Piper Apache and Cessna 182 landed on a dry lake bed, while the boats entered a cove marked by a crescent of red sea urchins.

To our misfortune, the wind blew a steady forty miles per hour for days. We ventured out in the boats, but even staying close, each still disappeared from the other in the swells. Then four of us chose to fly to the other side of the peninsula. We landed at a tiny village on the Pacific Ocean, and the fishermen there were luckier. One of their wooden boats was heaped with lobster. We negotiated and bought gunny sacks full for fifty cents a head. Our camp would not go another night without seafood.

When Ed got into helicopters, he came to North Texas to take delivery at the Bell Helicopter plant. I was in college at North Texas State University in Denton, and he invited me to join him. We discussed his plans. He wanted to spray cotton with the chopper and to use it in constructing the dam at Lake Powell, a project that incensed environmentalists because the beauty there would be submerged, a place no one knew to be made forever unknowable.

Ed decided to drop me off at school when he flew the helicopter home. It was a short trip to the campus, and, after circling, he chose to land on a parking lot in front of the president's home. I stepped out, waved goodbye, and he was off into the sunset. The president's wife was out tending flowers as I strolled past the big lawn on the way to my apartment. Word got out the next day that the president was curious about who came to school in a 'copter.

But it was in Eloy, where Ed and Ida lived, that I got a taste of using a helicopter to get to an office. We flew in the 182 to Flagstaff to meet a doctor-pilot for a round of golf one Sunday. We had a pleasant game on a course nestled in picturesque land formations, although the score was not memorable.

As we headed home from this brief outing, a storm boiled up toward Phoenix and further south toward the airstrip. The doctor invited us to spend the night, and the weather allowed us a swim—the host had swim suits in a number of sizes. I went to bed early, because I needed to go to the office the next morning. I was in a summer internship at the *Eloy Enterprise*, a weekly newspaper.

Up early, we flew by plane to the Picacho strip for a jazzy maneuver that would assure my getting to work on time. We taxied up to the helicopter and stepped out to change carriages. The new conveyance was like soaring in a bubble, and Ed put her down this time on a vacant lot across the street from the newspaper office, on time.

That could have spoiled me.

CHAPTER 25
TWILIGHT

THE WIND CHIMES THE SEASON as the blue jays return to my patio, with double doors flung open to my study. The flower bed has reverted to forest. Some would say it is unattended, and that is true, but I like the wildness that a straying oak, a triumphant shrimp plant, and clinging ferns evoke as lizards sun and dart.

The slender oak was possibly born on the bountiful tide of acorns from across the fence two years ago. It begets tolerance from crepe myrtles, firmly planted and enduring after twenty years (some with hard freezes) and busily producing green shoots for the delicate lilac blooms.

The shrimp plant, transplanted from my grandmother's wash pot in my parents' backyard, has tripled itself and wears its namesake headdress on all three plants.

The setting whispers when I write.

The words flow from contentment.

"COULDN'T GET *THE POST* to let me be a full-time writer," I said during a Continuing Studies course at Rice University.

"That was our loss," said Jackie Simon, the writing instructor.

In her remarks on assignments, she said my writing had "accuracy amounting to poetry" and "contained the number-one asset of memoirs, honesty."

As I went back over the transcript of *The Post* trial, I found the references to "lovely writing" and excellently written editorials, virtual raves about my work, yet the editor who fired me held little hope for my diseased mind to contribute more. And I lost hope, only now to dream again, from encouragement and recovery, to produce a few good reads.

My doctor has said I cannot work but has not vetoed the relaxed pace I keep at the keyboard. So I wish to light and hop in perches among friends, among my family. This would provide a geographic tapestry to meld into stories.

The possibilities are generous. They translate into contentment in my sixties. Orange trees flank a house trailer in the Arizona desert, inviting me to sit in a porch swing with a laptop, breezes whipping. In Washington state another writer's haven overlooks the San Juan Islands, with snowcapped Mt. Baker rising thirty miles inland. Quaint cafes serve coffee in Fairhaven, the old town, at the foot of the hill. And yet again, the orange-tiled roof of a Spanish-style home circled with flowers draws me to the hum of Los Angeles.

Meanwhile, there is the book within.

CHAPTER 26

ODYSSEY END

THE ODYSSEY WAS STILL THE BOOK WITHIN.

If I had been as wise as prize-winning author John Steinbeck, I would have known that the journey would end earlier than anticipated. He said before visiting Texas and the Deep South that his search for America "had been like a full dinner of many courses, set before a starving man. At first he tries to eat all of everything, but as the meal progresses, he finds he must forgo some things to keep his appetite and his taste buds functioning."

For whatever reason, maybe my familiarity from living in Houston—and loving it—I visited the cities and moved on, finding in the rural landscape a refreshing texture.

The tremendous beauty of the coastal region is not immediately apparent, I mused. Just as mountains were considered impediments to travel before artists and writers awakened us to their aesthetic quality, so the flat marshes and shallow bays pass monotonously before the untrained eye. It helps to read about the birds, grasses, and other life in those estuaries where such dining delicacies as shrimp mature rapidly and blue crabs thrive. You then possess something with which to contemplate the richness of the land. And it is rich. Roy Bedicheck, the state's foremost nature writer, said the Texas coast is a storehouse of natural wealth unparalleled elsewhere in the world in so little space. He noted the commingling of such natural elements as oil and gas, farmlands, harbors, climate, and the fishing industry.

And in the Coastal Bend, down near Corpus Christi, I found dreamers from the cities immersed in a space adventure. Others had dreamed there as well.

A HANDFUL OF TEXANS successfully launched the first space shot unsupported by government funds. This plucky band took its rocket, plopped it down next to a cattle tank amid yellow-blooming partridge peas and sunflowers, and let her fly. The launch has got to be the most remarkable accomplishment of man on the Coastal Bend of Texas—a spectacular statement in support of rugged individualism, free enterprise, and self-reliance.

When that thirty-seven-foot encasement of solid fuel streaked skyward, it seemed to assure the world of space services as common as the cargo of water.

The private launch was from Matagorda Island, a thirty-four-mile-long barrier island inaccessible by land vehicle. Barrier islands such as Matagorda stretch in a chain from Maine to Texas. They are the longest and best-developed string in the world, protecting the mainland and lagoons from direct wave attack by the sea. The earliest of Texas explorers passed Matagorda. Alonso de Pineda charted the coastline carved by the Gulf of Mexico in 1519 while looking for a water passage to India for Spain.

At the time of the launch in 1982, Matagorda Island was owned by three parties. The federal government possessed two-fifths, the state two-fifths, and Toddie Lee Wynne the remaining fifth. Wynne, eighty-four, was the principal investor in Space Services Inc. of America

(SST), which fired the rocket. He died just hours before he was to witness the liftoff from his ranch.

The region had trappings of a major space port. John F. Kennedy and Lyndon B. Johnson Causeways crossed nearby bays. Those U.S. presidents, of course, led the nation's quest for the moon. And with signs at shops in the nearby town of Rockport cheering the private launch, it didn't take much imagination to think of it as Rocketport.

Early on the afternoon of September 8, an international press gathered for a briefing at a Rockport motel. The launch had been postponed. This information was relayed by satellite from Matagorda. The voice was that of Donald K. "Deke" Slayton, one of the original astronauts and the pilot of the first international manned mission. "We're not sure exactly where the problem is," he said. "There's suspicion that it may be an instrumentation-type problem. Our master plan is to charge along toward a 10 o'clock launch tomorrow and hope we find our problem before the sun goes down."

With the designers of the platform, software, and telemetry at the site, the launch team pressed on. At 3 p.m. Slayton reported, "We're a little smarter than we were last time I talked to you. We've at least got our problem pinned down to two things. It's either our connector into the platform or a cable." So they put a new platform in and were checking the cable. "And if it all shakes out, why, we're about ready to go in the morning."

At 6 p.m. final checks for control of the payload continued. Other equipment tested out. Work remaining included mounting the gyro package, refilling a control system with gas, and recharging the battery. "We have a reasonably high degree of confidence that it is all going to flow," Slayton said. Meteorologists forecast isolated thunderstorms, making the shot indefinite for the two-hour launch window the next day. The Naval Air Station at Corpus Christi needed the range the following day, Friday. Weekend weather predictions were "lousy." A tropical storm in the Gulf of Mexico threatened to become a hurricane.

The Texas coast experiences some of the severest of hurricanes in September. The greatest natural disaster in U.S history occurred when one decimated Galveston on September 8–9, 1900. Six thousand lives were lost.

The private space shot lacked the hordes of spectators that show up at NASA launches. Still, 230 guests and 88 reporters sailed on the vessels Wharf Cat and Scat Cat for the island before dawn on Thursday, September 9. The fishing boats are normally berthed in Port Aransas. Another 44 members of the media flew out by helicopter. The spectators waited under a green and white tent, breakfasting on boiled shrimp and fruit, about a mile from the rocket, which stood on the southern tip of Matagorda. Scientists monitored the countdown in portable buildings between the tent and rocket. Flags flew at half mast in honor of Wynne. One of the launch-pad engineers, Hal Geise, used a felt-tipped pen to inscribe this message on the skirt of the rocket: "God bless you, Toddie Lee Wynne."

Cowboys interrupted their morning routine. They parked Star Brand Cattle Co. pickups on a rise near the tent. Rear-window racks carried rifles. Two horses saddled for work, Smokey and Diablo, would witness the launch. This was appropriate. The test launch was called Conestoga I. It took its name from the oxen- and mule-drawn covered wagons that transported pioneering Americans to the West in the mid-nineteenth century. A historian viewed those wagon trains as "free enterprise at its rawest."

A Life Flight helicopter from Houston set down at the launch site in case a medical emergency required transport to a hospital. "Three minutes, thirty seconds, and counting. The mission director has just confirmed that the roadblocks are up, the ground safety is operational, and the telemetry is ready to go." Thus Sallie Chafer, thirty-two, the resonant voice of Conestoga I, alerted viewers. "One minute, forty seconds, and counting. We have started the telemetry recorder. There will be a hold for two minutes at T minus one minute fifteen seconds. The mission director and the weather officer confirm that all FAA requirements are met, the weather is good, and all conditions are go for launch."

The countdown halted and then resumed for nineteen seconds before another hold was ordered for evaluation of the telemetry system. The count backed up a bit, resumed.

"This is Conestoga Launch Control. We are now at T minus fifty seconds and counting. The vehicle is now on internal power. The attitude control system and booster control system timer has been started. . . . T minus thirty seconds and counting. The control unit has been activated. ten, nine, eight (and all the spectators picked up the countdown) seven, six, five, four, three, two, one . . . ignition!"

"We see ignition. It's flying!" shouted a radio announcer. And indeed it was. Gathering velocity, but without a boom, the rocket climbed, trailing a brilliant yellow flame and white smoke. The crowd cheered wildly. The white spear poked no holes in clouds, because there were none. It seemed to arc toward the sun. At sixty-three seconds into the flight, the engine shut down. A forty-mile tail of smoke rippled and curled over the Gulf of Mexico. The rocket was no longer visible.

"T plus two minutes, and Conestoga I is now in space."

The crowd cheered, smiled broadly.

"We're coming up on T plus five minutes nine seconds. The vehicle should be at apogee (its farthest point from earth), at 195.9 miles altitude, 160.6 miles down range."

The 505-pound payload included roughly forty gallons of water. It was released and crystallized shortly after the descent began. The rocket reentered the atmosphere at 259.4 miles down range and at 51.3 miles altitude. And confirmation of Conestoga I's splashdown came after ten minutes forty seconds of flight. It was a quick $2.5 million adventure.

The man of the hour was David Hannah, Jr., toasted at the site with champagne and the focus of network television news and analysis. He founded SSI in 1981. A real estate developer in Houston, he had read a magazine article about space on a business trip six years earlier that changed his life. He and other investors pooled $1.2 million for an unsuccessful attempt to launch a liquid-fuel rocket the first summer. It blew up on the pad.

This successful firing demonstrated SSI's ability to organize, fund, and develop privately owned launch vehicles and sites. It advanced cooperation between the firm and government agencies, including the Federal Aviation Administration, Federal Communications Commission, State Department, and National Aeronautics & Space Administration. The thirty-one-member field team and management acquired operating experience. Engineering tests showed vehicle design integrity, the ability to separate stages and payload, and orbital insertion capability. The performance of guidance, navigational, and control systems was checked.

Hannah has proved himself a man of vision. By Texas standards he is not super-rich. Yet he tried and achieved what the state's billionaires have not. And in the long run he might also grow very rich. As Wynne, a man born in the last century who was helping lead the way into the next, once said, "I'll bet we make more money with this than that thing out there [an offshore oil rig]." The respected British newspaper *Financial Times* called Texas "a promised land in which the ideals of rugged individualism, free enterprise, and self-reliance still exist in their purest, and at times their harshest, form . . . There is nothing defensive, mean-spirited, or ultimately even conservative about the way that Texans embrace the spirit of capitalism. They do not regard capitalism primarily as a system for conserving their wealth and power. Rather it is a framework for risking wealth in the quest for further aggrandizement." Hannah possesses the ideals the *Times* recognized—the frontier spirit Americans cherish.

THE YEAR BEFORE the realization of the private space launch, two biologists, Steve Labuda of the U.S. Fish and Wildlife service and Ernie Kuyt of the Canadian Wildlife Service, became the first to track the migration of whooping cranes. The big birds, which number about 120 in natural habitat and in captivity, spend the winter in the marsh of a peninsula overlooking Matagorda Island.

Bedicheck, the naturalist, said the marshes are so extensive that they literally swallow up features. "Even the great blue heron and the American egret, two of this coast's largest waders, shrink almost into insignificance, while individuals of lesser species dwindle down to mere dots." He looked for something to complete the picture, something commensurate with the background and at home in the marsh. He found what was missing when he saw a family of whooping cranes. "Here is a double completion, for bird and marsh emphasize and enliven each other . . . Nothing less than such a marsh can frame a whooping crane; nothing less than a whooping crane is adequate for such a marsh."

When the scientists began following the whoopers in 1981, fire had just swept 80 percent of their summer nesting range in Canada's Wood Buffalo National Park. Feeding ponds in the park, which straddles the border between Alberta province and the Northwest Territories, also were drying up during a drought. The threat of malnutrition apparently restricted births that year to three.

In mid-September one of the chicks and its parents started south to Texas. They interrupted their travel to fatten up for the 2,600-mile journey in the wheat and barley fields of Saskatchewan. A farmer delighted in his feathered guests fluttering between field and pond for eighteen days. Then one hop proved fatal. The chick, knocked off course by a wind shift, hit a power line. Rushed by plane to a veterinary clinic, it died six days later. The parents continued their flight south.

Another whooping crane family, meanwhile, departed from the Nyarling River in the most northern nesting area. It, too, laid over several days in the grain stubble fields. Snow showers moved in. The whoopers took off in earnest. Powerful travelers, even with young, untried wings, they cover up to 470 miles in ten hours. In flight they spread their wings and spiral upward on vertical air currents. At peak altitude they tuck their wings a little and start long downward glides. Not until dusk, when thermal activity ceases, do they flap their wings as ducks and geese do. Flapping, as you might guess, drains more energy. And it was thirty days after leaving the Canadian sanctuary that the family of cranes from the Nyarling River arrived on the Texas coast. They sprinted to the Aransas National Wildlife Refuge, on an early November morning, with the father shrilly trumpeting, "Ker-loo! Ker-lee-oo!"

Some people feel we overspend on a bird likely to become extinct anyway. To them it is a case of when to pull the plug. But they are as nearsighted as the man who thought the joint U.S.-Canadian tracking team was trying to ambush a small herd of prized pronghorns.

The demise of the whooping crane would rob us not only of majesty but also of inspiration to endure adversity. A beautiful creature who spans a vast gulf between the ages of ice and space can soar with our souls.

A SHORT WAY DOWN the Texas coast, where the live oaks grow grotesque in salty breezes, George Ware Fulton had a wonderful window on the changing world of ships. A cattleman, he had participated in the transition from sail to steam by organizing a scheduled steamship service. And in old age he could witness steam's coming of age from the third-floor, corner bay window of a mansion study to which he retreated in an active household.

Fulton called the mansion Oakhurst. He and wife Harriet endowed their home with exceptional taste and innovations after building it on a small knoll next to Aransas Bay in 1874–77. Amid its splendor, they entertained lavishly. The couple was already advanced in age—Fulton was sixty-four—with four grown children. One grand occasion in the house was their fiftieth wedding anniversary in 1890.

Ideas for the architecture and furnishings were brought from the East Coast. The mansard roof was typical of French Second Empire architecture. Renaissance Revival furniture of walnut stood on richly colored Axminster and Brussels carpets, and chandeliers hung from high ceilings. The dining table was set with Gorham silver. Archways, nine-foot passages between rooms in place of standard doors, were trimmed in cypress and walnut, the stairs in ash. Tiles from Minton, the maker of fine English china, were laid in the foyer. A Victorian garden and conservatory were filled with roses, lilies, pansies, crepe myrtle, hibiscus, and rare foliage imported from Africa and the East Indies.

The mechanical ingenuity in the mansion far exceeded the standard for conveniences in Fulton's day. A basement furnace circulated air through ducts to decorative fireplaces on three floors—an early method of central heating. The warm air also flowed to a clothes dryer in the laundry. Hot water ran in tubs, cold moved through larder troughs to preserve milk and vegetables. A carbide gas plant fueled the chandeliers.

Today, the splendor of Oakhurst has been restored by the Texas Parks and Wildlife Department. Known as Fulton Mansion State Historic Structure, it sits in the town of Fulton, three miles north of Rockport. Tours introduce visitors to the style and mores of the era.

Should you visit, you may learn:

The Fultons literally rolled out the carpets for the fall social season. The carpets were very expensive. To protect them from the heat, dust, and insects, servants would roll up and store them in summer. Woven on twenty-eight-inch looms, the strips of carpet were hand-sewn together, a practice the park service repeated in restoration.

The sitting room was used by Harriet Fulton to entertain her grandchildren and to sew. Lace was her specialty as an accomplished seamstress. A piece of her work is in the dining room.

The couple indulged in only one closet, in the master bedroom, because some governments in those days taxed a house according to the number of rooms. A closet was considered a room. Even that closet didn't have hangers. Clothes were stacked or hung on pegs.

The Fultons had six servants. Researchers believe they were quite intelligent, because in one of her letters Harriet complained they were using too much kerosene reading at night.

When George stopped shipping his cattle on the hoof and just sent hides and tallow from his packing plant, the carcasses went into the bay. The odor borne on sea breezes permeated the family's clothing, necessitating disinfectant in the wash.

The children were potty-trained at three months.

"There isn't anything else in Texas like [the mansion]," said June Secrist, the park superintendent who guided the restoration. "It's decked, not framed. That's one reason it doesn't go anywhere during a hurricane. The things that went into this house that you don't see are the amazing things."

Ships from New Orleans brought huge quantities of pine planks. The one-to-five-inch boards were stacked and spiked on top of each other to make solid walls and floors. Steel rails, the kind used for train tracks, reinforced the house. Shells, not gravel, became aggregate in the concrete foundation and as soundproofing for the floors.

After departing the house, one may drive north along the bay on scenic Fulton Beach Road and reflect about the cultural heritage the park service has so meticulously preserved with revenue from cigarette taxes. In the restoration, the researchers even unearthed nursery receipts to decide what plants to put in the conservatory. And they buried a myth. It was previously thought that George Fulton was related to Robert Fulton, the first successful operator of a steamship in 1807. Genealogists found no link between the two other than their shared interest in steamships.

A natural beauty endures from Fulton's time. The striking deformities of live oaks grace mansion grounds and beach road alike. Breezes off the bay have leaned trunks inland. Salt spray has stunted limbs to windward, while branches to leeward appear to compensate by growing unusually long. On the drive at sunset, the trees embrace a mood of the past.

AS MUCH AS ANYONE, Charles Morgan, who pioneered in commercial steam navigation, put Houston and Indianola on the Texas map. Hurricanes, the bane of both, took the latter port away.

Morgan dominated Gulf of Mexico shipping in the 1800s. He dreamed of a steamship and railroad network linking the Atlantic and Pacific coasts and Latin America. Working toward this goal, the New Yorker tried to connect the port of Indianola on the middle Texas coast with a railroad leading west. The track never pushed beyond Cuero just sixty miles northwest. His venture was halted by the financial panic of 1873, waning government interest, and a deadly hurricane in 1875.

He would succeed later in Houston, where he dredged a ship channel at the city's request and acquired a railroad to join it to the hinterland. His transportation hookup shaped the economic development of Texas.

Morgan raised Houston's fortunes at the expense of Galveston. He did it for the same reason he earlier diverted his steamships from Port Lavaca to Indianola. Both Galveston and Port Lavaca had increased wharves fees. They wouldn't bend. So Morgan switched ports.

Indianola drew attention as the eastern end of the shortest land route to California. U.S. Army officers such as Robert E. Lee passed through town on their way to frontier outposts. Supplies followed as did contingents of animals unusual in numbers and kind. One shipment brought 2,000 horses. Camels used in a military experiment arrived in 1856.

The first mighty hurricane struck a bustling Indianola on Sept. 16, 1875. Gas lights flickered in hundreds of homes and in stores on the evening preceding the storm. Wealthy guests from upstate discussed the Civil War and Reconstruction at a bar in the Casimir House, an elegant hotel. Carts and wagons jammed the streets around Calhoun County Courthouse, where a sensational murder trial had recessed.

During the night, rain squalls and frothy waves lashed the town as the tide of Matagorda Bay rose. The sea rushed through the streets, floating a schooner into the telegraph office and isolating the community. As the storm built, houses drifted off their foundations. People on roofs and doors bobbed out across the flooded prairie.

Winds peaked at 150 miles per hour after midnight the second night. Then suddenly, the sea reversed itself and raced back into the bay with hapless people and buildings. Three hundred died. Some 75 percent of the buildings disappeared.

A second slammed into Indianola in 1886, wiping out with wind and water and an accompanying fire what little the earlier storm had left. The county relocated its courthouse to Port Lavaca.

Indianola's lifespan was forty-three years, having begun when Prince Carl of Solms-Braunfels led German immigrants ashore in

1844 to await development of a settlement in the Hill Country. But, like an unpolished shell that conceals beauty, this port site has little to show for its rich years of history.

Weekend houses on stilts and several beer-and-pool stops punctuate the narrow strip along the beach from the eastern tip of the townsite at Powder Horn Bayou to the western reaches known as Indian Point or Old Town. A chunk of granite at the eroded location of the courthouse and a cistern supposedly belong to the past. In the center of a cluster of covered picnic tables, a twenty-two-foot pink granite statue of the French explorer Rene Robert Cavelier, Sieur de La Salle, who came this way in 1685, provides a resting place for seagulls.

Farther inland, a cemetery is the only recognizable remains of the town. The few headstones emphasize the multiple deaths within families during plagues. Yellow fever, a disease caused by a virus transmitted by mosquitoes, raged up and down the Texas coast then. The year 1867 is chiseled on many headstones in the old cemetery. It was known in Indianola as the Year of Death. A couple of markers rise at graves of victims in the 1875 hurricane.

Grabbing at even the most naive expectations, my hopes rose when I came across Brown's Bait Stand & Cabins. The business was located where Brown's Addition had been in the 1850s. John Henry Brown, who developed the addition into Indianola's business and cultural center, had published the town's first newspaper and later served as a state legislator and mayor of Dallas. Unfortunately, no one anywhere near the bait stand claimed relation to or had even heard of John Brown and his addition.

THE BIGGEST FISH STORY told in Port Aransas, the Mustang Island village in the Coastal Bend, concerns not the length of a fish but a single scale mounted on the lobby wall of the Tarpon Inn. The story began the day President Franklin D. Roosevelt anchored his yacht Potomac nearby in the Gulf of Mexico with the 1,850-ton destroyer Moffett a short distance away.

Roosevelt had arrived on May 2, 1937, to troll for silver kings, or tarpons, which then migrated along the shore in huge schools. As is customary today, it was a working vacation. Shortly after arriving, he signed a broadened neutrality bill. It had been flown to Galveston from Washington. After two seaplanes ferrying dispatches to the president dragged anchor and collided in rough water, the bill was rushed the 200 miles by automobile and taken by small boat to the Potomac.

Port Aransas was a beer-guzzling little fishing village in those days—with its burgeoning skyline of condominiums nearly a half-century away. The famous people attracted to try their skill with the fighting tarpon stayed at the two-story Tarpon Inn. W. R. "Bill" Ellis, the owner when Roosevelt visited the area, enjoys reliving the golden years of 1925–40.

Clyde Beatty, the great circus animal trainer, slept in one of the inn's rooms with his pet lion. "Yes, he did. He absolutely did," Ellis said. "It was a cub—seventy-five to one hundred pounds. He had it, I think, in Room 30 on the first floor. I told the maid not to go in the room because there was a lion in there.

"The Tarpon Inn was a social meeting place for the United States," Ellis said. "Anybody who had a well-known guest, they would bring them here. We've had all kinds of politicians, a half-dozen movie stars. I've seen some tremendous poker games in there."

"University presidents from Iowa, Kansas, and Missouri came down," Ellis said. "We would accuse them of using Phi Beta Kappa keys to fish for tarpon . . . [The attendants] would remember the idiosyncrasies of guests. I think it was Duncan Hines [a restaurant critic] who liked ice cream on corn flakes."

When Ellis was helping make arrangements for Roosevelt, he tried to backstop for bad weather. An alternate plan was to take the president offshore snapper fishing in a large boat. A Fort Worth man berthed a sixty-foot yacht in Port Aransas, and it was considered seaworthy and very good for snapper fishing. So Ellis called the man and said, "Jack, in the event the weather is bad, we'd need something for backup for fishing here. Can we use your boat for Roosevelt?" The man replied, "Hell, no."

That pre-arrival incident not withstanding, FDR received a royal Texas welcome when Gov. James V. Allred landed in a plane on the beach and then boarded the presidential yacht a few hundred yards offshore.

There is controversy over who later guided the president in catching his first tarpon, but Ellis said emphatically, "Don Farley was the guide. He ran the boat. It was Don Farley's boat that they were fishing from." Don agrees. Other accounts ascribe the honor to Don's uncle, the late Barney Farley.

After Roosevelt landed his first tarpon, a ninety-pounder, in a twenty-six-minute battle, the presidential party cruised down to Port Isabel to try its luck. They lowered a runabout and later pulled alongside a shrimp trawler. Barney Farley was along again. In his memoirs he says he told the shrimpers his group wanted some fine Texas shrimp. The trawler crew started shoveling shrimp into the runabout. "The President was sitting there," Barney said, "shrimp in his lap, and all around him grinning."

By the time Roosevelt returned to Port Aransas, the press had caught up. He trolled in a choppy sea south of the South Jetty, a news conference imminent. "Barney, I'm hooked on a rock," he said. Barney read it differently. So did the boatman, Ted Matthews. The line trailed too far from the jetties to hook on rock. Matthews increased boat speed. The President came back hard. "A few seconds later a large tarpon exploded high in the air, the rod in a half circle and the reel singing," Barney said. The fish made a long run and another jump and stayed on. "We fought that tarpon (in front of the press) for an hour and twenty minutes, finally gaffing him near the lighthouse, a distance of more than two miles."

The manuscript of Barney Farley's fish stories is owned by James Atwill, an attorney who, at the time of my visit, owned and lived at the Tarpon Inn. He had remodeled some of the rooms and refurbished the restaurant behind the inn. Atwill had also added a historic touch to the inn, a place on top where he retreated to gaze out to sea. Some of the earliest homes in the area, including that of settler John G. Mercer about 100 years ago, were topped with a pilot lookout. Fathers and sons served as bar pilots, guiding schooners and steamers through treacherous sandbars in Aransas Pass. They perched on the lookouts awaiting gun or flag signals from ships for help.

Dredging and modern navigation lights ultimately eliminated the need for those lookouts. The fishing that lured Roosevelt has changed, too. Guide Don Farley's career began in 1925, the start of the resort's heyday. "Oh, we used to catch a lot of tarpon," he said. "When a good spell of weather came like it is now, the mackerel were out there by the millions. And tarpon, too. Just around the jetties. Nowadays the weather can get just perfect. And there's no mackerel out there and no tarpon, either."

Dr. Henry Hildebrand, a marine biologist in Corpus Christi, talks of years when 2,000 tarpon were caught at Port Aransas. "Our tarpon would come up each spring, accumulate, and go back in the fall," he said. "They would stay around in the passes till some would distribute back in the bays. And we have changed these bays and rivers so much that I don't believe the habitat is here anymore."

Early anglers found that a tarpon's leaping power makes it a catch requiring skill and perseverance. Only salmon can better the eight-foot jump. Scales measure more than two inches in diameter. The record tarpon caught on the Texas coast, more than seven feet long, weighed 210 pounds.

Tarpon still arrive after hurricanes. Hildebrand suspects it has to do with food. Boats game fishing for sailfish and white-and-blue marlin still operate out of Port Aransas. "Oh, the marlin, that's a great fish," Don Farley said, "and they're catching them, too. And the sailfish. They fish 100 miles offshore. Don't think anything at all of going 100 miles out, some of 'em 150. We didn't even know they were out there."

One more point about President Roosevelt's day at Port Aransas: There is no discernible controversy outside former inn owner Bill Ellis' business office over the claim that the President stayed at the Tarpon Inn. *Hurricane Junction*, a history of Port Aransas, notes the walls of the Tarpon Inn lobby have long been covered with signed scales from tarpon caught by guests, the latter status a requirement. A historical marker on the front lawn refers to Roosevelt as a patron. Every travel piece written over the years for newspapers, magazines, and guidebooks states Roosevelt stayed at the Tarpon Inn.

But a lot of people failed to ask Ellis. "He never touched foot on the shoreline," Ellis said. He did dock in Turtle Cove at Port Aransas, and he did autograph a scale from a tarpon to hang in the inn. But for the history books, Roosevelt never slept at the Tarpon Inn.

The inn itself marked its 100th anniversary some time ago. The original was built in 1886 on another site, and the main building in 1925. And the illustrious comings and goings of the hostelry, shelter to victims of hurricanes and famous guests, can withstand the truth along with the storms.

MY JOURNEY ALSO TOOK a nostalgic curve through East Texas. When I was growing up, my father sold drilling muds and chemicals, moving his family throughout the Texas oil fields before settling in

Beaumont, the site of the first major oil gusher. The oil well, the Lucas discovery well in the Spindletop field, had roared in January 10, 1901. Along the way, driller Curt Hamill needed to flush out the cuttings. He drove cattle into a nearby pond, and their milling-about produced the mud that, when pumped into the well, would bring up the cuttings. My dad didn't know his job, by then much more sophisticated, had developed almost in the backyard of our family home.

As I drove north through the pine forests, I searched out the first steel oil tanks and toured the East Texas Oil Museum at Kilgore, not far from where I had started school. My mother, with me along as a child, had stopped at roadside stands for produce. Now I sought fresh tomatoes, beans, and squash at farmers' markets in Lufkin and Tyler. Later I picked blueberries in an open field. An employee at a small restaurant in Jefferson was kind enough to wash and serve them with ice cream. And it is to Jefferson that I bring fellow travelers who long to taste the nostalgia for a simpler life during Texas's Victorian period.

Though it is located in far Northeast Texas, almost as far north as Dallas, Jefferson served as a major port during the mid-1800s. John Nance, a modern boatman, guided me over the route steamships navigated to and from bustling docks, coming several hundred miles upriver from New Orleans.

On a rainy fall day, he and I set out in a little wooden boat from Jefferson Landing, near the old turning basin on Big Cypress Bayou. As many as ten ships could dock there before it was filled in for construction of railroad and highway bridges. "This was almost always a one-way street for those river boats coming up here," he said, quieting the motor. "There was no place to pass for this last stretch, and they would have horseback riders coordinating river traffic."

We passed a crumbling stone building. "This magazine was built during the Civil War to store gunpowder away from town," Nance said. "There were once three of them spaced far apart in case one blew up. The other two were torn down for the brick in them."

Sweetgums on the banks brightened the overcast day with yellows, reds, and purples. Cypress had a reddish tint. During the steamboat era, paddle wheelers made their way up and down this waterway. Some carried passengers and light freight. The *Mittie Stephens* (a passenger ship on which more than sixty died when it burned and sank in 1869) was a side-wheeler about sixty feet wide. It was used during the Civil War as a supply boat. It could cover the 730 miles from Jefferson to New Orleans in six days.

"The cotton boats were a lot slower," the guide said. "The biggest one that came through Jefferson was 265 feet long. It carried out 4,500 bales of cotton."

After passing an inlet to Caddo Lake State Park, we entered the dark channels of Caddo Lake, fifteen miles from Jefferson. The unusual, shallow lake has thick stands of cypress draped with Spanish moss and acres of lily pads on its surface. A labyrinth of dredged channels crisscross it. The natives call the aquatic plants, which blossom in July and August, "yanquapin." They were identified from photographs as water lilies and lotus by an employee at Lilypons Water Gardens in Brookshire, near Houston.

Traffic to Jefferson ended abruptly in 1873 when the Army Corps of Engineers blew up a natural log and mud barrier on the Red River. The Great Raft had stretched more than 100 miles. When the Corps succeeded after years of trying, the depth of the lake and bayou was lowered by drainage to a shallowness unfit for larger riverboats. Other areas, including the port at Shreveport, benefitted.

Nance and I concluded our excursion on his favorite shortcut, Pirch Gap. "I think someone misspelled it," he said. Brooding trees in the narrow passage changed an already dark day into night.

A half century after the port of Jefferson's demise, another venture boomed on Caddo Lake because of Prohibition: moonshine liquor. Wyatte Moore, who remembers those days, lived at nearby Karnack, the childhood home of Lady Bird Johnson.

"In 1929, at the beginning of the Great Depression, I had been married about five years," Moore said as he reminisced in his living room. "We moved out on the south shore of Caddo Lake, and I built an old rough house. I stayed there fifteen years and eked out a living."

Besides hauling wood with a horse and wagon, "I fished, built boats, killed ducks and sold them, made whiskey, worked in the oil field, farmed a little, had hogs in the woods, and kept a couple of milk cows.

"Well, about '35 and '33 we had children," Moore said. "I hadn't made much liquor. I tried to get by without it. But I had old friends who kinda believed in me and insisted I might as well. Everybody else nearly was. I proceeded, and for about eight or nine years I kept a still going practically all the time."

He paddled up to 300 pounds of supplies and whiskey in a sixteen-foot boat, narrow and sharp on both ends. "I could paddle out in the lake where there were so-called islands," he said. "They weren't islands, but they were thick timbers up to 50 feet high and water through them about two-feet deep. And I had a platform.

"I had a low platform, and then I had kind of an upstairs so when the high water came, I could move higher," he said. "At one time I had a kerosene-burning, fifty-five-gallon drum up there, and I would fire it up and go on. I would hunt ducks and even go to town and watch them trying the other moonshiners at the courthouse while my still was still cookin' along."

Later, he enlarged capacity with a 110-gallon drum he fired with wood on a portable platform just off the bank. "Sometimes people came on a horse or a mule for liquor," he said. "I would take their mule or horse and ride down through some sorghum and out in the lake to the still to fill up the jugs. I mostly sold to doctors, lawyers, judges, preachers, and professional people who wanted a pretty good grade of liquor."

Did he ever get caught?

"The game warden was after me for fishing, hunting ducks, and selling them. The sheriff and revenuers were supposed to be after me for the still," he said. "I was nice to them. I'd give the game warden whiskey and the sheriff fish. I didn't feel like it was ethical to give the sheriff whiskey and the game warden fish . . . I got by . . ."

WATER PLAYS THE MUSIC throughout Texas—and under. It has created numerous caves in the easily soluble limestone.

The best of the seven open to the public is roughly seventy-five miles west of the usually recognized limits of the Hill Country. Caverns of Sonora near Sonora has been variously described as Ali Baba's treasure cave and "the most indescribably beautiful cavern in the world."

I toured it with Jack Burch, a developer and partner in its operation. "The tourist gets lost with the crystal patterns," he said. "He's overwhelmed, like he was inside a snowbank. If we had only one little spot like this at the entrance, people would say 'oh, oh' and photograph that one spot. But they come in here and they see it everywhere and they won't even take a picture. Why take a picture of a sand dune when you're in the middle of the Sahara Desert?"

In the midst of 100 percent humidity, we surveyed uncommon coral patterns on stalagmites, Texas-size "popcorn," and a unique butterfly constructed of helictites. Helictites are irregular and branching stalactites. "It's the only known butterfly in the world," Burch said. "It is actually two helictites that just accidentally grew side by side. With excess water coming through a central canal, minerals were deposited on the outside of it, and as the water was pulled by gravity on the underside, a drapery pattern became wings. These helictites are pure calcite. If they were broken, it would sound like glass breaking. I would give them a million years to grow a foot, and we've got them three feet long and still growing."

I was already convinced of the important role of water in caves when Burch and I met. But my understanding was muddy. We sat and talked. He said I was about 50 percent right when I noted caverns are really ancient passages of springs. "Caves do not have to have flowing water," he said. "They are mostly dissolved by solution. You have water that is high enough in carbon dioxide to start the chemical reaction. It will dissolve by releasing more carbon dioxide stored in the limestone itself. Springs are definitely associated with caves in limestone country."

Sometimes they do erode the caverns? I asked. "Oh yeah, oh yeah," he said. "And you can get alkaline water that's oversaturated so that instead of dissolving, it is going to deposit. That's how you get a stalagmite, for instance. You can have both solutions at the same time. That's why I say you are at least 50 percent right."

Carbon dioxide is very common in water. In solution it becomes carbonic acid, a weak, colorless acid. Rotting organic material such as leaves and grass produce it. "It's nothing super," Burch said. "This Coke has a lot more in it than our drinking water does. But [in hushed tones] it don't take much."

Caverns of Sonora captures the magical movements of the water symphony played in Texas. "Water has all in the world to do with caverns," Burch said. "You couldn't get a cave without water."

YOU CAN GO BACK IN TIME. There's a range as to how far back, from Texas caverns to the geologic ages of Utah, the final destination of this odyssey. I have also learned you can go back in time while skiing on the south side of the Matterhorn, in Cervinia, Italy, and hiking with a backpack in the San Juan Mountains of Colorado.

Then again, you cannot go back in time. You cannot be the man or woman you were a decade before. For me, hand tremors have robbed me of such trade skills as note-taking and slow-speed photography. I have found a slower method for writing, not in a long-shot a guarantee of income. I can still produce books from transcripts of taped interviews. But that's another story.

Steven Spielberg was a piker on the subject of the past in *Back to the Future*. With a trip through Utah, anyone can turn a car into a time machine good for 250 million exhilarating years. The premier attraction of Utah, after the fine snow for skiers has receded up the mountains, is its wondrous abyss of time open for exploration.

From the roadside, an immense and colorful canvas of layered cliffs, spires, and arches—the scenic rock of many geologic ages—awakens the senses to the power of time through erosion. But you'll have to get out of the car to reach an emotional peak. ". . . You can't see anything from a car; you've got to get out of the goddamned contraption and walk, better yet crawl, on hands and knees, over the sandstone and through the thornbush and cactus," writes Southwest author Edward Abbey.

As if to accommodate the author's suggestion, hiking trails easy enough for senior travelers and families toting infants weave through some of the most stunning geologic sights in Utah's national parks. Horses for hire and whitewater river rafts jack up the excitement.

It is as hard as rock to muster enthusiasm for the underlying reason for those magnificent earthen formations in southeast Utah. Certainly, you don't need to know why to appreciate the numerous national and state parks scattered westward from Moab, a recreation base for the region some 1,225 road miles from Houston but with gateway airports at Salt Lake City, Utah (239 miles) and Grand Junction, Colorado. (108 miles).

A simple one-mile hike to Delicate Arch in Arches National Park on the outskirts of Moab may alone make the trip worthwhile. It is an exquisite rock sculpture. Abbey, who pondered its significance in two seasons as a ranger at Arches, which he found to be the most beautiful place on earth, eloquently describes the arch in *Desert Solitaire*:

"A weird, lovely, fantastic object out of nature like Delicate Arch has the curious ability to remind us—like rock and sunlight and wind and wilderness—that out there is a different world, older and greater and deeper by far than ours, a world which surrounds and sustains the little world of men as sea and sky surround and sustain a ship. The shock of the real. For a little while we are again able to see, as the child sees, a world of marvels. For a few moments we discover that nothing can be taken for granted, for if this ring of stone is marvelous, then all which shaped it is marvelous, and our journey here on earth, able to see and touch and hear in the midst of tangible and mysterious things-in-themselves, is the most strange and daring of all adventures."

Delicate Arch does not stand alone in inspiration. More than 200 catalogued arches in this park range in size from a three-foot opening, the minimum considered an arch, to a 291-foot span. The 70,000-acre preserve boasts the greatest density of natural arches in the world.

The rocks, or deposited sediments, of Arches reveal 200 million years of geologic history. The arches themselves were carved in Entrada sandstone, a wind-formed layer about 145 million years old colored salmon, white, and red. Erosion exposed and then began working on it two million years ago. The abrasive action was helped along by earlier cracking of the earth in an uplift. The many parallel fractures were widened, leaving narrow walls, or fins, of sandstone.

The rock is composed of quartz sand cemented together by calcium. The mildly acidic nature of water from rain and snow dissolves that calcium just as it does the limestone in Texas Hill Country caverns.

Because the calcium is unevenly distributed, parts of the fins are more easily weathered, washed away, or popped off when the water freezes and expands behind flakes. The erosive forces eventually form holes, or arches, in some of the fins.

There remains, however, yet another major influence in this chain of events—the dominant geologic reason for the lay of the land—which has generated widespread enthusiasm among geologists for this part of the Colorado Plateau, a major topographical division of Utah. That element is salt.

Eons ago a 10,000-square-mile area in the region experienced subsidence just as we have had around Houston in recent years. That vanished depression has been named the Paradox Basin. In its time saltwater from an adjacent sea flowed in and then evaporated, leaving the salt. Erosion from the highlands that rim the basin later covered the salt.

Dr. Richard Mattox, professor emeritus of geology at Texas Tech University in Lubbock, said in a telephone interview that the Paradox Basin consists of an average 3,500 feet of salt, with the Salt Valley in Arches National Park sitting atop about 20,000 feet of salt.

"All those big, long valleys, Moab Valley and the valley in Arches, those are all anticlines that this salt created. They are just big folds that have later been faulted and downdropped."

The salt pushed up the overlying strata because it was lighter than the other rock. "It is just like you take ice and put it in water," Mattox said. "It is going to come up." The resulting upfolds, ridges with a core of salt, are called anticlines. Groundwater dissolved the salt in some and caused their collapse. But others up to thirty miles in length remain today. The trail to Delicate Arch leads up one.

"That is probably the finest area in the world to study those things," Mattox said.

The critical role of salt extends into Canyonlands National Park, less than twenty miles across U.S. Highway 191 from Arches.

In the spectacular triangle of canyons and desert biota between the converging Colorado and Green Rivers in Canyonlands, a new theory—which doesn't dilute in the least the dominant role of salt in the area—concerns a geologic structure called Upheaval Dome. About three miles in diameter, it is a dome with an eroded center in the middle of a ring syncline, a depression where rocks are folded down.

"It was discovered in the 1920s by geologists doing petroleum exploration in the Paradox Basin," said Dr. Eugene Shoemaker, a research geologist for the U.S. Geological Survey in Flagstaff, Arizona. "I had been looking at it for nearly forty years and finally realized what I was looking at."

Three years ago, he advanced a new theory, proposing that Upheaval Dome resulted from an impact crater caused by a small meteorite. He compared the crater to a collapsing hole dug in the ground by man. On the flanks of the hole, rocks slump toward the middle, and, where they meet, they rise up and form a separate peak. The dome is the central uplift, and the structurally detached region surrounding it is the collapsed region.

"The Colorado Plateau has been my geological stamping ground," Shoemaker said in a telephone interview. "So I was cruising along in a taxi just sort of thinking about it after giving a seminar and did the calculation in my head. 'There ought to be an impact structure exposed somewhere on the Colorado Plateau,' I thought. 'Where is it?' And then all of a sudden this dawning realization swept over me: 'Shoemaker, you dope, you've been looking at it all these years.'

"But, you see, there was something missing. I believed [an earlier geologist's] map, and I never should have done it. If it were an impact structure, there should be faults all around the edges."

To prove his calculation, Shoemaker took a graduate student with him to find the faults. "Three miles before we got to the dome," he said, "we looked into a canyon with its beautiful exposures, and there they were. No one had ever bothered to look. I hadn't looked at the outside; I had always looked at the inside."

In coming to grips with how the West was young, a traveler may complement his sightseeing with leisure and meals in Moab, population 5,333. In the 1950s, uranium made it a boomtown. Now, the tourist economy stimulated by the creation of the national parks has built enough small motels and cafes to give its main street the charm of a strip shopping center. A large number of whitewater rafting outfitters book trips from here, and jeeps for rugged tours of the back country may be rented.

If there is anything like seclusion at a national park, and there is, Capitol Reef National Park, located 140 miles west of Moab, offers it. One of the least visited in the system, it, too, can awe you with unusual geologic structures, plus introduce the visitor to some downhome richness.

A painter working under a brightly colored umbrella on the desert floor emphasized the artistry of the park. He was at work near an unpaved pioneer wagon road that parallels the soaring, sun-drenched western face of a 100-mile-long landmark of the plateau area. He could draw his strokes from a natural palette of grays, purple, gold, red, green, and browns.

A proper introduction to the landmark wall of rock—a single earthen fold, or monocline, called Waterpocket Fold—is delivered at a small theater in park headquarters. A narrated slide show is presented beneath a window view of a dramatic 1,000-foot bluff on a tributary of the Fremont River, which cuts through the heart of the fold. The names Capitol Reef and Waterpocket Fold assume clarity as you start to fathom this 241,000-acre park's 250-million-year slice of geologic time.

Within a couple of miles of the visitor center grow thousands of fruit trees. They are a remnant, along with a one-room school, of settlers who began arriving on the site of the Fruita community in the late 1870s. For a small charge you may pick cherries, apricots, peaches, pears, apples, and a few nuts in this eighty-acre orchard. The produce starts ripening in June, and various trees bear through October.

Bob Reynolds, the personable superintendent at Capitol Reef National Park, talked to us one evening about the magnificent seclusion of the park, recounting that "day after day people say, 'We had no idea you were here; we were on our way to Bryce [Canyon National Park].' They are just amazed. We now have a road that is a direct shot from Bryce, one of the best-known parks. It is a world-class scenic drive, about 100 miles."

That was all we needed to hear. Reynolds met us the next morning before dawn for a twenty-mile drive up State Highway 12 to a 9,200-foot summit in Dixie National Forest. As day broke, we stopped on an overlook to gaze at the horizon about 150 miles east, in the vicinity of the La Sal Mountains. The only distraction was mosquitoes. A rising sun silhouetted the distant peaks, and filtered softly across mountain file after mountain file. The fiery ball emblazoned the clouds, a wide crimson band with a streak of gold. It was intoxicating, and we would soon discover that nature had lost its head as well on this road.

On the homeward descent, after a brief, sobering view of a power plant belching smoke over in Arizona, we balked time and again, first at a herd of deep brown elk in a dark green meadow and then at several groups of browsing mule deer moving among the white trunks of aspen.

Coming off the mountain, we ate breakfast at the Sunglow Motel and café in the nearby ranching community of Bicknell. It had generally good food, particularly pies that sounded forbidding at first. One of the favorites in a tasting binge was the pickle pie (I swear) topped with whipping cream. If you wished, you could trade one of your own offbeat pie recipes for one of pie maker Cula Ekker's, though she was not sure how the sweet pickle concoction would end up at lower elevations.

CHAPTER 27

DOING SIXTY

It is autumn, and it is dusk for the fortunate until the hard cold drives in.

The wind chimes for me today, on the hearth of my writing, the patio. As is habit, I let the outside in—the trees, they play a chord from childhood.

I still feel the East Texas forest at Lake Cherokee when I was eight. We had one of the first weekend houses there with a cypress dock and wooden boat propelled by a five-horsepower motor. But I roamed a sandy path in the woods more than the water's edge. What was burned in my soul was a stand of sweet gums, their colors splashed to brilliance by fall sunshine. Now they may not have been sweet gums; no matter. It is the feel that stays with me, as strong today as that wire and pipe fence that my dad erected around our place a half-century ago.

A couple of years passed, and the boyhood was out at Kountze, nearer the coast. A red-haired lad drove me out a sandy road into the heart of the Big Thicket in a jeep, the top off. It was a joyous ride into adulthood.

In my early teens, visiting my maternal grandparents (the George W. Porters) in the Central Texas town of Troy, I hiked to the early family farmhouse and to a nearby creek with limestone banks. The shade likely came from elms—the creek was Little Elm, and I felt on the loose. Thereafter, a spiritual awakening occurred on a path through brooding cypress and white oak. They stood between a church camp and Village Creek, part of the Big Thicket. The shadows of the thick woods emitted as much or more power than a man possessed. To walk there was to mature.

Some say the Saratoga Light shines from railroad days in that tunnel of trees. They can see it as I see a light at the end of my line, at the end of my tunnel.

I have grown to appreciate, to like and to love a former high school classmate, Beaumont South Park, '59. We are doing sixty with entertainment madness—from Willie Nelson to James Taylor. The pace, I find, is just right.

The woman with whom I have shared so much fun and happiness is Judy Cunningham (her real name). She was mixing cornbread to go with a pot of gourmet beans and sausage last night, and she showed her skill in the kitchen, heating the eggs so they would blend.

After reading my manuscript, she concluded that our strongest common interest would be nature. And I embraced all that that said, all the promise of that bond.

She doesn't know it, but we share a fondness of hotels. She lives in a tower overlooking the striking Houston skyline, the next closest thing to a hotel one can find. For years I have sought out when traveling a Driskill in Austin or a La Mansion in San Antonio. It is a certain elegance that soothes. And with someone you care for, it is the fireworks on the Fourth of July.

Judy can turn up her intellect in a conversation, impressively. She dug right in to the sexist religious right the other night in a next-door conversation with other tower dwellers. She phrased our sentiments well, and I just sat there pleased to be on her side of the fence.

Commitment. Judy agreed in the early days of our relation to three months hence visit the Vowells in Los Angeles for a golfing weekend. It was a promise unbroken until the terrorists struck the World Trade Center two days before our departure. The promising friendship has stayed intact.

Is there more than friendship? There have been rumblings of attending a marriage course at Rice University. It would satisfy the goals of both even if we went our separate ways. I cannot dally longer, do not want to, and would immediately become a partner to this engaging friend. We reason together, embrace similar tastes, have compatible energy (mine less than hers), and yes, love.

"I love you, too," she said.

But she may not want a union because of past missteps. Or me.

"Just keep doing what you are doing," I would reply.

EPILOGUE

AT AGE 65, I moved from behemoth Houston to the tiny and usually peaceful Terlingua in far West Texas, at the western edge of Big Bend National Park and 10 miles from the Mexican border. If stress were my foe, this appeared a healthy bastion away from mental illness. How wrong I was. Within the first eight years, to 2014, I succumbed to another three manic episodes. The lifetime count had climbed so high I had to guess—about 20. However, the latter episode was fought on a different turf. I was not hospitalized, and my doctor, Dr. Terry Rustin, treated me by way of a television hookup from his office in Houston to Alpine, a small college town 80 miles north of Terlingua.

Rustin fought the monster by increasing my dose of Risperdal and seeing me by appointment. He believed hospitalization was a last resort for a bipolar patient.

In an email message later, he listed three reasons for hospitalization: 1) If the patient were of immediate danger to self or others; 2) if there were a psychosis that renders the patient unable to manage in society; and 3) if there were a danger of rapid deterioration due to mania or depression that cannot be managed as an outpatient.

Unfortunately, my treatment did not harness all wild activity. I was able to get a bank loan of $6,000 to put Terlingua musicians in big-city venues. I also started a magazine blog. Both ventures folded when I came back to reality.

Still, there had been successes in Terlingua when my mind was clear. I wrote and published two books, *Carlton Leatherwood's Big Bend People,* featuring some 100 people. Mike Perry, publisher of the online Alpine Daily Planet, was the instigator, adding me to his staff to write a column on those folks. Earlier, I wrote another, skinnier book, *Why Terlingua.*

Dori Ramsay, of Terlingua, pointed to those successes as proof for loved ones that they can fight against mania and win. Voni Glaves, another "local," said amen. And with many more of my friends in the community, there was resolution to take the illness in stride, often offering help during crisis "because you are my friend, and I care."

After the last episode, there were residual feelings. I no longer had the hope that there would not be another, and I had lost the drive to write.

But for my caring friends, one in particular, and my doctor. I might not have continued to write. To them I owe my world.

A final look at Risperdal: Generic is now available for less than $15 a month.

In the message from Rustin, an MD who is a consultant in internal medicine, addiction medicine, and psychiatry, he listed discoveries about the manic depressive illness in the past 20 years. That is the period of time after expert witnesses addressed the illness in my discrimination trial. Here are the findings:

1. Bipolar disorder is a biological condition and is not caused by childhood experiences, parental behavior, or other life experiences;
2. Bipolar disorder has a 35% heritable component and is present in 3% of the general population;

3. Individuals with bipolar disorder are more likely than others to be creative, artistic, musical, literary, and dramatic (this supports earlier findings);
4. Individuals with bipolar disorder have a high rate of substance abuse and addiction, independent of their bipolar disorder—about 40 percent:
5. Bipolar patients stabilize when they follow an orderly, consistent regimen—sleep, eat, work on a schedule;
6. Exercise benefits patients when they are depressed;
7. According to some studies, suicide is the number one cause of death in bipolar patients;
8. When using substances, bipolar patients tend to use mood-congruent drugs rather than mood stabilizing drugs. That is, they may say they are using drugs/alcohol to control their mood, but that is not correct. When manic, they use stimulants (cocaine, tobacco, coffee, amphetamines) which enhance their manic mood. When depressed, they use depressants (alcohol, marijuana, Xanax) which further depress their mood. So, the drugs they use exacerbate, rather than ameliorate, their mood.

Throughout this memoir I have included my writing, and now is no exception. I will borrow two features from the People books, though the selections are like choosing from your children. But they illustrate the decency and intellect I have found in a community that I hope is the terminus of my moves.

Here is one of the interviews from the first People book:

> Pardon me, but I thought until today that every drop of religious water or wine had been wrung out of our schools. It is revelation to find that is not so.

Pardon me, if my blame of misunderstanding is heaped on the extreme right or those who speak that political wing's language. Maybe, just maybe, those who speak out are an uncontrolled fringe. But I have not been in a classroom for 50 years, and so as those years rolled by, I perceived that God was dead to young ears. That was the uproar I heard.

Then along came Martha Stafford, an English teacher for all four grades of high school in Terlingua Common School District's small education halls. She had played the lead, Miss Amelia Evans, in *The Ballad of the Sad Cafe* a few years back, and I had a small part in that Last Minute Low Budget Productions play. Our paths rarely crossed after that.

I was pleased to see her helping out at the altar for the Episcopalian Christmas Eve service in the Lajitas chapel. And I knew from her invitation to a Sarah Palin white trash party that she had an outspoken political side.

However, it was only a few days ago that she landed on all fours on the back of a social media zealot.

"If teachers can't teach anything related to the Bible," she responded to him, "how can they teach Beowulf, King Arthur, William Blake, Grendel, Keats, Shelley, Tennyson . . . (way too many to list here)."

Well, I wanted to know more about the modern classroom, and she said she would love to visit. So a meeting was arranged for Easter afternoon. Again she had helped at the altar for what she called a High Church service, which she said they didn't normally do. Father Mel, retired minister from Redford, "had me ringing bells which I rang at the wrong time, and we had the wrong lesson to read, and so there was a lot of stopping and starting and Father Mel whispering instructions . . . a very patient man."

That sounded like a refreshing effort akin to students giving their all to a one-act play, which she also directs. And did I forget to say she is librarian at the school and is coordinator of academic contests in the University Interscholastic League?

Enough background. Here's the serious part of this discussion, the age of enlightenment in my later years.

"So much of literature is biblical allegories," Stafford said. "With Beowulf the monster is Grendel. Well, he's a descendant of Cain. If the kids don't know Cain and Abel, then they don't understand he has been an outcast his entire life.

"It goes on throughout literature, and when I first started teaching in 1985, you just had to say Cain and Abel, or the Great Flood, and all the kids knew it. A lot of that I think was growing up in small towns where everybody went to church every Sunday.

"Now that has changed; kids don't go to church. And so they don't have these basic stories, and so as a teacher you have to give them the background, and nine times out of ten, it's biblical. Otherwise, they are not going to understand the importance of 12 men with Beowulf, and one betrayed him, and these type of things.

"You have to explain it all to kids. And so when people talk about you don't mention God or Christianity or any of that sort of thing in school, they're wrong. They are just flat out wrong." She added that, of course, there is a lot of literature without any kind of biblical reference. "My faith and spirituality have grown in great bounds," she said, "but I don't bring my personal belief system into the classroom. Society has changed.

"I don't think it means that we've become godless at all," she said. "I don't think parents put the emphasis on biblical stories that they used to. Maybe we are a more literate society so that there are other examples to draw from than just the Bible. That's way beyond what I know." There is a saying among teachers, she said: As long as there are tests, there will be prayer in school.

Stafford has stayed close to home, except for a sojourn to Montana. She is a Marfa native and went to Sul Ross State University.

There were a couple of quick questions left, and short answers.

Is there a Bible in the library?

"Yes, there is, in the religion section, the 200s.

Is there a Koran?

"I do believe we have a Koran."

And yet another interview:

The primary focus of my interview was on my guest's silver smithing, but when he surprised me by saying he owned three AR-15s, that sharpened my attention. Those rifles had come to the front in the gun control issue, otherwise this gun-leery person wouldn't have known about them. The pronouncement wasn't shrill, so I was at ease but wondering. It followed the question which was something like, "What do you do in your spare time when you aren't working with silver?" And the answer was, "I'm a rifle shooter."

Then I asked Paul Wiggins, "Do you have an AR-15?" And he was a straight shooter.

At home I did a little research on the rifle and called Wiggins back. "They must be different," I said, "different manufacturers or variations."

"They are chambered differently, he answered. "One is for sport, and two are for competition. I'm not a survivalist, nor do I fear a tyrannical government. Life is very sweet."

But Wiggins' tenure along the Rio Grande precedes competitive shooting, to a score of years with silver and to fun times in the '80s when a hot bath came in a barrel and when beers were drunk around campfires, not in bars.

He had lived at Redford in the 1970s, and that changed suddenly, and he found himself on the road.

"I was doing bead work in Santa Fe, and I met a man who suggested that knowing how to work silver would be a great addition to my bead work," he said. "He was right, and I had wanted to do some buckles and hardware for my belts, and he convinced me to look into it."

In '84, Wiggins moved to Terlingua Ranch and began to work with silver.

"I really did my first piece in '92, the first piece that I was proud of," he said, "the first piece that I knew was a product, a star concho. And I did several belts early on, when silver wasn't so expensive, and sold them right here to my friends."

Since that time, that's pretty much been Wiggins' livelihood.

Technically, smithing is really forming silver with hammers, and melting and casting. "There's a lot of silver jewelry making," he said, "but there's not many craftsmen doing smithing. I do just enough to say that I do, but I haven't made the classic teapot or done any real vessels. That's really smithing. What Paul Revere did was silver smithing, and now there's some done in the Orient.

"I love to hammer." he added. "I do some forming, but by the time you smith out a silver goblet or a silver plate, it costs a bloody fortune. That's because silver is so expensive."

What have you made recently that you call smithing?

"These bracelets that I do, these heavy cuff bracelets. The Navajo called them filed bracelets," he answered. "They require me to cast a slug; then I hammer it and roll it out, bend it and carve with files, and stamp it. It's real basic smithing.

"I enjoy making chains," he continued. "I love to make chains, and there's not many people doing that."

Wiggins doesn't do much bead work anymore and hasn't made a beaded belt in years. "I could, I could," he said. "I think about it sometime, getting back to it, but it didn't prove very lucrative for me. I lavish a lot of effort on the beadwork, and the color decisions take time. It's stitching right into the leather."

He used to make more heavy silver belts, but that's not happening so much now because they would cost a fortune—that would be way over a $1,000—"and most of my market here is in the $100–$300 range." he explained. "I'll be doing more overlay silver on brass and copper, at less expense, and it's beautiful."

In that "spare time," the last five or six years, Wiggins has been learning to shoot competitive rifle—service rifle and high power.

"I've had a real good time doing that," he said. "I've spent a lot of money on it, and I'm shooting a lot better now. I don't have a lot of company in this. A deputy sheriff is rated high master. He and I always swap ideas."

As for the AR-15s, Wiggins said, "One of them I can't get bullets for, another's at the gunsmith's, and the third one I'm just trying to buy brass and keep it up. The whole shooting fraternity is in dutch right now over politics and the tragedies that have happened, the poor way the NRA has represented itself, and the mistakes they made."

Is there middle ground in gun control? "I believe some things need to change. I believe there is some middle ground," he answered.

"But when you get people who love guns and people who hate guns together, you don't go anywhere. I enjoy shooting, but I don't see any tyrannical government out there, and I'm not a fanatic about the Second Amendment. I think the issues are going to devolve to the states. You can already look at what New York and California have."

Wiggins doesn't think the assault weapons ban is going to get too far but that existing laws are going to be enforced with more vigor and that there are going to be some changes in the idea of private sales.

"I think there is a very quiet majority that is not going to let Congress fool around too much with the basic rights," he said, "and this thing about self-loading rifles is a nightmare to get into.

"We already have perfectly reasonable restrictions on automatic weapons and other specialized military weapons," he emphasized. "I just think the self-loading rifle, its innovation, is the way this is going, is the way rifles are going. I don't think you are going to succeed at prohibiting innovation."

The AR-15 is a semi-automatic rifle that fires a single round each time the trigger is pulled. It is also known as a self-loading rifle, successor to earlier rifles that required manual-cycling of the weapon after each shot, such as the bolt-action rifle.

Wiggins concluded by saying, "The target shooting discipline in America is really coming to be built around the self-loading rifle. The AR-15 has very recently outperformed a very high-tech bolt rifle in a national match, and that's a 200-, 300-, 600-yard shooting line."

And he was philosophical: "Freedom always courts disaster."

But I didn't want to let an "old timer" get away without hearing more about early baths here. Several people had mentioned Wiggins' early bathing option.

"I haven't done that in many years," he obliged. "I just used to fill a barrel up with water and build a fire under it, then invited my friends to come over for a good soak. It became a little legendary. Some people had a hard time squeezing into a barrel."

Did this take the place of showering at La Kiva in the old days?"

"Oh, those damn showers would give you a shock," he answered. "The coin boxes were all wired, and before they were taken out, it wasn't uncommon to get a little jolt. That was '80, '81. "There weren't many places to take a bath or shower. We all pretty much roughed it here.

"Didn't have any bars to go to, but had campfires. There really was a time when the only bar was the Lajitas Trading Post. It was the only place to sit down and drink."

67623826R00170

Made in the USA
Middletown, DE
23 March 2018